A NATURAL HISTORY
OF THE
MONTEREY BAY NATIONAL
MARINE SANCTUARY

A NATURAL HISTORY OF THE

MONTEREY BAY

NATIONAL MARINE SANCTUARY

Foreword by Julie Packard

Monterey Bay Aquarium
in cooperation with the
National Oceanic and Atmospheric Administration
Sanctuaries and Reserves Division

Contributing Authors:

Chapter 1: *The National Marine Sanctuary* by David G. Gordon
Chapter 2: *Oceanography* by Christina Slager
Chapter 3: *Geology* by Lou Bergeron
Chapter 4: *Wetlands* by Pam Armstrong, Mark Silberstein, Eileen Campbell
Chapter 5: *Beaches and Dunes* by Jerry Emory
Chapter 6-9: *Rocky Shores, Reefs and Pilings, Kelp Forests, Sandy Seafloor* by Alice Cascorbi, and *Kelp Forest* features by Dr. Judith Connor
Chapter 10-11: *Open Waters, Deep Sea* by Michael Rigsby

Scientific Reviewers and Contributors: Alan Baldridge, Chuck Baxter, Kurt Buck, Dr. Francisco Chavez, Dr. Judith Connor, Natasha Fraley, Mark Furgeson, Dr. Gary Greene, Dr. Eugene C. Haderlie, Dr. Randy Kochevar, Liz Love, Dr. Dan Orange, Dr. Bruce Robison, Dr. Frank Schwing, Mark Silberstein, Dr. Mary Silver, Diedre Sullivan, Dr. Steven Webster

Managing Editor: Nora L. Deans
Senior Editor: Michael Rigsby
Project Editors: Roxane Buck-Ezcurra, Lisa M. Tooker
Design & Production: Lawrence Ormsby, Carole Thickstun and Lorna Miller

Published in the United States by the Monterey Bay Aquarium Foundation, 886 Cannery Row, Monterey, CA 93940-1085. www.mbayaq.org

Library of Congress Cataloging in Publication Data:
(A Natural History of the Monterey Bay National Marine Sanctuary   p. cm.
Includes bibliographical references and index.
ISBN 1-878244-11-6
1.   Monterey Bay National Marine Sanctuary (Calif.) 2. Natural
history–California–Monterey Bay Region. I. Monterey Bay Aquarium Foundation. II.
United States.
Office of Ocean and Coastal Resource Management. Sanctuaries and Reserves Division.
QH91.75.U6N38 1997   508.36432–dc21   97-7956   CIP

Cover and back cover photos: Kip Evans and Charles Seaborn

Printed in the United States on recycled paper.

MONTEREY BAY
AQUARIUM®

*"What better gift can we give the next generation
than a passion for
science and discovery, and a
commitment to caring for the natural world?"*

JULIE PACKARD

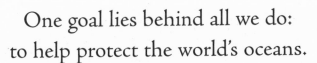

One goal lies behind all we do:
to help protect the world's oceans.

MONTEREY BAY AQUARIUM

Our mission is to
manage marine areas of special
national significance to protect
their ecological and cultural
integrity for the benefit of
current and future generations.

NATIONAL MARINE SANCTUARIES

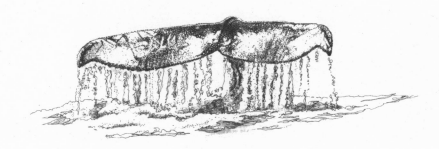

CONTENTS

FOREWORD

DESIGNATION OF MONTEREY BAY AND THE SURROUNDING WATERS as the nation's largest marine sanctuary is one of the most significant conservation achievements of the 1990's. The remarkable richness and diversity of marine habitats within the sanctuary are evident to all who visit the coast. The jewel-like tide pools of Fitzgerald Marine Reserve, the raucous elephant seal breeding grounds at Año Nuevo Point and the teeming bird life at Elkhorn Slough are only some of the most obvious sights. The waters below hide even greater abundance: pastures of plankton that cloud the water in spring and summer, great spawning shoals of squid, silver schools of anchovies, dense kelp forests and a deep sea fauna we're only beginning to explore.

This rich natural history has shaped a cultural history built around prolific fisheries and steeped in the sea. And in recent decades, the sanctuary waters have become an important center of marine research, with a growing number of institutes, laboratories and educational institutions, including the Monterey Bay Aquarium, dotting the coast.

The Monterey Bay National Marine Sanctuary provides a haven for this diverse ocean life. But a marine sanctuary doesn't preserve an area in a pristine state. It serves instead as something akin to a wet national forest: it allows for multiple human uses of the resources here and seeks to sustain those resources for the future. Real protection of this sanctuary will come from implementation of strong laws to regulate activities within its boundaries and from effective research and education programs. Through research we can better understand the sanctuary's ecosystems and how they're affected by natural processes and human-induced pollution. Education, directed especially at the next generation, will help assure that future caretakers of the sanctuary are wise and knowledgeable environmental stewards.

This book is one step towards this goal of greater understanding. The culmination of a partnership between the sanctuary office and the aquarium, it grew out of course materials used to teach and inspire the aquarium's volunteer guides about the bay and its rich habitats and sealife. We hope it will inspire others to understand and care.

Why should we care? Because, ultimately, our own future is linked with the sea. From the air we breathe to world food supplies, the oceans provide vital services that sustain human life. Yet they encompass the largest and least-known habitats on Earth. Already, our activities are altering ocean systems in ways we don't understand. If we are to live in ways that will both sustain human needs and preserve Earth's natural systems, we must have a better understanding of life in the oceans. And, we must accord the marine environment the protection it deserves. I encourage you to become actively involved in protecting our oceans for future generations of ocean wildlife and humankind.

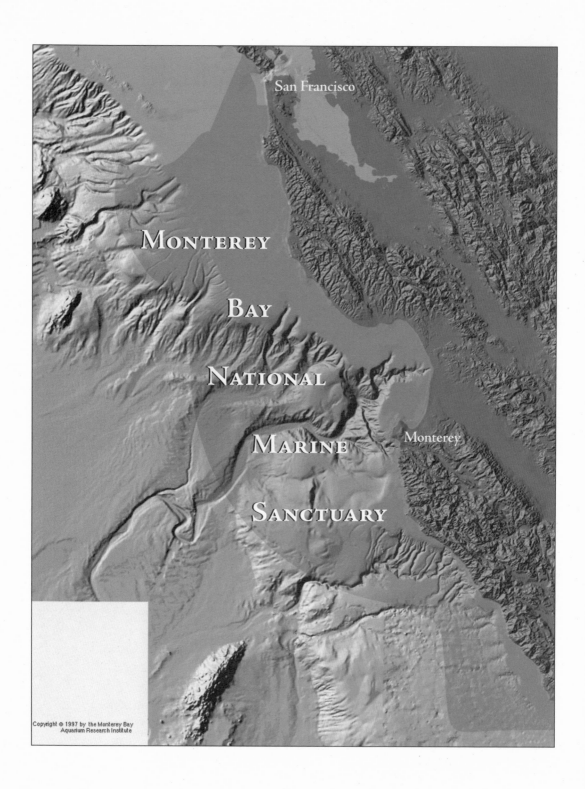

San Francisco

MONTEREY

BAY

NATIONAL

MARINE

SANCTUARY

Monterey

CHAPTER ONE

THE MONTEREY BAY NATIONAL MARINE SANCTUARY

*"Today, marine sanctuaries are places in the sea, as elusive as a sea breeze,
as tangible as a singing whale. They are beautiful, or priceless, or rare bargains,
or long-term assets, or fun, or all of these and more. Above all, sanctuaries
are now and with care will continue to be 'special places.' Each of us can have
the pleasures of defining what that means. "*

DR. SYLVIA EARLE

FROM DEEP WITHIN THE TURQUOISE WATERS of this
jewel in the nation's crown of sanctuaries, life radiates with the
ebb and flow of the tides. Gulls and pelicans soar overhead,
slicing through the sea mists on their long, gracefully arched
wings. Harbor seals lounging on offshore boulders exhale with audible
sighs. Forests of giant kelp undulate in the currents, while silver clouds of
fish sweep through the dappled light and darkness of the deep. Thousands of
colorful and camouflaged anemones, crabs, shrimp, urchins, and sea stars turn the
seafloor into a mosaic of undersea life.

Monterey Bay's aura of biological richness has shown brightly throughout the millennia. Only recently, however, have measures been taken to ensure that this light will continue to shine, brightening the lives of the many thousands of people who live, work, or travel along the central California coast. While it took nearly three decades to enact these measures, the wait was well worth it.

WHY MARINE SANCTUARIES?

IN THE PARTS OF THE WORLD where no protective actions have been taken, the life thriving in marine waters has waned. Along some parts of our country's ocean coast, sea life has been smothered by human pursuit of offshore oil and mineral deposits. And without catch limits or seasonal closures to control the takings, many local populations of shellfish, fish, and marine mammals have disappeared. At other sites, the very constituents of underwater habitats—limestone, for instance, from tropical coral reefs—have been taken for construction and road-building projects. Even where other sources of building materials are available, reefs have suffered: the Florida Department of Natural Resources estimates that, in the recent past, more than three tons of live coral and coral-encrusted rock were leaving Miami International Airport each day, bound for home aquariums and pet shop displays.

Just as detrimental to shoreline and offshore habitats are the pollutants stemming from land-based activities: the litter and debris from shipyards and marinas, contaminated runoff from roads and farmlands, toxic residues from the lawn- and garden-care products sold for home use. In many large coastal cities, outmoded sewer systems still mix wastewater with rainwater. These systems aren't big enough to carry the volumes that collect during strong storms, so some of the effluent (and along with it, everything from insulin syringes to Styrofoam cups) pours into the ocean without treatment. Add the barge loads of residential garbage and occasional barrels of nuclear waste that humankind intentionally dumps into the sea.

Confronted by this vast assortment of environmental threats, the scientists and policy-makers of several nations began to explore ways to save the world's oceans. Inspired by the existing network of national parks and preserves, they quickly embraced one solution: the establishment of marine sanctuaries, within which the impacts to ocean resources could be carefully monitored and controlled.

What better place to test this new concept than the Great Barrier Reef of Australia, the most massive coral cathedral on the face of the earth? Created in 1975, this 135,000-square-mile marine sanctuary off the coast of Queensland is the home to six different species of sea turtles, over 1,500 species of fish, 240 species of

birds and 350 species of hard coral. This unrivaled abundance lures visitors, as many as a thousand a day, from all corners of the globe.

Other world powers have followed Australia's lead, compiling a rich roster of places where underwater communities can thrive with minimal interference from humankind. Among the most recently protected locales are the crenelated coral formations of Tunku Abdul Rahman National Park in Malaysia, the sunken hillocks and valleys of Kenya's Shimoni Marine Park, the submerged plateau of Tubbataha Reef in the Philippines, and the isolated islands of the Galapagos.

U.S. SANCTUARIES AND SAFEGUARDS

IN THE UNITED STATES, the first federally established marine sanctuaries were dedicated in 1975, the same year that Australians celebrated the birth of their magnificent marine park. One of a pair of new federal protected areas, the *USS Monitor* National Marine Sanctuary, was little more than a dot on the map— one square nautical mile off the coast of North Carolina. Within this small reserve, which today remains under the care of the federal government, are the rusted remains of the legendary Civil War-era ironclad warship. The nation's second marine protected area, the 100-square-mile Key Largo National Marine Sanctuary off the coast of Florida, was considerably larger, bestowing protection on a sizable chunk of the third largest reef in the world. In recent years, this sanctuary and its sister preserve, the Looe Key National Marine Sanctuary, have merged, extending their protective boundaries over the full length of Florida's barrier reef, a distance of 220 miles (350 kilometers).

Guided by the Marine Protection, Research, and Sanctuaries Act and working from a master list of prospective sites, the U.S. Congress enacted legislation to create additional national marine sanctuaries, one or two at a time, off the coasts of California, Massachusetts, Texas, Georgia, Washington, Hawaii, and American Samoa. As of 1997, a pair of sites—the Northwest Straits in Washington and Thunder Bay in Michigan—were being considered for sanctuary designation. Formally approved, these two would raise the current total of national marine sanctuaries to fourteen.

Responsibility for the National Marine Sanctuary program lies within the Sanctuaries and Reserves Division of the Office of Ocean and Coastal Resources Management, a branch of the National Oceanic and Atmospheric Administration (NOAA). This division is also responsible for the overall management of sites once they become national marine sanctuaries. Written goals of the program encourage staff to "support and promote scientific research," "enhance public awareness," and "coordinate conservation and management of these regulatory authorities— protecting the conservation, recreational, ecological, educational, and aesthetic values of these important marine areas."

To be included in the sanctuary program, a site must possess certain natural or cultural resources. These can include unique or unusual natural habitats, sensitive or endangered animal species, and the presence of shipwrecks or other archaeological relics. It must also be determined that the protection and use of these resources will benefit from the comprehensive planning and management that sanctuary status brings. The socio-economic effects of sanctuary designation and the overall manageability of the site must also be explored.

As with nearly all federal programs, the principal user groups and the public at-large are invited to participate at various stages in the decision-making process. Naturally, not everyone shares the same vision for a prospective marine sanctuary; indeed, some individuals and interest groups may be actively opposed to such a notion, fearing that sanctuary regulations may place restrictions on fishing, seaweed or shellfish harvesting, and other commercial or recreational uses of a site.

Surprisingly, such views only strengthen the designation process, for it is only after all of the environmental and economic concerns are adequately addressed that a new national marine sanctuary can be born.

Sanctuary personnel prefer to speak softly but they can carry a big stick. The new rules they create seldom place limits on fishing or other existing uses of a sanctuary's resource (an exception is the Florida Keys National Marine Sanctuary, whose regulations prevent treasure hunters from removing relics from archaeologically

Chart of National Marine Sanctuaries

Monitor NMS   1975   one square nautical mile

Wreck of the Civil War ironclad, U.S.S. Monitor, which sank in 225 ft. of water.

Channel Islands NMS   1980   1,252 square nautical miles

Surrounds the four northern Channel Islands and Santa Barbara Island; rich kelp forests and fisheries resources; extensive pinniped and seabird assemblages; important migration corridor for gray, blue and humpback whales.

Gray's Reef NMS   1981   Approximately 17 square nautical miles

Submerged live bottom (limestone reef) area; highly productive and unusual habitat for a wide variety of corals, fishes, sea turtles, and other marine species; migratory passage for the Northern right whale.

Gulf of the Farallones NMS   1981   948 square nautical miles

Provides important habitat for pelagic fishes, plants, bottom-dwelling invertebrates, marine mammals; includes the largest concentration of breeding seabirds in the continental U.S..

Fagatele Bay NMS   1986   163 acres

Contains unique deepwater coral formations on a submerged volcano; habitat for a diverse array of tropical marine plants and animals, including endangered hawksbill and threatened green sea turtles.

Cordell Bank NMS   1989   397-square nautical miles

Granitic formation, providing habitat for an unusual assortment of marine fishes and subtidal invertebrate species, including colonies of purple hydrocorals.

Florida Keys NMS   1990   Approx. 2,600 square nautical miles

Coral reefs, seagrass beds, and related mangrove and other shoreline habitats of the Florida Keys ecosystem; encompassing previously established Key Largo and Looe Key National Marine Sanctuaries.

Flower Garden Banks NMS   1991   Approx. 42 square nautical miles

Two separate submerged features (the East and the West Flower Garden Banks) comprising the northernmost coral reefs on the North American continental shelf.

Monterey Bay NMS   1992   4,024 square nautical miles–

Currently, the largest National Marine Sanctuary. One of the deepest and largest submarine canyons on the west coast of North America, rich in natural resources; breeding, feeding and migration areas for over 26 species of marine mammals; significant prehistoric cultural sites as well as over 300 shipwrecks.

Stellwagen Bank NMS   1992   638 square nautical miles

Highly productive feeding and nursery grounds for more than a dozen cetacean species, including the endangered humpback, northern right, sei and fin whales.

Hawaiian Islands Humpback Whale NMS   1992   Approximately 1,300 square nautical miles

One of the major areas used by the endangered North Pacific population of humpback whales for breeding, calving, and nursing.

Olympic Coast NMS   1994   2,500 square nautical miles

Submarine canyons, marine mammals, seabirds, rich intertidal communities, fisheries, gray and humpback whale migration corridor.

The Monterey Bay Sanctuary's Key Rules

To protect the resources within the Monterey Bay National Marine Sanctuary, certain activities are prohibited:

➤ Exploring for, developing, or producing oil, gas, or mineral resources Designating new sites for the disposal of dredged materials

➤ Discharging or depositing any materials (with the exception of fish parts or bait used in fishing operations, water incidental to vessel operations, engine exhaust, or dredged materials for which the appropriate federal permits have been obtained)

➤ Moving, injuring, or possessing any historical resources

➤ Altering the sea bed or constructing any structures on the seabed (unless incidental to anchoring vessels, harbor maintenance, dock repairs, installation of navigation aids, fishing operations, or anchoring)

➤ Injuring or harassing marine mammals, sea turtles, or sea birds (unless permitted by regulations under the federal Marine Mammal Protection Act, Endangered Species Act and Migratory Bird Treaty Act)

➤ Flying motorized aircraft below 1,000 feet along portions of the coast

➤ Operating motorized personal watercraft (e.g. jet skis, water bikes, hovercraft, etc.) except within established operating areas

➤ Attracting white sharks by any means within State territorial waters of the Sanctuary.

Additional state-adopted restrictions (such as catch limits for fish and shellfish) are also enforced within the sanctuary.

important shipwrecks). Instead, they focus on activities that could lead to the injury, loss of, or destruction of these resources. Should this occur, violators may be penalized for their actions according to specific sanctuary regulations.

New rules are meaningful only if they can be enforced. As with many government branches, budgets are usually tight, so few sanctuary staff can be hired. Because of this, sanctuary managers often rely on the existing infrastructure of state-run and locally operated programs. For example, at the newly created Florida Keys National Marine Sanctuary, federal enforcement officers are assisted by members of the Florida State Marine Patrol, the U.S. Coast Guard, and the staff of John Pennekamp State Park, an extremely popular tourist destination at the sanctuary's northeasternmost tip.

Partnerships with area schools and environmental groups, like The Nature Conservancy and the Center for Marine Conservation, are equally helpful for informing people about sanctuary rules and fostering local support for resource protection.

MONTEREY BAY: A WEALTH OF HABITATS WORTH PROTECTING

ESTABLISHED BY CONGRESS IN 1992, the Monterey Bay National Marine Sanctuary is the largest federally protected area in the lower 48 states. Encompassing 5,300 square miles of open water (4,024 nautical miles), an area much larger than either Yellowstone or Yosemite national parks, its boundaries span nearshore and deep ocean habitats, extending from the high tide mark to as far as 53 miles (85 kilometers) offshore. The seaward boundary averages 30 miles (48 kilometers). Its landward edge spans one-fifth of the California coast, from Rocky Point, seven miles north of the Golden Gate Bridge in Marin Headlands, north of San Francisco, to a mile south of Cambria Rock, in San Luis Obispo County, due west of San Simeon— a distance of 360 miles (480 kilometers). The deepest point in the Sanctuary lies 10,663 feet (3,250 meters) below the surface in the Monterey Submarine Canyon, which is twice the depth than the Grand Canyon.

Sheer cliffs, wave-swept rocky beaches, and placid sandy beaches are all popular attractions with visitors to the sanctuary along the coasts of Monterey, Carmel, Big Sur, and Half Moon Bay. But more important, these coastal habitats afford important feeding, breeding, and resting areas for the many mammals, birds, reptiles, and amphibians that stop over or live here year-round. Some of their inhabitants, including the Santa Cruz long-toed salamander, are listed as endangered; others, like the California sea otter, are classified by wildlife authorities as "threatened" or "sensitive" species, warranting protection under state and federal law.

Offshore habitats are equally as varied and supportive of life. A stone's throw from shore, lush stands of 100-foot-tall giant kelp rise from the seafloor. These swaying pillars of Monterey Bay's underwater forest provide permanent or temporary shelter to an array of creatures—from tiny marine snails to silvery anchovies and leopard sharks. To the bay's resident population of California sea otters, the kelp forests serve as sun-dappled hunting grounds, rich with crabs, snails, urchins, octopus

and a multitude of fishes. This habitat once represented the last refuge for these marine mammals, who, at the turn of the century, were nearly eliminated by the fur traders' zeal to acquire the most luxurious of all animal pelts.

Farther from shore, the seafloor becomes a featureless field of sand and mud, a barren landscape that is occasionally broken by granite outcroppings, shale reefs, or the remains of shipwrecks. Colorful communities of fishes and invertebrates congregate in and around these structures. Sablefish, lingcod, boccaccio, jack mackerel, market squid, Pacific sardine and hake are only a few of the species of fish pursued by commercial and recreational fishermen. Yearly catches at the sanctuary's submerged sites are valued in the millions of dollars.

One of the most significant features of the offshore environment is also the least understood: a massive sunken canyon often likened to Arizona's Grand Canyon, although different in size. One of the deepest and largest submarine canyons on the west coast of North America, its eroded rock walls fan out from Moss Landing across Monterey Bay, meandering over 60 miles of seafloor, dipping down two miles into the oceanic abyss. Most of the creatures at this depth can be observed only by remote operating vehicles (ROVs) and state-of-the-art submersibles such as the *Alvin* or *Deep Rover*. Many, including the small, gray catsharks with highly reflective green eyes or the orange clusters of plump pincushion seastars, bear obvious resemblance to life forms in shallower seas. However, canyon dwellers such as the 90-foot-long siphonophore, a distant relative of the Portuguese man-o'-war jellyfish, look like aliens from another planet. On almost every expedition into the sanctuary's dark abyss, scientists gain insights and understanding into the mysteries of deep ocean life.

All told, the sanctuary boasts a vast diversity of sea life, with 26 species of marine mammals, 94 species of seabirds, 345 species of fish, 4 species of turtles, 31 phyla of invertebrates and more than 450 species of marine algae.

Cultural resources abound as well. Within the unpredictable waters of the sanctuary lie 1,276 reported shipwrecks, and along its shores, 718 prehistoric sites.

THE MONTEREY SANCTUARY IS BORN

THE ORIGINS OF THE MONTEREY BAY NATIONAL MARINE SANCTUARY can be traced to the late 1970s, when the State of California nominated Monterey Bay and nine other locales along the Pacific Ocean coast for consideration by the Sanctuaries and Reserves Division of NOAA. Three sites—the Monterey Bay area, the Channel Islands, and Point Reyes-Farallon Islands—were later selected from this list and, based on favorable public response, declared active candidates for designation.

Sanctuary status was bestowed on two of the candidates, which became the Channel Islands National Marine Sanctuary in 1980 and the Point Reyes-Farallon Islands National Marine Sanctuary (later renamed the Gulf of the Farallones National Marine Sanctuary) in 1981. However, demands on staff time from the two new sanctuaries thwarted any progress on the proposed Monterey Bay site. Recognizing that similar resources were already protected by California's two new sanctuaries and realizing that a sanctuary of Monterey Bay's size would carry an even heavier administrative burden, NOAA chose to drop this site from its list of active candidates in 1983.

NOAA's decision was unpopular with many California residents. They refused to let the idea of a sanctuary for Monterey Bay die. It took five years of grassroots campaigning and the tireless support of Congressman Leon Panetta before Congress directed NOAA to reinstate Monterey Bay as an active candidate for sanctuary status. After four more years of public meetings and preparation of several detailed planning documents, the actual ribbon-cutting ceremony for the Monterey Bay National Marine Sanctuary took place on September 21, 1992.

> **The Monterey Bay National Marine Sanctuary**
>
> *Phone:* (408) 647-4201
>
> *Fax:* (408) 647-4250
>
> *Email:*
> mbnms@ocean.nos.noaa.gov
>
> *WWW:*
> http://bonita.mbnms.nos.noaa.gov

The sanctuary's headquarters are presently located in Monterey. Entrusted with such a vast area of coastal ocean, and required to play host to thousands of sanctuary visitors each day, these hardworking government servants have wisely recruited outside help. A Sanctuary Advisory Council advises and assists the sanctuary manager and staff. A nonprofit organization has been established to help sanctuary programs and raise funds to supplement the sanctuary's budget. Sanctuary staff are also working with other nonprofit groups, regional chambers of commerce, visitors bureaus, hotels, and watersport businesses—important lines of contact for reaching people who might not have heard about sanctuary rules, state fishing and shellfishing regulations, or beach etiquette.

Hundreds of marine scientists at both public and private institutions around the bay provide an ideal framework for the sanctuary's research goals. By collaborating with these scientists and their students, sanctuary managers can inexpensively compile a detailed picture of the region's biological, geological, oceanographic, and cultural resources. This information will be crucial for making informed science-based decisions as the sanctuary's management plan continues to evolve.

Waves and fog along the California coast

CHAPTER TWO

OCEANOGRAPHY

"For all at last returns to the sea—to Oceanus, the ocean river, like the everflowing stream of time, the beginning and the end."

RACHEL CARSON, THE SEA AROUND US

IF YOU WALK THE BEACH ON A SUMMER DAY surrounded by a dense, gray fog, just skirting the cold and biting edge of the surf, your eyes automatically follow the tumbling waves back into the bay. Endlessly rolling and churning, they swell until finally breaking on the beach. What drives these powerful gray curtains of water? From what distant source did they originate? Where do the waves begin and the swells stop?

Why Is the Ocean Salty?

SEA WATER IS A COMBINATION of water and many dissolved materials, including inorganic substances like salts and gases as well as organic compounds from living organisms. Traces of almost all natural elements are found in sea water—even gold. This amalgam of materials is the accumulation of eons of solvent action by water on soil and land rocks, diffusion from the atmosphere, and substances from the earth's interior discharged into the ocean via underwater vents or outfall from volcanic activity. Of all these elements, chloride and sodium comprise about 85% of the solids and they're what gives sea water its salty taste.

To understand the bay, and the incredible diversity of life that dwells beneath these waves crashing at your feet, you need to know a little about the forces of nature at work. The ocean is constantly in motion, moving and mixing. While familiar processes like waves and tidal changes are readily visible, many physical forces we can't see profoundly influence atmospheric and ocean conditions. These agents of ocean movement are complex and sometimes unfamiliar processes including currents, global winds, the Coriolis effect, upwelling, downwelling and a global conveyor-belt of sorts. All of these complex physical processes are happening simultaneously—occurring over thousands of years or in only a microsecond. These phenomena, as well as heat from the Sun and the gravitational pull of the Sun and Moon on Earth, cause oceanic movements that affect not only the sanctuary but all the oceans and the atmosphere of this planet.

THE ATMOSPHERE AND THE OCEAN

BEFORE WE CAN UNDERSTAND MOTION IN THE OCEAN, we must understand the physical processes governing that motion—many of which are actually controlled by the atmosphere. Either directly or indirectly, all water movement is affected by the complex interaction of the atmosphere with the ocean. In constant contact, meeting of air and ocean affects surface temperatures, influences weather and climate, and creates most ocean waves and currents.

The atmosphere above Earth is not constant. In the form of high and low pressure areas, and their associated winds, it flows in large patterns molded by the seasonality of solar heating, and the rotation of the Earth. In the Northern Hemisphere, cold, dense air above the land masses of Canada and Siberia sinks and forms areas of high atmospheric pressure above the northern continents. Air over the Bering Sea, which is warmer than the adjacent land masses, form an area of low atmospheric pressure. Air naturally flows parallel with lines of equal pressure, with the highest pressure on the right.

The distribution of highs and lows changes with the seasons as well as on shorter daily or weekly time scales, leading to storms and other changes in our weather. Sometimes, these general patterns of atmospheric circulation changes are dramatic and long-lasting. The Southern Oscillation is one such shift, as is El Niño. During El Niño, the atmosphere shifts from the normally low atmospheric pressure over the western Pacific and normally high pressure over the eastern Pacific. This reverses or weakens the trade winds, which in turn influences the flow of currents and causes warm, nutrient-poor El Niño currents to flow eastward to South America. El Niño and Southern Oscillation events are so frequently linked that they are commonly referred to as ENSO phenomena.

Other long-term shifts in atmospheric pressure patterns have only recently been noticed and studied. These patterns can occur in seasonal cycles that seem to repeat themselves year after year, and on time scales lasting ten to twenty years. A major cause of changes in global heat distribution, it can take an entire decade for equilibrium to be restored. While oceans were once thought to be a steadying influence on climate, it's possible that they are linked to long-term and abrupt climate shifts and indicate other pending climate changes. The global scale of these shifts affect the entire planet, including Monterey Bay.

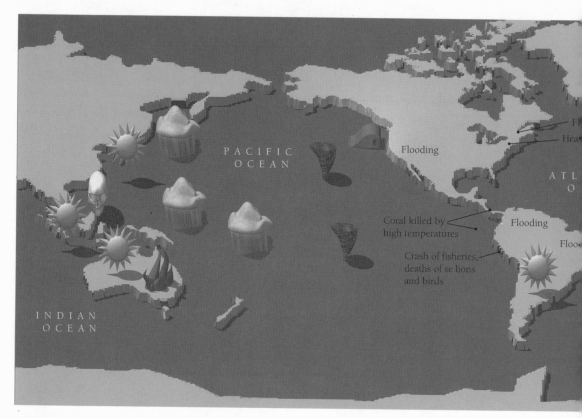

Flooding

ATL
O

Coral killed by
high temperatures

Flooding

Floo

Crash of fisheries,
deaths of se lions
and birds

PACIFIC
OCEAN

Flooding

Fl
Hea

INDIAN
OCEAN

Cyclones

Drought

Famine

Fire

Heavy
rainfall

High surf

Events linked to El Niño

What is El Niño?

EL NIÑO is the term for unusual oceanic and atmospheric conditions in the eastern tropical Pacific Ocean. Typically in the eastern Pacific, cold, nutrient-rich water wells up along the South American coast. During an El Niño however, westward-blowing tradewinds subside and warm water slowly moves eastward along the Equator, interrupting the cold-water upwelling. Although originating in the tropical Pacific, El Niño events have global ramifications and influence oceanographic, atmospheric, biological, and economic conditions around the world.

First noticed in Peru almost 500 years ago, El Niño—Spanish for "The Child"—was so-named because it usually occurred around Christmas time. Its counterpart, unusual cooling of the eastern tropical Pacific, is called La Niña. Historically, El Niño referred only to a warm current that moves along the coasts of Ecuador and Peru and its disastrous effects—reduced harvests of fish and seabird guano, coastal erosion and flooding, and rain-induced hordes of insects. It wasn't until recently however that scientists began to realize the global significance of El Niño's climatic anomalies.

Locally, El Niño impacts the sanctuary with warmer surface waters low in nutrients, higher than normal sea levels, and sometimes sweeps uncommon plants and animals into the area. Although El Niños usually occur in this region every three to five years, with a major event about every ten years, they don't always cause the same conditions. One year an

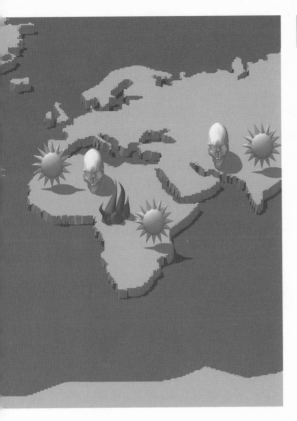

LOCAL WEATHER

THE WEATHER around the shores of the sanctuary is milder than in the country's, interior, moderated by the neighboring ocean. Usually, annual temperatures range only from 50°F to 60°F. Local weather is dominated by interactions between the North Pacific High Pressure System and the Aleutian Low Pressure System. The North Pacific High Pressure area is a large, sausage-shaped mass of air that lies off the southwestern United States and extends across much of the North Pacific Ocean. It moves north and south in response to the seasons and other conditions, and as it moves, it affects local weather.

Like all high-pressure areas in the Northern Hemisphere, the North Pacific High Pressure System produces southward winds on its eastern side, adjacent to the North American coast. During the spring, the system grows stronger and expands northward producing powerful coastal winds conducive to ocean upwelling. These winds frequently continue into the fall. But as many locals know, atmospheric storm systems moving into the sanctuary often cause daily to weekly fluctuations in local winds and temporary changes in upwelling intensity.

The Aleutian Low Pressure System is an area of low atmospheric pressure centered in the Bering Sea. In the winter, the pressure drops and the low expands southward, pinning the sanctuary between the North Pacific High and the Aleutian Low. In the summer, the sanctuary is on the

El Niño may mean abundant rains, but the next occurrence might produce a drought.

El Niño's large-scale changes of atmospheric and oceanographic conditions are now believed to influence a variety of global weather events including torrential rainfall, devastating droughts, and searing heatwaves. Dust storms in Australia, drought in India and brush fires in Ghana are just a few of the problems attributed to its climatic changes. El Niños can also be biologically and economically damaging. Fishery failures in South America impact the world food market and have other far-reaching effects. As a result of the 1972–1973 El Niño, anchovy availability declined causing a permanent switch from anchovy meal to more soy meal. This change initiated the clearing of vast sections of the Amazon rainforest and North American wetlands for agriculture.

eastern edge of the North Pacific High and is not influenced by the Aleutian Low. The seasonal interaction between these two pressure systems usually causes winds that tend to blow southward in the summer.but eastward in the winter.

Seasons in the sanctuary are generally less distinct than those of other locations, particularly on the East Coast. Winters tend to be wet, summers are dry. Most of the rain falls in January and February, while July and August often are completely dry. Even these rainfall patterns vary strongly from year to year, as well as from location to location. For example, Monterey receives an average of about 15 inches (38 centimeters) annually, while 45 miles (72 kilometers) away in Santa Cruz, the rainfall averages about 28 inches (71 centimeters) each year.

During the spring and summer, fog is a common seasonal occurrence in the sanctuary. Heavy in the morning, it tends to clear as the air warms during the afternoon. Fog is created when the moist maritime air is cooled by the cold, upwelled water along the coast.

WAVES & TIDES

LIKE SEASONAL FOG, waves and tides are obvious to all who visit the shores of the sanctuary, and result from the many forces contributing to the continuous circulation of the ocean.

For most of us, surface waves are perhaps the most familiar of the ocean's complex movements. Wind blowing over the water's surface forms the waves. Size is determined by the wind's speed, duration, and span of water (or fetch) over which the wind blows. Strong winds blowing for long periods build larger waves. Varying in size from tiny ripples to monumental storm waves as high as 90 feet (27 meters), waves move away from the area where they form and help to mix surface waters.

Tides are another facet of ocean circulation familiar to most of us. Tides are the periodic rising and falling of the ocean caused by the gravitational pull of the Moon and the Sun and by Earth's rotation. Tides usually range from two to ten feet (less than one to three meters), although they can reach over 50 feet (15 meters) in some enclosed coastal regions such as the Bay of Fundy in eastern Canada. In Monterey Bay, the typical tidal range is about three to six feet (one to two meters).

There are two general tidal periods. The semidiurnal tide produces two high-water and two low-water tides in a period slightly longer than one day. Diurnal, or daily tides have only one high-water and one low-water tide per day. We experience mixed tides in the sanctuary. That is, we see approximately two high-water phases and two low-water phases each day, but the consecutive highs have different heights, which is obvious when you look at a typical tide table for this area.

SURFACE CURRENTS

WHILE WAVES AND TIDES ARE POWERFUL FORCES of ocean circulation, it's surface currents, powered by the warmth of the Sun and the force of the winds, that are the most dynamic water mixers. Some surface currents are swift and river-like, bearing distinct boundaries; others are slow-moving and diffuse. As they circulate, they influence weather and climate, spread nutrients and organisms, and transfer heat from tropical to polar regions.

Surface currents are largely the result of the frictional drag of the wind on the ocean's surface. The primary global surface currents are formed in conjunction with the earth's major wind currents. In the Northern Hemisphere, three major wind belts affect currents: 1) the trade winds in the tropics blowing from northeast to southwest,

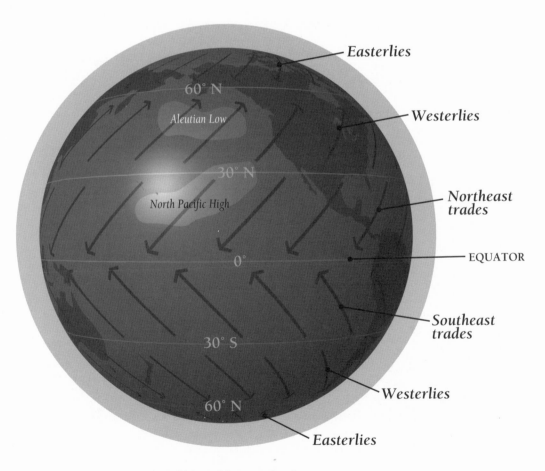

Major wind belts and their prevailing directions

within about 30 degrees of the equator; 2) the westerlies of the middle latitudes, which blow primarily from the west to southwest; and 3) the polar easterlies that blow from the east at very high latitudes. The southern hemisphere has a mirror-image counterpart of all these wind belts. These wind belts and the currents they create have a significant effect on the rate of heat transfer from tropical to polar areas, and on the distribution of the marine life.

Surface currents effectively distribute many more things than the plants and animals that live in the sea—they carry oil spills, sewage and, in a well-chronicled mishap, even shoes. In May 1990, a freighter traveling from Korea to Seattle accidentally spilled 60,000 pairs of athletic shoes into the North Pacific Ocean. The sneakers floated east, and by that winter began to wash up on the beaches of Washington, Oregon and British Columbia. By early 1993, some of the same shoes were washing up on Hawaiian beaches. This "shoe spill" was the largest at-sea release of human-made objects to date, and it provided oceanographers with valuable new information for charting the movements of ocean surface currents.

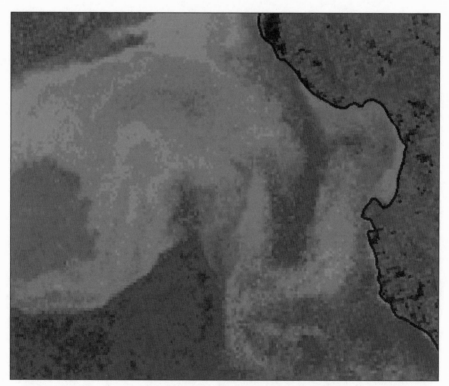

Satellite "ocean color" image of chlorophyll, an indicator of plant plankton. The differences in light and dark areas represent different concentrations of plant plankton. The light gray areas are chockfull of plants; the dark gray areas aren't. Higher concentrations are generally found in recently upwelled nutrient-rich water.

Contrary to what you might think, currents pushed by the winds do not move parallel to the wind. The rotation of Earth causes water, or artillery shells, footballs and anything else in motion, to drift sideways due to a phenomenon called the Coriolis effect. The Coriolis effect deflects surface currents to the right of the wind in the Northern Hemisphere, and to the left in the Southern Hemisphere (but does not affect the direction your toilet bowl water flushes!). The net effect of this pattern of deflection is a system of wind-driven surface currents that flow primarily in an east-west direction. Periodically, however, exceptional surface currents arise which do not flow in the prescribed manner; Monsoon currents in the northern Indian Ocean and the periodic El Niño currents of the Pacific are familiar examples. Along the California coast, the Coriolis effect teams with the predominantly southward winds to create an offshore surface current and a vertical water movement called upwelling.

UPWELLING AND DOWNWELLING

WATER IN THE OCEAN does not just move horizontally. It also moves from the surface to the depths and back to the surface. Most vertical water movements are caused by water masses sinking and upwelling. The Coriolis effect on the predominantly southward winds along California creates an offshore surface current. The upwelling process moves nutrient-rich colder water closer to the surface, where it replaces the original surface waters. You'll find upwelling in coastal regions along the eastern boundaries of all ocean basins. It was once thought that the Monterey Canyon itself was the source of most of the bay's upwelling. However, there's very little evidence to support that theory and scientists no longer believe that the principal source of upwelling comes from deep within the canyon. The cold waters in the bay actually upwell near Año Nuevo and then move south into the bay, and so are a product of traditional coastal upwelling.

A counterpart to the phenomenon of upwelling is the process of downwelling. Near Monterey Bay, for example, although the winds generally blow from the northwest, storms and other atmospheric conditions can cause winds near the earth's surface to slow down, or relax, and even reverse direction. As more water piles up at the coast, a downward vertical movement develops. Downwelling moves surface water into deeper parts of the ocean, and also moves warmer water closer to the coast.

OCEAN LAYERS

DESPITE THE HORIZONTAL AND VERTICAL MOVEMENT of ocean water, the ocean still tends to separate according to the different densities of the water masses. More simply put, the ocean can be divided into three layers: the surface layer, the intermediate layer, and the deep and bottom layer.

The warm surface layer extends as far down as 660 feet (201 meters), although in the Monterey Bay area it is more typically about 30 to 150 feet (9 to 45 meters), depending on the season and recent solar heating and wind conditions. Sometimes called the mixed layer, it is regularly mixed by wind, waves, and currents. The intermediate layer occurs to a depth of about 5,000 feet (1,500 meters) and contains the main thermocline, a zone of transition between the warmer waters above and the colder waters below. The main thermocline is a much more massive version of the smaller thermoclines often encountered by scuba divers swimming through sudden temperature changes when descending or rising in the water. The deep and bottom layers begin below about 5,000 feet (1,500 meters).They are uniformly cold, usually less than 39°F, and contain the oceans' densest waters.

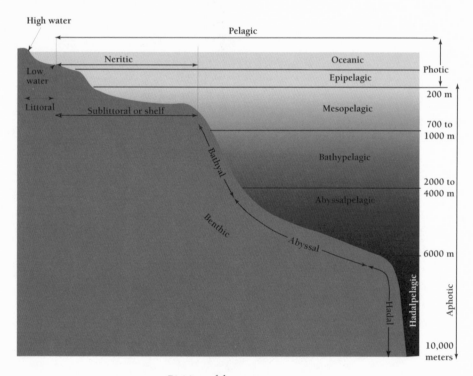

Divisions of the ocean

THE CALIFORNIA CURRENT

IN THE SANCTUARY AND IN MONTEREY BAY, many complicated and intricately connected processes affect ocean movement and circulation. Of all these, the California Current has a great impact on local ocean, weather and atmosphere.

The California Current is an eastern boundary current that is part of the vast clockwise circulation of the north Pacific Ocean. At higher latitudes, water moves eastward across the Pacific, driven by the force of the prevailing wind field. Near the coast of North America this flow divides into two branches. One branch flows northward toward the Gulf of Alaska. The other branch forms the California Current.

The California Current is a generally southward movement of cool surface water along the West Coast of the United States. It is accompanied by the nearshore California Undercurrent which flows northward underneath the California Current. Although once thought to be shallow, slow and constant, recent studies suggest that in reality the California Current is much more complex and highly changeable.

The major Pacific Ocean surface current systems

Scientists have found that the California Current is simultaneously variable and dynamic. Its meandering flow is embedded with rotating eddies and injected with rapidly flowing jets—it is anything but a solid, uniform movement of water. Instead, at various locations, particularly in offshore regions, the current flows south, while in other areas its flow is oriented perpendicular to the coast. At certain times, and in some locations, parts of the current flow northward. At any time, currents only a few miles apart can be flowing in opposite directions.

The California Current transports water low in salinity and temperature but high in nutrients and dissolved oxygen from subarctic regions toward the tropics. As it continues south, it mixes with warmer and saltier subtropical water from the west and south. All this energetic movement causes waters of contrasting temperatures and salinities to collide, creating powerful ocean fronts that serve as collectors of marine life—both predators and prey.

Concentrations of phytoplankton and zooplankton mark the areas where water types flow together and interact. This moving aquatic "salad bar" attracts animals that feed on the plankton, which in turn attracts many other types of predators, including people.

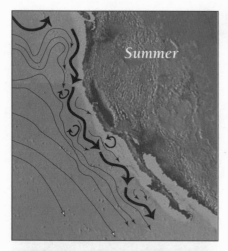

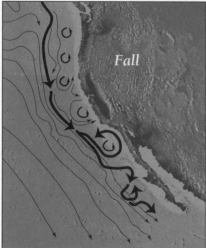

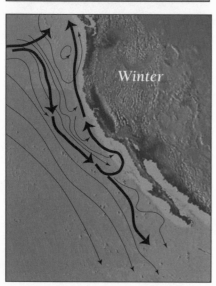

Seasonal variations in California Current

A CURRENT FOR ALL SEASONS

As MARK TWAIN OBSERVED, "Everybody talks about the weather but nobody does anything about it," and if you're a resident or a frequent visitor to the sanctuary, you're probably familiar with certain seasonal stereotypes discussed by locals and tourists alike. Summer is "foggy, cold, and windy." Fall—always described as "our best season"—is sunny and clear. Winter is "rainy with brief periods of clear skies."

These three weather "seasons" are largely controlled by annual variations in the atmosphere, especially changes in the winds that blow along the central California coastline. Due to the complexities of the California Current and variations in the weather, it's not completely accurate to assign specific and sharply defined "seasons" to water movements in the sanctuary. Nonetheless, three patterns of movement are generally associated with these seasons, and it's convenient to term these patterns the upwelling period, the oceanic period, and the Davidson Current period. Handy as these monikers are, it's important to remember that any of the conditions ascribed to these three periods can and do occur every month of the year in the sanctuary.

The upwelling period, also called the cold-water phase, occurs from spring to late summer, when cool, upwelled surface waters prevail in the bay. The surface water temperature generally ranges from 50°F to 55°F and the cold water chills the overlying air, contributing to fog banks and cool summers near the coast.

From late summer to early fall, during the oceanic period or warm-water phase, warm offshore water flows into the bay as the winds that bring upwelling gradually subside. The winds are weak and usually the water surface temperatures are at their highest during this period, ranging up to 60°F.

During the Davidson Current period, referred to as the low thermal gradient phase by the more esoteric,

22

SPRING AND SUMMER
(March-July)
*In spring and summer, temperatures in
the outer bay often drop into the 50s.
That is when driving winds push
warm surface water offshore, allowing
colder water from below to rise up in
its place.*

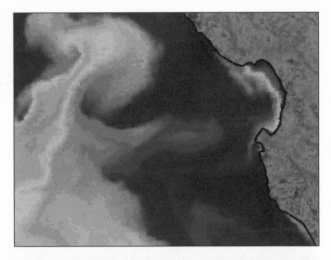

the current is northward and
surface temperatures are fairly
uniform throughout the area.
Some oceanographers believe
this current, once popularly
called the Davidson Current, is
better described as a surface
flow reversal of the California
Undercurrent. Regardless of
terminology, this period is
associated with our rainy season
lasting from late fall through the
winter and with highly variable
winds caused by storms.

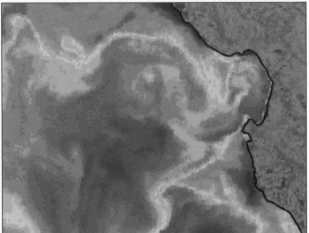

FALL
(August-October)
*When coastal winds subside in fall,
warm water from miles out in the
Pacific flows into the outer bay. Still,
65 degrees is about as warm as it gets.*

WINTER
(November-February)
*During winter, a north-flowing current
sweeps into the outer bay, bringing
relatively warm water close to shore.
Temperatures range between 50 and 60
degrees.*

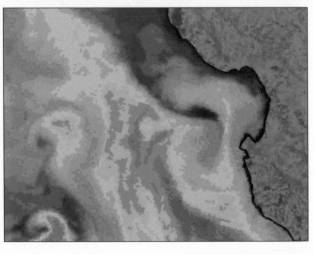

*These satellite pictures show how surface water
in the outer bay changes temperature from
season to season: the water is coldest during
spring and summer.*

CIRCULATION IN THE BAY

TO SOME DEGREE, water circulation in Monterey Bay is an extension of the
California Current and of the effects of coastal upwelling. While the bay's circulation
is influenced by a variety of processes, including internal waves, tides, local heating
and river discharge, water circulation in the outer part of the bay is a continuation
of the southward flow of local upwelled water and the California Current. When
offshore winds are steady, the water in the upper 300 feet (90 meters) in the
"pocket" of the bay circulates around the bay in a clock-wise fashion. However,
when the winds change direction or weaken, the recirculation pattern can become
complicated or even reversed.

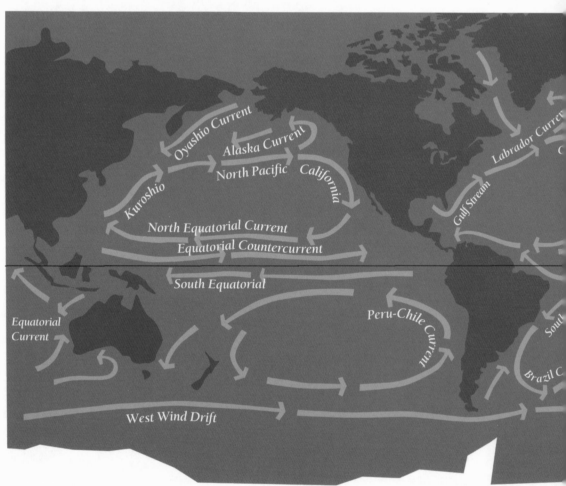

THE GLOBAL WEB OF OCEAN CURRENTS

THE BAY IS NOT A CLOSED SYSTEM. When you dip your toe in Monterey Bay, you are linked to all the world's oceans because the earth's sea water is basically one continuous mass. Not stationary nor uniform, major ocean current systems move surface waters around the planet driven by the major wind belts.

Major ocean currents are not a recent discovery. Ancient sailors were familiar with the currents, and as early as the fifteenth century used them to speed ocean crossings. By 1753, even non-sailors like Benjamin Franklin were knowledgeable about the power of these currents. While serving as America's first postmaster, Franklin noticed that it took mail ships two weeks longer to return from Europe than it took them to get there. After questioning expert sea captains about surface currents, Franklin learned that outbound ships sailing with the Gulf Stream gained

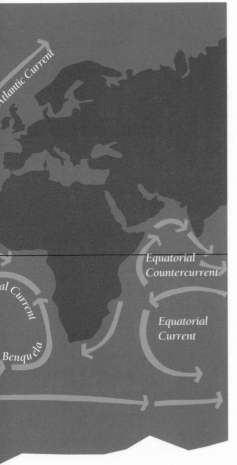

Eastern Boundary Currents

EASTERN BOUNDARY CURRENTS, such as the California Current, form at the eastern edge of ocean basins along the west coast of continents. Generally, these currents are broad, slow-moving, and carry cold, upwelled water toward the equator. This upwelled water is rich in nutrients and supports a variety of marine life.

This abundance of marine life makes eastern boundary currents biologically and ecologically important. Some of the richest fishing grounds on the planet occur in the four eastern boundary currents. These major currents—the California Current off western North America, the Canary Current off the Iberian Peninsula and northwestern Africa, the Benguela Current off southwestern Africa, the Peru–Chile(or Humboldt) Current off western South America—account for almost half of the world's fisheries' catch.

The flow of eastern boundary currents compensates for the faster poleward-moving western boundary currents, such as the Kuroshio in the north Pacific and the Gulf Stream off the eastern United States.

The eastern and western boundary currents are connected in a number of gyres, the large elliptical circles of circulation which dominate ocean surface flow and contribute to the movement of the ocean conveyor belt.

The major Pacific Ocean surface current systems

The Global Conveyor Belt

In addition to surface currents, water moves through the deep ocean. Termed thermohaline circulation by oceanographers, this deep-water movement is driven primarily by heat and salinity differences, while the Coriolis effect, gravity and friction shape its direction and volume. Thermohaline circulation moves water like a global conveyor belt re-distributing solar heat from the tropics to the poles.

The conveyor belt begins with dense, cool water that sinks, or forms, near the poles, then travels through the deepest reaches of the oceans and surfaces in the Pacific, Atlantic and Indian Oceans. It continues along the surface back to the poles where it sinks once again. As it transports huge volumes of water around the planet, the conveyor belt also moves tremendous amounts of heat, which dramatically affects the climate of the continents. In western Europe, for example, the climate is milder than off eastern Canada at the same latitudes because the Gulf Stream transports warm water from the Caribbean and the North Atlantic to the European continent.

During periods of large scalel warming or cooling, the global conveyor belt redistributes heat around the globe, mitigating the effect of changing air temperature on land masses. It also helps to move carbon dioxide from surface waters to the deep ocean, thereby reducing the concentration of the gas in the atmosphere. Additionally, it contributes to the important effects of upwelling. As the belt moves water masses, it also moves great amounts of oxygen and nutrients from cold, deep water up to the sunlit surface waters. This upwelling creates ideal growing conditions for a variety of marine life, and many animals take advantage of these extra nutrients by breeding during periods of peak upwelling.

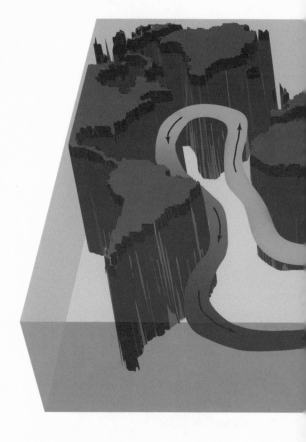

speed, but returning ships lost speed as they struggled against it. Franklin subsequently published the first nautical chart of the Gulf Stream and included instructions on how to avoid it when sailing back from Europe.

Major surface currents move enormous volumes of water that both affect and are affected by the world's climate. They move huge masses of warm water to cold regions and return to warm regions with cold water. As these currents flow along the edges of ocean basins, they combine to form gyres (from the Greek

gyros meaning circle). Gyres are typically a combination of a western boundary current, an eastern boundary current and two transverse currents. For example, the California Current, the Kuroshio Current, the North Pacific and North Equatorial Current combine to form the North Pacific Gyre.

To comprehend the complexities of the ocean, it's vitally important to understand how its physical factors are intricately woven into an elaborate matrix of patterns, cycles, and long-term changes affecting every living thing on Earth. With our persistent consumption of resources and our escalating global population, we continue to stress the marine environment and affect the ocean and atmosphere on a planetary scale. Without a requisite understanding of physical oceanography, it will be impossible to ever control or balance or possibly repair the damage already done by marine pollution, habitat destruction, ozone depletion and global warming.

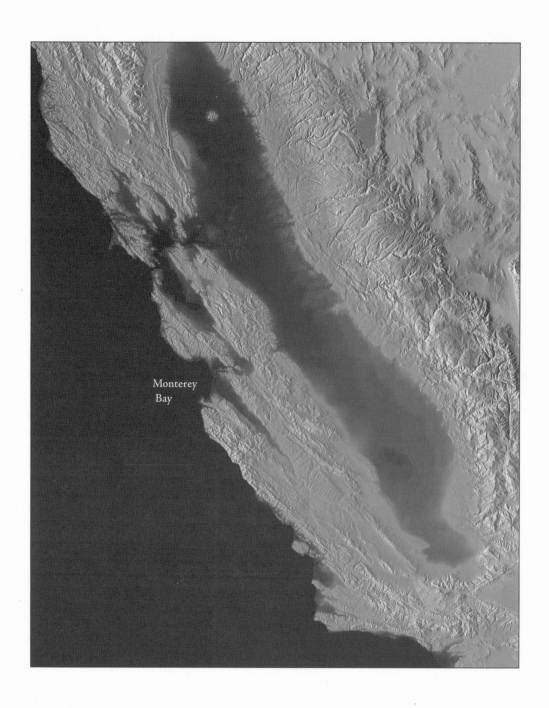

Monterey
Bay

CHAPTER THREE

GEOLOGY

"All the coast passed this day is very bold, there is a great swell and the land is very high. There are mountains which seem to reach the heavens and the sea beats on them, sailing along close to land, it appears as though they would fall on the ships... At their beginning there is a cape which projects into the sea which they named Cabo de Nieve (Cypress Point)."

CABRILLO, 1542

THE CYPRESS POINT OF CABRILLO'S EXPEDITION could easily refer to the promontory of land we call the Monterey Peninsula. If you visit Monterey on a sunny summer day, take a stroll through Shoreline Park along the seaside path just west of the Monterey Bay Aquarium and Stanford University's Hopkins Marine Station. As you look out at the water, what probably catches your eye first is its constant motion. An endless series of waves comes rolling in from the sea, breaking and washing up onto the beaches or crashing against the rocks. If you pause on one of the granite outcrops, letting the sea breeze wash over you, smelling the salt air and watching the motion of the waves, the whole ocean seems to be a maelstrom of ceaseless activity. Direct your gaze landward, and the contrast couldn't be more striking.

While the ocean teems with energy, the land seems remarkably static. The bluffs that loom above the water seem impervious to the waves beating against them, and the gnarled cypress trees, looking like oversize bonsai, seem as though they've been growing out of their perches atop the weathered granite for eternity. But contrary to appearances, the land is not motionless. Even as you stand there surveying the scene, the landscape around you is changing.

On scales ranging from a single grain of sand to the entire continent, the earth and rock around and under you are in motion. Each breaker that sweeps up the beach pushes some grains of sand a little farther along. Each wave that crashes into a rocky headland erodes just a tiny bit more from the cliffs. And, when the gigantic tectonic plates of the earth's crust lurch past each other in an earthquake, the coastal mountains are boosted upward and the entire Monterey Bay edges northward.

It is the motion of the tectonic plates that has brought the coast of central California to its present location. Sandwiched between two major fault zones, the bay and surrounding land have been slowly moving north along the west coast of the continent for millions of years. Were you to journey back in time far enough, you would not even find a Monterey Bay. Step forward into the future far enough, and you would again enter a world without the bay. For all its seeming permanence, Monterey Bay will ultimately prove to be little more than a shimmering jewel glimpsed during a brief moment of geologic time.

During the time Monterey Bay has existed, the forces of nature have worked ceaselessly to modify the landscape, eroding the mountains even as tectonic forces push them skyward, building sandy beaches, sculpting cliffs and carving the immense submarine canyons, in a complex interaction of geologic energy with wind and rain and sun.

The varied landscape that you see when you visit the sanctuary is part of the thin outer layer of the earth called the "crust." In comparison to the rest of the planet, the crust is about as thick as the skin of an onion. But the overall structure of Earth is perhaps more like that of a cantaloupe than an onion. Deep in the center of the earth, where a cantaloupe would be filled with seeds, is the "core." The core is a dense ball composed mainly of iron and nickel and measuring roughly 4,000 miles (6,440 kilometer) in diameter. Geophysicists believe that the inner core is solid and the outer core fluid. Surrounding the outer core, where the succulent flesh of the cantaloupe would be found, lies the "mantle," a not-so-succulent layer of mostly solid iron- and magnesium-rich rock about 1,800 miles (2,898 kilometers) thick. Wrapped around the mantle is the crust, which at its greatest is probably never more than about 40 miles (64 kilometers) thick. But unlike either the rind of a cantaloupe or the skin of an onion, the crust of the earth is not seamless.

The Earth's crust is broken into large pieces called "plates." Seven huge plates cover most of the Earth's surface, with the rest covered by about a dozen smaller ones. The larger plates are immense. Almost all of North America, along with a healthy portion of the northern Atlantic Ocean, sits on just a single plate. All the plates are constantly shifting around, their motion generally thought to be related to slowly moving currents in the mantle. Although the mantle is mostly solid, it is still capable of flow, albeit at a pace that makes a snail look speedy. But because the entire surface of the globe is covered with plates, their movement is restricted. Like guests standing shoulder to shoulder at a crowded cocktail party, it is impossible for one plate to move without jostling another.

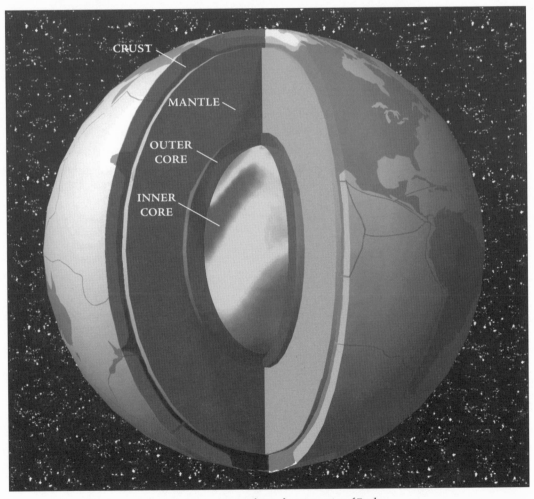

An artistic rendition of a cross-section of Earth.

CONTINENTS UNDER CONSTRUCTION

AS THE PLATES SHOULDER THEIR WAY ACROSS THE SURFACE OF THE PLANET, they interact along their boundaries in one of three ways: bumping into or squeezing past each other or splitting apart. Just what happens along a boundary where plates meet depends partly on whether the plates involved are composed of oceanic or continental crust.

Oceanic crust is mainly basalt, produced by partial melting of the mantle. It is darker (almost black) and heavier than continental crust because it contains much greater amounts of dark, dense minerals rich in iron and magnesium. Basalt is most commonly extruded onto the ocean floor at long, high ridges that form where plates are pulling apart. Called "spreading centers," these ridges are plate boundaries where new oceanic crust is created.

As new oceanic crust forms at a spreading center, old oceanic crust is being consumed elsewhere, at a plate boundary called a "subduction zone." A subduction zone forms where plates collide and one plate is shoved beneath the other. When continental and oceanic crust collide, the lighter continental crust rides up over the denser oceanic crust, which is forced down through the crust and into the mantle.

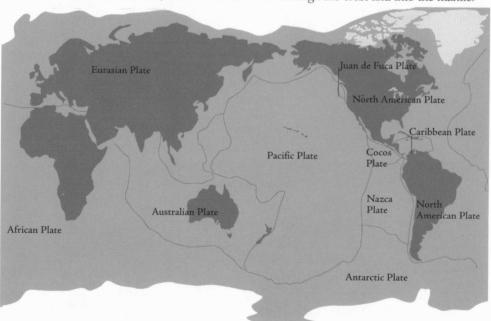

The surface of the earth is broken into constantly shifting "plates."

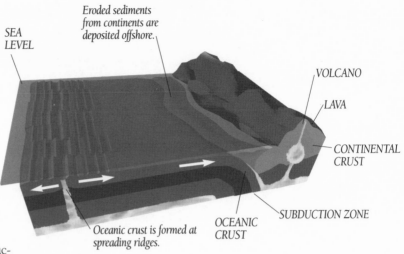

Volcanic activity and earthquakes deep within the earth are associated with collisions of spreading centers and plate boundaries.

SEA LEVEL

Eroded sediments from continents are deposited offshore.

VOLCANO

LAVA

CONTINENTAL CRUST

Oceanic crust is formed at spreading ridges.

OCEANIC CRUST

SUBDUCTION ZONE

Even as subduction consumes old oceanic crust, it also produces new continental crust, in a continuing cycle of creation born of destruction. As the old ocean floor sinks into the mantle, it heats up, and materials with low melting points liquefy into magma (molten rock formed within the earth). The relatively buoyant magma moves upward along fractures in the continental crust. As it journeys upward, its heat melts some of the nearby crust, adding to the magma and altering its composition. Continental crust thus has a much more complex history and variable composition than oceanic crust, but in general the continental crust, also called "granitic crust," is rich in silicon and aluminum, making it lighter in color and less dense than basalt. Sometimes the magma is extruded onto the surface as lava; other times it cools and solidifies while still underground. Granitic magma that cooled underground is what formed the extensive granite rock of the Sierra Nevada and the granitic outcrops around Monterey. Magma that is still working its way to the surface is what fuels the volcanoes of the Cascade Range, like Mount St. Helens.

Subduction also produces continental crust in another way. As the ocean floor travels from a spreading center to its eventual demise in a subduction zone, particles of sediment settle onto the seafloor and accumulate on top of the basalt. When the seafloor is subducted under a continent, the dense basalt sinks into the mantle and the sediments on top of the basalt are scraped off by the continental crust, piling up like snow before a snowplow. One of the principal rock formations along the California coast, the Franciscan Assemblage, formed in such an "accretionary wedge."

Two plates trying to move past each other have a third effect. As they grind along "rubbing shoulders," a transform, or strike-slip, fault develops and slices across the landscape. Usually the transform boundary so formed consists not of a single fault, but a whole system of staggered, parallel faults, all showing movement in the same direction. The San Andreas fault is one such fault.

Fault Types

A FAULT IS A BREAK OR FRACTURE IN ROCK along which there has been movement of one side relative to the other.

Geologists use the direction of movement on the fault plane to classify a fault. A fault with mainly vertical motion is called a dip-slip fault, whereas a fault that shows mostly horizontal motion is called a strike-slip, or transform fault.

The terms dip-slip and strike-slip derive from the way geologists describe the orientation of a planar surface. The intersection of a planar surface with an imaginary horizontal plane is called the strike, thus a fault with horizontal movement is called a strike-slip fault. The direction of the steepest slope on a surface is called the dip, so a fault with vertical movement is called a dip-slip fault. Strike and dip are always perpendicular.

There are two types of dip-slip faults. When a body of rock is being pulled apart, like at a spreading center ridge, the movement on a fault is of the rock on either side of the fault moving away from the other side. Such faults are called normal faults, and result in a lengthening of the rock body. When a rock body is being compressed, the movement on a fault tends to shove one side over the other, resulting in shortening of the rock body. This is called a reverse fault.

Strike-slip faults, too, categorized according to the direction of motion along the fault plane. The way to determine motion on a strike-slip fault is to look at

something that's been offset by the fault; a fence, road, or stream. Imagine yourself standing on one side of a fault, by an offset fence. Look across the fault to the location of the fence on the other side. If the fence on the other side of the fault is to your right, the movement on the fault is right-lateral. If the fence is to your left, the movement is left-lateral. Were you to cross over the fault and look at things again, the sense of motion would remain the same. Try it with the illustration, just by rotating the book to alter your vantage point.

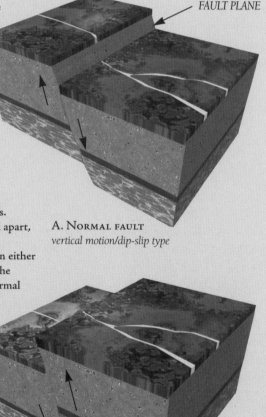

FAULT PLANE

A. NORMAL FAULT
vertical motion/dip-slip type

B. REVERSE FAULT
vertical motion/dip-slip type

Faults occur on all scales, from the megascopic scale of tectonic plates to the microscopic dislocations in the structure of a single crystal. In general, the larger a fault is, the more complex it is. Large faults usually don't have a single discrete fault plane, but produce a fault zone, consisting of a band of broken and sheared rock, sometimes over a half-mile (or a kilometer) wide. Most of the major faults along the transform boundary between the North American and Pacific plates are more accurately described as fault zones. Taken together, all these fault zones constitute a larger fault system, (the San Andreas fault system), a series of overlapping, sometimes discontinuous, faults, roughly parallel to each other.

C. Strike-slip fault
horizontal motion/strike-slip type
(left lateral)

Motion on a fault plane occurs when pressure builds up so much that the rock can no longer withstand it, and must deform. When a large fault succumbs to the pressure, a noticeable earthquake is triggered. The faults of the San Andreas fault system periodically produce extremely noticeable earthquakes, and it is during these events that the landscape is uplifted.

D. Oblique-slip fault
horizontal motion

The motion on all the faults of the San Andreas fault system is right-lateral, from the mostly underwater San Gregorio-Hosgri fault zone on the west, to the Hayward and Calaveras faults to the east. Together, these faults constitute one of the most-studied fault systems in the world, a system that's played an integral role in the development of the landscape of the Sanctuary.

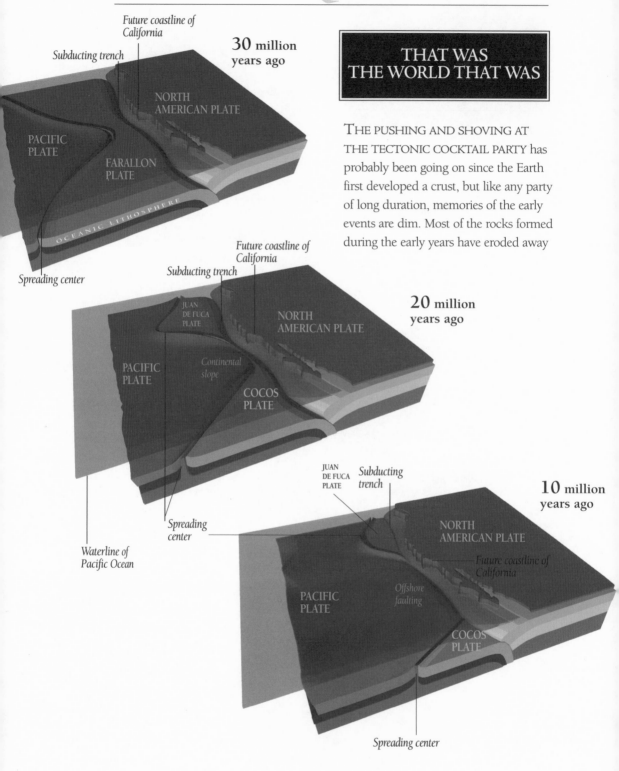

Future coastline of California

Subducting trench

30 million years ago

NORTH AMERICAN PLATE

PACIFIC PLATE

FARALLON PLATE

OCEANIC LITHOSPHERE

Spreading center

THAT WAS THE WORLD THAT WAS

THE PUSHING AND SHOVING AT THE TECTONIC COCKTAIL PARTY has probably been going on since the Earth first developed a crust, but like any party of long duration, memories of the early events are dim. Most of the rocks formed during the early years have eroded away

Future coastline of California

Subducting trench

20 million years ago

JUAN DE FUCA PLATE

NORTH AMERICAN PLATE

PACIFIC PLATE

Continental slope

COCOS PLATE

Spreading center

Waterline of Pacific Ocean

JUAN DE FUCA PLATE

Subducting trench

10 million years ago

NORTH AMERICAN PLATE

Future coastline of California

PACIFIC PLATE

Offshore faulting

COCOS PLATE

Spreading center

or been consumed in subduction zones. But geologists can reconstruct the movements of most of the last 200 million years fairly well by examining the basalt on the ocean floor. Basaltic lava contains metallic minerals which become magnetized with the same orientation as Earth's magnetic field as the basalt cools. Thus, the ocean floor preserves a record of the magnetic field at the time it formed.

Studying the pattern of magnetism recorded in the seafloor allows us to deduce past plate motions. This is how we know that by 60 million years ago most of the continents were nearing their present positions and there was a subduction zone along the western coast of North America. Two oceanic plates, the Pacific and the Farallon, were moving toward the North American plate, and the Farallon plate was sliding underneath the continental crust. At the same time, the oceanic plates were also pulling apart along a spreading center called the East Pacific Rise.

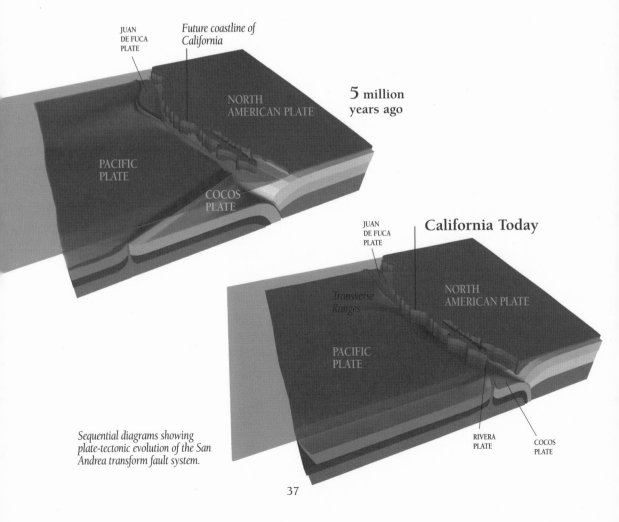

Sequential diagrams showing plate-tectonic evolution of the San Andrea transform fault system.

CALIFORNIA TAKES SHAPE

CALIFORNIA BEGAN TO DEVELOP SOME OF ITS PRESENT FEATURES approximately 60 million years ago. The Sierra Nevada had been uplifted and intruded by granitic magma, and the sediment eroding from the mountains was being deposited in the Central Valley, which was then covered by a shallow sea. Some of the rocks that would build the modern central coast had formed, though they were still far south of their location today.

Approximately 30 million years ago, continued subduction of the Farallon plate brought part of the East Pacific Rise to the coast of California in the vicinity of Los Angeles, where it descended into the subduction zone. This event changed the nature of tectonic activity along the coast dramatically. As the spreading ridge was subducted, the Pacific plate came into contact with the North American plate. Because the Pacific plate was moving northward, roughly parallel to the plate boundary, a transform fault developed along the new plate boundary.

And with development of the transform boundary, some of the rocks of the North American plate found themselves on the west side of the fault system and began moving north with the Pacific plate. As different faults in the transform system moved at different speeds, pieces of the continental crust were shifted northward at varying rates, and the jumbling of the coastal rocks began in earnest.

Most of the motion along the transform boundary today occurs on the San Andreas fault system, a complex, 800 mile (1,288 kilometer) long network of faults, most of which are oriented northwest-southeast and show right-lateral offset. This fault system is approximately 50 miles (81 kilometers) wide in the Monterey Bay area. Although the most well-known fault in the system is the San Andreas fault, other major strike-slip faults include the Hayward and Calaveras faults and the Palo Colorado–San Gregorio fault zone. Each of these faults has the potential to generate a major earthquake.

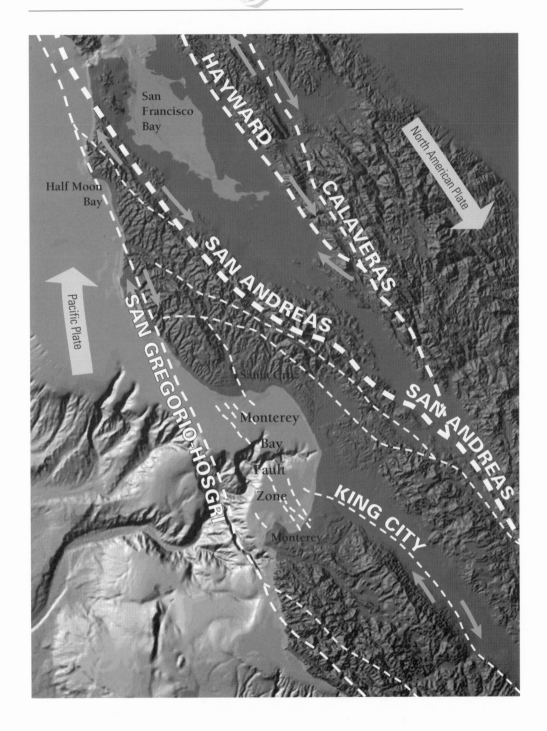

A JOURNEY OF 350 MILES

BY APPROXIMATELY 21 MILLION YEARS AGO, the transform fault extended north far enough to reach the vicinity where Monterey Bay was developing. Of course, 21 million years ago, the bay was not where it is today nor was it a bay. Back then it was about halfway between the location of Los Angeles and the early proto-Bakersfield, near where Santa Barbara is today. As the transform fault developed, it cut into the granitic rocks of southern California and of the Sierra Nevada, slicing off a chunk which was then "rafted" on the Pacific Plate northward. This chunk of crust upon which Monterey Bay sits is called the "Salinian block."

Most of the rocks exposed at the surface of the Salinian block today are sedimentary, but the majority of the rocks that lie beneath the sedimentary strata, known as "basement rocks," are granitic. These rocks are similar in composition to granitic rocks of the far southern Sierra Nevada, evidence that has helped convince many geologists that the Salinian block originated in southern California.

The Salinian block's journey exposed it to many and varied influences. Ebbing and flowing tectonic pulses produced periods of subsidence, then uplift. At the same time, the worldwide sea level rose or fell during the ice ages in response to the retreating or advancing glaciers. This complex interplay of tectonic and climactic forces alternately drowned and exposed the block, resulting in episodes of deposition alternating with erosion. And the splitting and shuffling action of the long, parallel faults of the San Andreas fault system pushed different slivers of rock at different speeds within the block, creating numerous offsets to further complicate the situation.

Estimates of the rate and amount of offset on the various faults in the San Andreas fault system vary. Faults don't necessarily move at a constant rate, so unless they offset distinct

NORTH

Sur-Nacimiento Block

Salinian Block

San Andreas Fault

CALIFORNIA

rock formations that can be easily correlated, making accurate estimates of motion can be quite challenging. This is especially true if most of a fault lies underwater, as in the case of the San Gregorio fault. But evidence suggests that the combined total of movement on the San Andreas fault system could be as much as 350 miles (about 560 kilometers) since it formed, and the present rate of motion is estimated at about two inches (five centimeters) per year.

For much of its northward journey, the Salinian block has had a traveling companion. To the west of the block, on the far side of the Palo Colorado–San Gregorio fault zone, is another tectonic block, the Sur-Obispo composite terrane. A terrane is a grouping of rocks that share similar characteristics, including a common history, that set them apart from the rocks around them. When a fragment of crust is split off from the area in which it formed, transported to another location and reattached to a continent, it is called an "accreted terrane." Both the Sur-Obispo composite terrane and the Salinian block are accreted terranes.

The Sur-Obispo composite terrane includes old seafloor formed 70 to 150 million years ago and rocks of the Franciscan Assemblage, formed approximately 72 million years ago. The Franciscan Assemblage is notorious for its complicated origin and marked instability, a pronounced tendency toward landsliding and easy erosion. This jumbled-up mixture of disparate rock types, with broken fragments of all sizes immersed in a sheared matrix of mud and shale, like chunks of different fruits suspended in a gelatin salad, has been slivered and shuffled in an accretionary wedge, the tectonic equivalent of a food processor.

Today, onshore exposures of the Franciscan Assemblage within the sanctuary are limited to the southern part, between Point Piedras Blancas and San Simeon, but undersea exposures are extensive. The Franciscan Assemblage is the basement rock along the west side of the Palo Colorado–San Gregorio fault zone from Cape Mendocino south almost to Point Sur, and it underlies more than half the waters of the sanctuary. Between Point Sur and Point Piedras Blancas, a wedge of the old seafloor is exposed along the coast.

In spite of the tremendous complexity and variation in the geologic history of the sanctuary's rocks, scientists have identified certain trends. The northwest-southeast orientation of the transform boundary produced faults with the same orientation. The persistent northerly motion of the tectonic blocks along the faults in turn created the pronounced northwest-southeast orientation of the mountain ranges and valleys in the region. Owing to the compression created by the faults' motion, uplift of the Salinian block has recently dominated over subsidence, as evidenced by the outcrops of formerly marine strata exposed in the sea cliffs and mountains around the sanctuary.

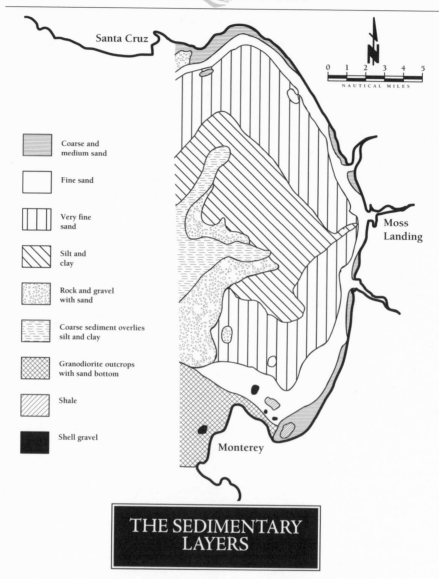

Legend:

- Coarse and medium sand
- Fine sand
- Very fine sand
- Silt and clay
- Rock and gravel with sand
- Coarse sediment overlies silt and clay
- Granodiorite outcrops with sand bottom
- Shale
- Shell gravel

Santa Cruz

Moss Landing

Monterey

0 1 2 3 4 5
NAUTICAL MILES

THE SEDIMENTARY LAYERS

BETWEEN 21 AND 65 MILLION YEARS AGO, the proto-Salinian block spent some of its time as an underwater basin. Rivers washed in sediment eroded from the southern mountain ranges, depositing many of the older sedimentary rocks now exposed in the Santa Cruz, Gabilan and Santa Lucia mountains, though subsequent erosion has removed most of what was deposited.

During the Salinian block's trip up from southern California starting around 21 million years ago, most of the sedimentary rock formations now exposed along and under the waters of the bay were deposited. Fine-grained rocks like shale and mudstone were laid down in calm, deep water. In shallower, more turbulent water

42

closer to shore, the fine particles stayed in suspension, and only coarser sediments like sand or gravel settled out.

As geologists map the floor of Monterey Bay in greater detail, they will doubtless discover more complexity than current maps show, but it presently appears that just a few sedimentary rock formations cover large expanses of the floor, in addition to the substantial outcroppings we see on the shore today.

The Monterey Formation, thin beds (layers) of shale and mudstone deposited in deep water from 11 to 17 million years ago, crops out over large areas under the bay and in the Santa Lucia and Santa Cruz mountains. Some of the beds within this formation are rich in silica, the cellular and skeletal remains of billions of tiny one-celled plants and animals, diatoms and radiolaria, that lived in the sea. Buried by overlying sediments, some of the silica formed chert, a hard, dense, microcrystalline form of quartz that the Ohlone Indians used to make arrowheads and tools. The tiny plants and animals of millions of years ago contributed to the formation of new rocks that today are home to rock-boring clams and mussels, along with dozens of species that live on the eroded undersea surface.

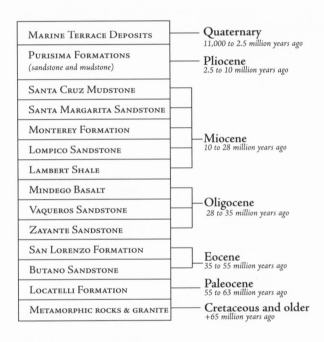

MARINE TERRACE DEPOSITS	**Quaternary** *11,000 to 2.5 million years ago*
PURISIMA FORMATIONS *(sandstone and mudstone)*	**Pliocene** *2.5 to 10 million years ago*
SANTA CRUZ MUDSTONE	
SANTA MARGARITA SANDSTONE	
MONTEREY FORMATION	**Miocene** *10 to 28 million years ago*
LOMPICO SANDSTONE	
LAMBERT SHALE	
MINDEGO BASALT	
VAQUEROS SANDSTONE	**Oligocene** *28 to 35 million years ago*
ZAYANTE SANDSTONE	
SAN LORENZO FORMATION	**Eocene** *35 to 55 million years ago*
BUTANO SANDSTONE	
LOCATELLI FORMATION	**Paleocene** *55 to 63 million years ago*
METAMORPHIC ROCKS & GRANITE	**Cretaceous and older** *+65 million years ago*

Ancient diatoms and radiolaria produced another substance appropriated by humans: oil. Quickly buried by sediments, their remains slowly decayed and were transformed into petroleum. Many of the oil derricks off the coast of Santa Barbara are pumping oil out of the Monterey Formation.

Two other formations are the Santa Cruz Mudstone and the Purisima Formation. The Santa Cruz Mudstone is a fine-grained, deep-water formation deposited five to seven million years ago that crops out offshore and in sea cliffs from the west side of Santa Cruz to Point Año Nuevo. The Purisima Formation was deposited one to three million years ago, during a period of fluctuating sea levels, and so consists of layers of both sand and finer silts. The relatively porous sand layers of the Purisima Formation act as an aquifer, storing groundwater throughout a large part of the Monterey Bay area. In addition to providing a source of water for crop irrigation, it may play a role in forming some features of the Monterey Canyon.

Outcrops of all three formations also occur just outside the northern boundary of the sanctuary, at Point Reyes. For about the past 10 million years, rock on the west side of the San Gregorio fault has been moving northward at rates generally estimated at about four-tenths of an inch (one centimeter) a year relative to the movement of the Salinian block. Parts of these three formations that were deposited west of the San Gregorio fault have been rafted up to 94 miles (more than 150 kilometers) farther north than the same deposits on the Salinian block.

Most of the rest of the floor of Monterey Bay is covered either by younger, mostly unconsolidated sediments laid down in the last few million years or by crystalline igneous rocks, mainly granites, whose history we are just starting to unravel.

COASTAL PROCESSES

THE ACTIVITY OF THE PAST 200 MILLION YEARS provided the raw material out of which the landscape of today has been carved, uplifting the mountains and wearing them down, depositing their eroded sediments in the basins to form new rocks and uplifting them in turn, and moving the entire coastline north along the transform boundary. The actual sculpting of the shore and nearshore into the shapes we see today has been done by forces collectively known as "coastal processes." Coastal processes encompass not only the forces already described, but also the combined power of waves, tides, wind and rain. But the biggest influence on the location of any beach, big or small, is sea level. Worldwide sea level has risen and fallen many times as the glaciers melted or advanced during the ice ages, and the location of the shoreline along the sanctuary shifted with the ocean. Eighteen thousand years ago, during a low sea level, the beaches were several miles west of where they lie today. Some 125,000 years ago, when sea level was almost 30 feet. (more than nine meters) higher than today, many beaches would have been much farther inland, shortening the trek considerably for whatever species of weekend beachgoers was then inhabiting the inland valleys.

The Internal Structure of Earth

THE INTERNAL STRUCTURE of Earth developed early in its evolution, probably within the first few hundred million years of its approximately 4.5-billion-year life to date.

According to current theories, the planets of our solar system formed from an immense disk of interstellar dust and gas that rotated about the Sun. This disk was itself the remnant of an even larger rotating cloud of dust and gas from which the Sun evolved. In the same way that raindrops form around minute particles of dust, so the gases in the disk probably condensed around the grains of cosmic dust. The dust and gas coalesced, first into tiny snowballs so small you could hold them in your hand, then continued growing into preplanetary bodies called planetesimals, some of which may have been several hundred to several thousand kilometers in diameter. The planetesimals in turn combined into planets through collisions with other planetesimals.

Although the planetesimals are thought to have been relatively cold, as they accreted to form the inner, terrestrial planets, the evolving planets began heating up. The warming resulted partly from heat generated by the force of the impacting planetesimals, partly from compression of the increasingly large mass under the force of gravity, and partly from the decay of radioactive elements. The heat generated from these three sources eventually became great enough that much, perhaps even all, of the planet became molten.

During the molten period, most of the heavier elements in the planet sank toward the core. This process of differentiation, during which the elements separated out according to their relative densities, produced the layered structure of our planet. The inner core, composed primarily of iron and nickel, and perhaps about 10 percent sulfur, appears to be solid, based upon the speed with which it transmits certain types of waves generated during major earthquakes (and the occasional nuclear explosion). These same waves travel through the outer core at a significantly slower speed, indicating the outer core is liquid. Together, the inner and outer cores of the planet constitute roughly one third the mass of Earth.

As the heavier elements sank deep into the heart of the planet to form the core, lighter elements were displaced outward to form the mantle, which accounts for roughly two-thirds of the mass of Earth, and the crust. The crust, for all its importance to we who dwell upon it, constitutes a very modest portion of Earth's mass, less than one percent.

As anyone who has ever stumbled and fallen outdoors can attest, the crust of the earth is quite solid. Most of the mantle is also fairly rigid, but there is a portion of it that is partially molten, and therefore capable of flowing. This ability to flow plays a vital role in the movement of the tectonic plates that constitute the outermost layer of Earth, and ultimately the origin of Monterey Bay.

CARVING THE CLIFFS

ALONG MUCH OF THE SANCTUARY BOUNDARY, the most dramatic and striking landforms are the steep coastal bluffs. Sea cliffs on certain stretches of the coast, notably around Big Sur and in the Devil's Slide area north of Half Moon Bay, tower hundreds of feet above the water. The main force in the creation of the bluffs is tectonic movement pushing the mountains up and out of the sea during earthquakes. Although uplift along the coast has not been uniform across the land or over time, during the last 1.5 million years average uplift along the central California coastline is thought to have ranged from six inches (about 15 centimeters) to a maximum of two feet (about 61 centimeters) per thousand years, a relatively rapid rate, geologically speaking.

But tectonic movement is not solely responsible for these landforms. The erosive action of the waves also assists in the creation of the sea cliffs and the broad, flat benches extending seaward from the base of the cliffs ("wavecut platforms"), which develop simultaneously with the crashing of powerful winter storm waves, laden with sand, gravel, boulders and even uprooted trees, against the cliff. The relentless waves slowly grind and batter a notch into the base of the cliff, until eventually the notch undermines the cliff face and the face collapses. As the cliff retreats, the bedrock under the surf zone is planed off by the sediment-laden waves, producing the gently sloping (about one degree) surface of the platform.

To see a wavecut platform being cut now, stand (not too) near the edge of a bluff and look down at the beach. Almost anywhere along the coast from Santa Cruz to San Francisco you can see this happening, but easily accessible locations are Año Nuevo State Park and the path along West Cliff Drive in Santa Cruz. Under the sand and water lies the almost planar wavecut platform, tilting gently out to sea and extending well offshore. During a low tide you may see places where the platform is exposed.

This process occurs with greatest effect in the winter months, when the ground is saturated and waves are large. Storm waves smashing against a cliff can generate pressures well in excess of 1,000 pounds per square foot. Where cliffs are composed of sedimentary rock, the average rate of erosion along the California coast is 6 inches (about 15 centimeters) to one foot (about 30 centimeters) per year. If the rock in a cliff face is weakly cemented or highly fractured, the average erosion may be far greater, and big storms can take out huge amounts. A series of large storms in January 1983 eroded 46 feet (about 14 meters) of bluff top from one cliff in Santa Cruz.

The violent shaking that accompanies major earthquakes also accelerates sea-cliff erosion. The 1989 Loma Prieta earthquake (magnitude ~7.1), which shook for 15 seconds, triggered numerous coastal landslides on cliffs along the sanctuary's boundary, including some bluffs that were protected from wave attack. But even as an earthquake tears down the cliffs, it also raises the landscape out of the water.

As the land is uplifted, wavecut platforms may be raised above sea level and stranded above the active surf zone. Once high and dry, they are called "marine terraces." The most extensive and well-preserved marine terraces are cut during rises of sea level, when the power of the waves is maintained across the increasing width of the platform. As noted earlier, sea level is seldom, if ever, constant when considered over the vast length of geologic time. The actively eroding platform at the base of sea cliffs today started forming during the last rise of sea level that began 16,000 to 18,000 years ago.

The presence of sea cliffs along a coast tells us that the coastline is being eroded by waves. But when waves stop attacking a cliff, the cliff still erodes, albeit more slowly, and the debris that it sheds piles up at the base of the cliff. Without waves to carry the debris away, it eventually obscures the cliff face completely. Thus, even a towering sea cliff is an ephemeral feature and will vanish unless maintained by the waves. Eventually, either uplift out of the surf zone or a lowering of sea level will lead to the demise of the cliffs we see today.

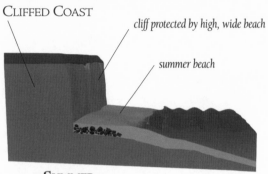

CLIFFED COAST

cliff protected by high, wide beach

summer beach

SUMMER

beach removed by waves attacking base of cliff

WINTER

Atop the elevated marine terraces lies a loose conglomeration of sand and gravel. These "terrace deposits" are the remains of the beach sand and coarser nearshore sediments that were on the platform when it was uplifted.

If you look around the central California coast, you can find marine terraces, like giant steps leading up the side of a great pyramid, elevated above sea level on the slopes of the Santa Cruz and Santa Lucia mountains. Each was cut by waves and is now elevated above sea level, a clear indication that either sea level has fallen or the land has risen. In fact, we know from other evidence that although the sea level has indeed fluctuated over time, the land has been raised.

Regardless of where you are on the coast, the terrace lowest and closest to the coastline is the youngest. Older terraces along the coast have already been elevated and moved inland. If you drive on Highway 1 along the base of the Santa Cruz or Santa Lucia mountains bordering the sanctuary and find yourself on a broad, flat expanse of agricultural fields or meadows that extends to the ocean, you are driving on a marine terrace.

SPREADING THE SAND

THOUGH THE CLIFFS ARE DRAMATIC, it is the relaxing, sun-soaked sand of a summer beach that attracts many visitors to the coast. But even the apparently placid beach is the scene of abundant geologic activity. Gentle summer waves wash sand onto the beach, building the beach out into a broad, flat expanse. In winter, powerful storm waves pull the sand offshore and pile it in bars at the edge of the surf zone, leaving only a narrow beach or none at all.

The movement of sand is more than just a simple routine of going from beach to bar and back again. Waves usually approach a beach at an angle, propelling sand up or down the coast in the direction of the swell. Even gentle summer waves move sand across the face of a beach, but most of the movement occurs during winter, when the sand is off the beach. Once offshore, the sand is caught up in the longshore current and transported along the coast from beach to beach. For most of the sanctuary, the prevailing current is to the south, though it varies with the season.

Studies of sand movement along a coastline have found movement rates on the order of 0.6 mile (one kilometer) per year when there are no obstructions. Sand you see this year on New Brighton State Beach may have summered last year on the beach in Capitola. But the journey of sand along much of the sanctuary coast faces many obstructions. The rocky headlands jutting out from shore also extend under water, acting as barriers to sand moving down the coast. Only powerful winter storm waves can push sand over or around these ridges, which are usually 10 or 15 feet (3 to about 4.5 meters) above the sandy floor but may tower as high as 40 feet (about 12 meters). Human-made obstructions affect sand flow as well, sometimes with unforeseen consequences. Construction of the jetties at the mouth of the Santa Cruz harbor in 1965 widened Seabright Beach just upcoast of the harbor but also starved the beaches downcoast, increasing erosion rates on the sea cliffs and threatening homes and property. It took 10 years for Seabright Beach to widen enough for sand transport past the jetty to resume. In 1985, the cost of dredging the sand that fills in the harbor entrance channel was estimated to exceed $500,000 per year.

As sand journeys down the coast, it sometimes encounters a barrier that it simply cannot overcome, like Monterey Canyon, which divides the circulating sand into "cells." From the Golden Gate by San Francisco down to the head of Monterey Canyon is the Santa Cruz sand cell, and from the canyon to Point Pinos on the Monterey Peninsula is another. From the peninsula south may be another, but the continental shelf here is so narrow and discontinuous that sand may not be able to move along it. Sand circulation along the southern coast of the sanctuary is not well understood at this time, and it may also be that sand enters the Santa Cruz cell from farther north than the Golden Gate, but this, too, is still being studied.

Beaches not only vary from season to season but also from place to place. The region of Monterey Bay between Aptos and Monterey has long sandy beaches that stretch uninterrupted for miles. Other areas, like San Mateo and northern Santa Cruz counties, have an abundance of tiny "pocket" beaches that build up in small, sheltered coves between rocky headlands. Along the steep sea cliffs of Big Sur, even pocket beaches become rare.

The type of beach that forms is partly the result of the rock types along the coast, but mainly of the amount of sediment being pumped into the beach, which depends on the pre-existing landscape and geology. The biggest beaches tend to be found where rivers enter the ocean and drain areas of sedimentary rock. The Salinas and Pajaro rivers eroded broad, flat valleys during a prior low stand of sea level. As the sea level rose, the ocean invaded the valleys and found unconsolidated river deposits, an excellent source of sand. Near a river mouth there is also a yearly infusion of new sediment into the environment. If you stand on a bluff overlooking a river mouth after a winter storm, you can see the large brown plume of sediment, brought down from the mountains by the river, dispersing into the bay. Estimates of the sources of sediment along the California coast ascribe 75 percent of the sand to inputs from rivers and only 20 percent to that garnered from the erosion of the sea cliffs. Where the cliffs are granitic, the contribution from cliffs to the beaches is probably even less.

The angle of wave attack along the coast also influences beach formation. Large beaches tend to build up on the windward and upcurrent sides of large headlands, such as at Point Año Nuevo and southern Monterey Bay. If enough sand accumulates, fields of dunes may form along the shore and migrate downwind. Where the shore is oriented so that most of the winter waves don't attack it directly, or where a protective headland dissipates some of the wave energy before it reaches the beach, a large beach is more likely to persist.

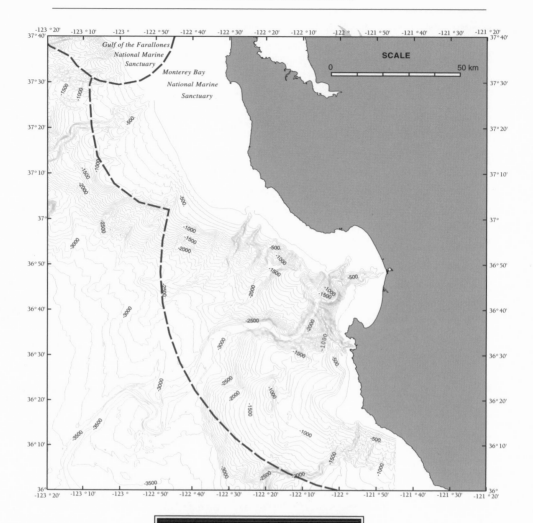

SIGHTS SUBMERGED UNDER THE BAY

WHILE THE CLIFFS AND BEACHES BORDERING THE SANCTUARY are certainly dramatic, the landforms underwater are even more so. The broad, flat continental shelf that abuts the shore gives way to a steep continental slope, dropping down to the deep abyssal plain of the ocean. In the northern part of the sanctuary near San Francisco, the shelf extends over 25 miles (about 19 kilometers) but narrows to eight or 10 miles (about 13 or 16 kilometers) as it approaches Monterey Bay, and it is increasingly incised by deep submarine canyons. South of Big Sur the shelf narrows so much it barely exists in some spots and is seldom more than a mile or two wide.

ORIGIN OF THE SUBMARINE CANYONS

THE MOST STRIKING FEATURE OF THE UNDERWATER TOPOGRAPHY is the series
of canyons carved into the continental shelf and slope, the greatest of which is
Monterey Canyon.

First described in
1897, Monterey Canyon
puzzled geologists for years.
The popular theory was that
submarine canyons had
been eroded by rivers when
the continental shelf was
exposed during periods of
low sea level. But there was
no large river emptying into
Monterey Bay, so the
question of how such a deep canyon could

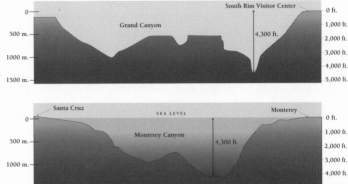

*Comparison of elevation variations between the Grand Canyon
of the Colorado River and Monterey Canyon*

originate without a great river to carve it was perplexing. Some suggested that the
Sacramento River might once have flowed south from San Francisco Bay and out to sea
through the canyon, but there were numerous problems with this and other hypothe-
ses. It took the advent of plate tectonic theory in the 1960s to provide new insight.

The same geologic evidence that supports the northward journey of the Salinian
block also argues for a southern origin of Monterey Canyon. Twenty-five to 30 million
years ago the site of the canyon was at the western end of the present-day. Transverse
Ranges, a series of small, fault-bounded mountain ranges that cut directly across the
dominant northwest-southeast structural grain of California. The canyon is thought to
have eroded along an east-west trending fault that cut the granitic basement rock of the
Salinian block, raising the south side of the fault. This fault probably formed the
channel for a river that drained the great shallow marine embayment that filled the
Central Valley, thus initiating canyon formation.

But the most powerful erosive forces carving out the canyon were, and are, dense,
sediment-laden flows of water called "turbidity currents." Named for the turbulence of
the fluids, these currents start when a mass of sediment shakes loose from the walls or
head of the canyon. Like an avalanche of sand and mud, the heavy currents rush down
the canyon and fan valley, scouring the floor. Turbidity currents measured on the
continental slope off Newfoundland in 1929 were estimated to move at velocities up to
40 to 60 miles (64 to 96 kilometers) per hour, based on the rate at which they snapped
telephone cables on the Atlantic slope.

During their northward journey, many canyons, especially Monterey, were alternately drowned and exposed several times as tectonic forces ebbed and surged and sea level rose and fell. When submerged, additional sediments were deposited in the canyon and on the adjacent seafloor. When the continental shelf was elevated above sea level, erosion was still concentrated in the canyon, thus perpetuating the canyon, even as new sediment built up the walls around it.

The canyon also suffered occasional amputations during its long trek. As strike-slip faults seaward of the San Andreas fault rafted pieces of the continental crust north at a faster pace, several times the deeper outer portion of the canyon was sliced off from the head. Like halves of a severed flatworm that each grow into another complete worm, both parts of the canyon regenerated. The truncated canyon segments slowly drifted northward along the fault to begin incising heads at new sites along the continental slope while Monterey Canyon started cutting another lower canyon. Pioneer, Ascension, Año Nuevo and perhaps Cabrillo canyons are all thought to have developed this way, shifted north by the Palo Colorado–San Gregorio fault zone.

WITHIN CANYON WALLS

THE UPPER REACHES OF MONTEREY CANYON, which begins only about 110 yards (100 meters) offshore from Moss Landing, are similar to a mountain river valley, its steep walls and a narrow floor giving it a V-shaped cross section. As the canyon reaches the lower continental slope, the floor widens, and in many places sediment has cascaded down from the walls, lessening their steepness. Where the canyon opens onto the "continental rise," the gentle incline that comes up from the deep ocean floor to meet the steeper continental slope, the sediments washed down the canyon are deposited in a huge submarine fan. The other canyons along the continental slope are similar in their features, though not as developed. The Monterey Fan contains enough material to fill the canyon almost 100 times and is itself incised by a fan valley that is a continuation of the canyon. Whether a turbidity current deposits sediment on the fan or cuts deeper into the valley depends on how much energy the current has when it reaches the fan.

SLUMPS AND SEEPS

THROUGHOUT THE LENGTH OF THE CANYON and fan valley are steep erosional scars on the walls where saturated sediments have slumped onto the floor. These slumps can be triggered by shaking during earthquakes or undercutting of the toe of the slope by a turbidity current. The 1989 Loma Prieta earthquake on the San Andreas fault caused large areas of slumping along the upper canyon wall. Vast numbers of tube worms and other creatures living in the sediments of the canyon wall were exposed by the slumps, triggering a feeding frenzy among the fish. Slumps also occasionally occur at the head of the canyon, bringing the head ever closer to Moss Landing, and millions of years ago they may have had a role in initiating the canyon.

Another driving force behind slumping is the expulsion of fluids from the rock and sediment in the bay. Because they are under hundreds or thousands of feet of sea water, rock and sediments are fully saturated, with water in every pore and fracture. If they are squeezed, either by tectonic pressures or the weight of overlying sediments, the fluid within them is expelled. On steep canyon walls the expelled fluids carry along some of the sediment. Even without squeezing, water may emerge from the sediments if it becomes enriched with gas, rendering it less dense than the surrounding sea water. Gas originating from the decomposition of organic matter buried in sediments or the older, lithified rocks of the Monterey Formation is thought to be the source of some of the "cold seeps" found in the bay.

Slumps can also result from groundwater migrating from land to sea through porous rock like the sandstone layers of the Purisima Formation, whose beds extend from the San Gregorio fault zone on the west to the San Andreas fault on the east. The slight seaward dip of the Purisima, resulting from the uplift of the Santa Cruz Mountains, creates a natural conduit for groundwater flow into the bay. Especially during a winter of heavy storms, these porous sands may funnel rain down from the mountains and out into the bay, to discharge where the sandstone crops out on the canyon walls or on the shallow bay shelf.

Groundwater normally flows under the influence of gravity, and thus has a natural tendency to move from the coastal mountains down to the sea, but there are exceptions to this norm. In the Watsonville area of the Pajaro Valley and Castroville area of the Salinas Valley, heavy pumping of groundwater for agricultural irrigation has reversed the flow, and saltwater intrusion into some of the freshwater aquifers has become a serious problem, reaching almost to Salinas.

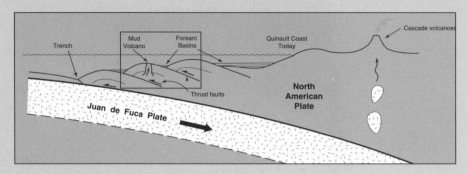

Cold Seep

ONE OF THE MORE UNUSUAL and fascinating geologic puzzles currently being investigated in the sanctuary is the origin of some cold seeps found in Monterey Bay. Water enriched with sulfide and sometimes methane gases is percolating out of the rock at the seeps, which occur both within Monterey Canyon and on undissected portions of the continental slope. The sulfide in the seep waters has given rise to some unusual clams and tube worms that use the sulfide to create food in a process similar to the way most plants use sunlight during photosynthesis.

The sulfide and methane gases are probably byproducts of decomposed organic matter in the rocks and sediments that lie under the waters of the bay. The Monterey Formation, rich in petroleum, is a likely source for some of the seeps, and the Purisima Formation may be a source as well. The unconsolidated sediments of the Monterey Fan Valley are also home to several seeps, and probably also contain abundant decomposing organic matter.

As mentioned elsewhere in this chapter, water can be expelled from rocks or sediments by several mechanisms. Pressures from the grinding of the tectonic plates can cause fluid expulsion, as can differences in pressure within an aquifer, pressure from overlying sediments, or just the natural buoyancy of water enriched with gas.

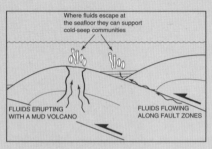

To sustain the creatures living by a cold seep, there must some sort of conduit that allows large volumes of gas-enriched fluid to pass through the rock and sediment to the surface. At seeps within the San Gregorio fault zone, the conduit appears to be the fractured rock along fault planes. The relatively porous sandstone aquifer beds of the Purisima are thought to serve as a conduit for some of the seeps east of the San Gregorio fault.

When a large volume of fluid moves upward as a coherent mass, and comes to the surface in an area covered with unconsolidated sediment, a mud volcano is born. A mud volcano erupts muddy water and gas, and it, too, can support cold seep organisms. One of the larger cold seep communities sits by a mud volcano on the wide, smooth ridge between Monterey and Cabrillo Canyons.

The origin of the cold seeps is a complex puzzle, and won't be solved without a lot more study. But each new grain of knowledge gained in the quest sheds new light on the origin and evolution of the underwater world of the Monterey Bay National Marine Sanctuary.

FLEXIBLE BOUNDARIES AND AN UNCERTAIN FUTURE

THE FLOW OF GROUNDWATER illustrates again the nebulous nature of the boundary between land and sea, pointing out the need for care when humans interact with the land. Anything we apply to the surface can end up out in the bay, whether by surface runoff or by percolating down to an aquifer and flowing out underground. Pesticides and herbicides, automotive fluids, household cleansers and anything else we might spray, spread or toss in the trash can end up in the bay even if our action took place miles inland. Building a dam on a river in the mountains reduces the amount of sediment that enters the bay and causes the beaches to shrink. Building a jetty to hold sand on one beach ends up starving the beaches downcoast of sand. Pumping groundwater out of an aquifer encourages sea water intrusion into that aquifer. No action is devoid of consequence.

Although in the long haul of geologic time, the forces of nature will dominate the eventual fate of the sanctuary, in the short term of human existence, our actions will play a pivotal role in the evolution of its landscape.

Elkhorn Slough (seen from above) is the largest coastal wetland between San Francisco Bay and Morro Bay.

CHAPTER FOUR

WETLANDS

But in the estuary as in most of nature, the visible is but a shallow foot-print of a larger and more elusive truth.

STEWART T. SCHULTZ 1990

WINTER HAS ARRIVED at Elkhorn Slough. The early morning air is crisp, and the first glimpse of sunlight peeks over the distant hills of California's coastal mountains. It's peaceful, quiet. Suddenly, a willet's shrill cry pierces the stillness as it flies off to another muddy spot in search of food. High overhead, strings of geese parade by, headed south for a reprieve from the icy winter in the north.

It is during this time of the year, from late fall to winter, that Elkhorn Slough (pronounced "slew"), like all wetlands, serves as a stopping place for hundreds of thousands of migratory birds traveling south to Mexico and beyond. It is here that they refuel, finding food and rest to continue their long journeys. Come spring, the birds will stop again as they head back north to their summer breeding grounds in Alaska and Canada.

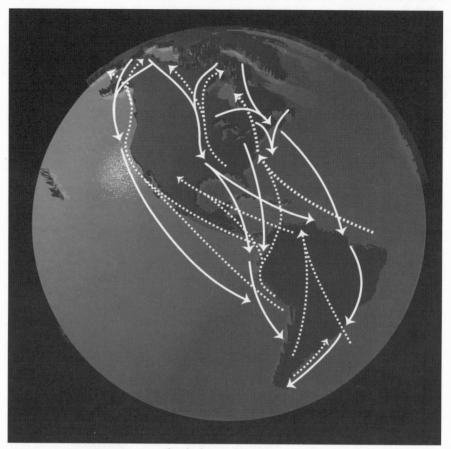

Shorebird migration patterns

Though the slough teems with migratory birds in winter, other animals come to the slough throughout the seasons. In spring, snowy egrets and blue herons nest in treetops, while fat innkeeper worms spawn down in the mud. Leopard sharks and bat rays swim into the slough in summer, give birth to live young, then return to the sea. There is a seasonality to plankton, too. These plants and animals—most of them very tiny—drift with the water currents. Each spring and fall, during the plankton bloom, they multiply in great numbers and enrich the slough's waters.

Elkhorn Slough is one of California's few remaining coastal wetlands. Sitting on the central California coast about 100 miles (160 kilometers) south of San Francisco, it marks the middle of the curve of Monterey Bay. A narrow arm of the sea, it reaches seven miles (about 11 kilometers) inland, bends north at an elbow and ends in a thin finger. Though it is one of the

Snowy egret
Egretta thula

largest remaining coastal wetlands in California, its several thousand acres of tidal land would be dwarfed by many of the world's other marshes.

The slough is part of the Monterey Bay National Marine Sanctuary, but it differs rather significantly from the adjacent ocean. Where waves pound and lash furiously at the ocean's shore, the slough is placid and serene. Water currents in the slough are, for the most part, generally quiet, and there are no waves. But the steady tidal current can be quite strong—up to three knots—challenging even experienced kayakers when paddling against it. As the tide rises, sea water enters the slough, gently flooding its banks and extending to its far reaches with subtle determination. Most plants and animals that find shelter in this quiet haven wouldn't survive the ocean's strong, pounding waves.

WHAT IS A SLOUGH?

ELKHORN SLOUGH IS CONSIDERED A SLOUGH because it's a narrow, winding waterway edged with muddy and marshy ground. A slough can be salt water or fresh, open to the sea or separated from it. A slough is a kind of wetland. Wetlands are a broader category that include all kinds of land-and-water environments.

Elkhorn Slough is a full-time slough but only a part-time estuary. An estuary is a protected embayment, and unlike a slough, it's a place where fresh water flows in from the land (as from a river) and tides come in from the sea. It's a region where fresh water and salt water mix, and where salinity rises and falls with the tides and amount of fresh water runoff. In simplest terms, it's an inlet where a river meets the sea. But unlike San Francisco Bay, which drains the Sacramento and San Joaquin

rivers, the slough has no year-round
freshwater flow. It's only in winter,
when the rains run off the
adjacent hills, that Carneros Creek
fills, then rushes

California newt
Taricha torosa

down the valley to empty into the slough giving it the status of part-
time estuary. This addition of fresh water can dilute the slough's
saltiness to half that of the bay, creating a brackishness that's typical
of estuaries. In spring, the creek slows, then dries up completely.
The summer sun evaporates the still backwaters of the slough,
concentrating them to a saltiness greater than sea
water. This greater inflow of fresh water in winter
gives Elkhorn Slough its seasonal estuary character.

Western pond turtle
Clemmys marmorata

Red-legged frog
Rana aurora

60

CHANGES OVER TIME

MANY VISITORS EXPECT TO FIND A RIVER associated with Elkhorn Slough. The slough's lower end, where it meets the ocean, looks like a river mouth, and its snakelike form is rather like that of a river. But there is none here today, although the slough itself can be considered a fossil river. Perhaps as long as a million years ago, a sizeable stream flowed through this area to drain into Monterey submarine canyon. On its way, it carved out the valley that is now the slough. At some point, movement along the San Andreas fault to the east changed the course of the ancient river, leaving the slough as a valley with one end opened to the sea and the other enclosed by land.

Elkhorn Valley remained a small drainage of water until about 15,000 years ago, when the last ice age began its thaw. As the great glaciers that covered Europe and North America melted back toward the poles of the Earth, their meltwater ran to the ocean, raising sea level hundreds of feet. During this time the sea crept into Elkhorn Valley, refilling the ancient river course with salt water. Slowly, as sand and mud washed down from the uplands and accumulated in the valley, mudflats and then a saltmarsh began to grow along its margins.

BEFORE 1908 **1908-1946** **1946-PRESENT**

 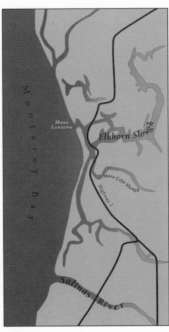 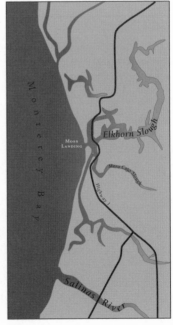

Historical maps show changes in the Salinas River and mouth of Elkhorn Slough

PEOPLE AND THE SLOUGH

BUT NATURE IS ONLY ONE CAUSE OF CHANGE at Elkhorn Slough. People, too, are part of the ever-changing ecosystem and have had their hand in shaping Elkhorn Slough. The Ohlone Indians began making the slough their home more than 4,000 years ago. Over the centuries, people's effect on the slough has progressed with the technological advances of humankind. In the 1700s, the Spanish grazed their cattle on the slough's native grasses. In the mid-1800s, Americans began logging and farming the uplands, causing erosion and introducing nonnative species. Then in the 1940s we began introducing pesticides–all of these problems continue to affect the slough today.

In the mid-1900s, engineers moved the slough's mouth. Originally, the slough's water slowly flowed north, winding behind the sandy beach and dunes north of Moss Landing before connecting with the bay. Sediments washing down from local hillsides slowly filled the slough. But with the construction of the new Moss Landing Harbor, engineers moved the slough's mouth a bit to the south, dredging a permanent opening through the beach and dunes and opening the slough to the sea. This allowed water to flow in and out of the slough with greater force, scouring the channel's banks and eroding the saltmarsh and mudflat communities. Over time, we've also diked the marsh to hold back the tides, and we've rechanneled the streams, shaping the slough to fit our needs.

Historical view of the Salinas River flowing past a ferry at the mouth of the slough.

PRODUCTIVITY

ELKHORN SLOUGH IS VITAL TO THE GREATER SYSTEM OF HABITATS that surround it, and it is one of the most productive. Interestingly, productivity doesn't rely on a great diversity of species to make one habitat more productive than another. Rather it's how efficiently and rapidly new living matter is produced, and that's based on the availability of resources like sunlight and nutrients. With its shallow waters to maximize sunlit water and daily tides to replenish nutrients, the Elkhorn Slough system remains highly productive.

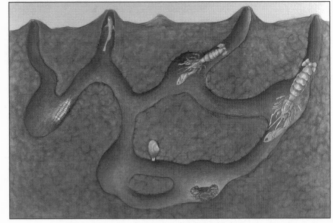

Ghost shrimps shelter other species, like crabs and fishes, in their burrows.

Protection from ocean waves further contributes to the slough's high productivity. Estuarine plants—a handful of species adapted to tolerate the changing, salty conditions of a slough—are well adapted to their environment and are extremely productive. Hence, these plants, in particular the seaweeds and eelgrass, produce three to four times as much new living matter as the average production of corn or wheat fields in the United States.

Readily available nutrients and protection from waves combine with one of the greatest keys to the slough's productivity: the abundance of tiny particles of decaying plants and animals floating in the water. As the plants die and decompose, their fragments provide food for countless protozoa and bacteria. These microscopic decomposers and micro-grazers, suspended in the slough's water along with bits of decomposing plants, make a rich soup called detritus. Unlike many marine habitats, where plants and phytoplankton serve as the base of the food web, it is primarily detritus that supports the diversity of life in Elkhorn Slough and other coastal marshes. Most of the detritus comes from within the slough, primarily from the marsh plants, though some of it is brought in from the bay with the tide. A tremendous number of animals, from fat innkeeper worms to bent-nosed clams and skeleton shrimp, thrive on this rich and nutritious fertilizer, supporting a food web of thousands of different kinds of animals.

Detritus

THERE'S A BUSTLE OF ACTIVITY taking place in nature all the time that's too tiny for us to see with the naked eye. It's the work of bacteria, one of life's simplest forms, constantly breaking down tiny bits of dead plants and animals and subsequently, releasing nutrients essential to the growth of new life.

These tiny bits of dead plants and animals are called detritus, and they, along with the associated bacteria, form the base of the food chain for many animals.

Detritus is mostly dead plant material. (Only about 10 percent of all plants are ever consumed by herbivores—the rest becomes detritus.) Most dead plant material contains carbohydrates like lignin and cellulose that are difficult for many animals to digest. Thus, a piece of detritus alone isn't very nutritional to them. But bacteria and fungi have enzymes that do digest these tough structural materials, helping to break them down. A host of animals feeds on the bacteria, from microscopic protozoans and ciliates to invertebrates and other larger animals. The larger animals feed on these detritus-bacteria particles, digest the outer coating of nutritious bacteria and fungi, then defecate the hard-to-digest detritus. A new wave of bacteria and fungi then colonize the particle, and the process of breaking down detritus continues.

Salt marsh

Lowest tide -0.6m)

SLOUGH HABITATS

TODAY, ELKHORN SLOUGH is composed of four different subhabitats, each supporting its own community of plants and animals that are specially adapted to live there. The four main subhabitats in Elkhorn Slough are the main channel or waterway, the mudflats, the saltmarsh and the uplands. These subhabitats of Elkhorn Slough provide home to a diversity of life—more than 80 species of fishes and 270 species of birds live in this habitat during some part of their lives.

Northern anchovies
Engraulis mordax

Average low water (0.0m) ——— Channel

Highest tide (2m)

WATERWAYS

The main channel is quite wide and deep—700 feet (about 212 meters) across and 25 feet (about 7.5 meters) deep at its mouth. Even at the lowest of tides, water still fills the channel. As the channel extends inland, it gradually grows narrower and shallower until it ends in a marshy expanse. Fishes swim into the channel from Monterey Bay; bat rays glide along just above the mud, their winglike fins stirring up sediment to unearth clams and other burrowers to eat. Leopard sharks, flatfishes, anchovies and sardines enter to feed on small fishes or plankton. Many species find the channel to be a calm, safe place to lay eggs and raise their young. Flatfishes (like flounders) and other commercially valuable species are among those that replenish their numbers in the slough's nursery.

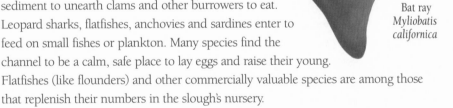

Bat ray
*Myliobatis
californica*

Pacific sardine
Sardinops sagax

MUDFLATS

Past the first bend in the main channel, side streams begin emptying into it, cutting through the marsh to flow across the mudflats. At high tide these channels, "tidal creeks," fill with the incoming salt water. Like branching arteries, they carry tidal flow up into the farthest reaches of the saltmarsh, then reverse to drain it off as the tide drops.

Twice-daily tides sweep into and out of the slough. The incoming tides bring clean, cold, salty bay water, while the outgoing or ebbing tides flush out the silty slough water. But the slough's long, narrow shape and lack of fresh water flow limit this exchange. The turning tide acts like a giant piston, compressing the ebbing waters and pushing them back to the slough's upper reaches before they can escape to the bay. These waters languish in the upper slough: complete replacement with bay water may take weeks, whereas in the lower slough it takes only days.

Tidal creek with exposed mud

As a result, the slough is almost like two bodies of water. The upper slough waters are saltier in summer and fresher in winter than lower slough waters; they're murky with suspended mud and nutrients; and, surprisingly, they often contain more oxygen because of the masses of photosynthesizing algae in them.

Animals and plants respond to these differences. Toward the mouth of the slough, where exchange with the sea is greatest, oceanic species like lingcod, halibut and some species of surfperch are abundant. Farther up the slough, backwater species like staghorn sculpins and gobies are more common.

Staghorn sculpin
Leptocottus armatus

In winter, when fresh water flows into the slough, the incoming tides create another seemingly invisible boundary. Fresh water, which is less dense and viscous than sea water, tends to float on top of the salty sea water, vertically and horizontally separating the water into two bodies of water. The size and shape of these two bodies of water changes depending on the amount of fresh water entering the slough and on whether the tides are coming in or going out. Again, plants and animals respond accordingly, living in salinity levels appropriate to their needs.

As the water flows into and out of the slough, it carries with it silt and clay—which geologists define as particles of soil that are smaller than sand. (Clay and silt are 0.001 millimeter to 0.01 millimeter in size, while sand is 0.1 millimeter to 1.0 millimeter.) The slow currents of Elkhorn Slough are calm enough to allow these finer materials to sink and settle to the bottom. They accumulate there—especially along the edges of the channel, forming broad expanses of mudflats composed of fine, organically rich particles. This directly contrasts with the coarser, low-nutrition-al value of the sands that form the ocean's wave-swept beaches. At Elkhorn Slough, this accumulation of particles has created mudflats up to as much as 20 feet (6 meters) thick.

Twice daily the tide recedes, and when it does, it exposes on both sides of the channel the rich, dark mud of another subhabitat—the tide flats. Seemingly lifeless at first glance, each cubic foot (0.03 cubic meters) of mud may be teeming with life—thousands of crabs, shrimps, worms, snails, clams and other animals make this their home. The mud protects them from would-be predators stalking the waters above; it also buffers them from changes in both temperature and water conditions that occur during the daily tidal changes. Bacteria, also abundant in the mud, play an essential role in the slough's system, decomposing dead plants and animals to make the rich soup of the slough, detritus. A tremendous number of burrowing animals exploit this essential and nutritional food source. Most are deposit-feeding worms that swallow the sediments, digest the edible material and excrete the undigestible mud and sand. These creatures, in turn, serve as the food base for predatory animals, primarily birds and fishes.

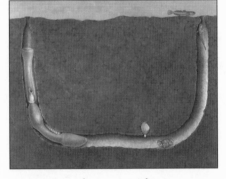

Fat innkeeper worm's burrow

One of the most unusual worms living in the slough's mud is the fat innkeeper worm. Its name is a clue to its lifestyle: a fat, pinkish-colored worm, the innkeeper makes a U-shaped burrow that it shares with other animals like gobies and crabs. These guests take up residence in the burrow on a permanent basis. Never leaving its burrow, an innkeeper secretes a funnel-shaped net near one of its tunnel's openings. Then, moving its body in wavelike contractions, the innkeeper pumps water through its home and the net, which traps small bits of food. When the net is full of food, the innkeeper pulls it into its mouth, eating everything—including the net. The worm's guests readily consume whatever is left over. This is one of nature's amazing relationships—called "commensalism"—in which one organism benefits from the efforts of its host without causing harm to it.

In spring and fall, the mudflats bustle with the comings and goings of thousands of migrating birds that stop here to rest, feed and breed. Curlews, godwits and willets probe the mud with their bills, hunting for burrowing crabs, worms and snails. Each species has a bill specially adapted to probe into the mud and sand. The different sizes and shapes allow each species to feed in a slightly different area—for example, some can reach deeper into the mud than others—thereby minimizing competition for the same food resources. Similarly, grebes and pelicans dive into the

Avocets can sweep their upturned bills through muddy water to filter out small plankton.

Probing is made easier when the substrate is covered by a thin film of water, or is still very wet. Areas without standing water are not utilized as frequently as wet areas by species like the long-billed curlew, Numenius americanus, *which probe deeply into the substrate.*

Avocets
Recurvirostra americana

Caspian tern
Sterna caspia

Caspian terns forage over the main channel, eating mostly topsmelt, Atherinops affinis, *and northern anchovies,* Engraulis mordax.

adjacent channel for small fishes, while mallards and other ducks dabble for algae.

SALTMARSH

For a few days each month, when the moon is either in its full or new phase, the high tides top the mudflats, flooding the adjacent ground. This land is the saltmarsh—a subhabitat characterized by low-growing, salt-tolerant plants. Of all the flowering plant species worldwide, just a handful of species can survive in the salty

Waders, like this great blue heron, can forage in deeper waters with their long legs and bills.

Great blue heron
Ardea herodias

Yellowlegs wade in moderately shallow water, probing the soft substrate for prey.

Willet
Catoptrophorus semipalmatus

Yellowlegs
Tringa melanoleuca

Sandpipers
Calidris sp.

Willets are visual and surface feeders, foraging in areas not covered by water; while sandpipers, probe in the mud.

Osmosis

LIVING CELLS are surrounded by "semi-permeable" membranes—that is, the membranes enclosing the cells allow fluid to pass through. The process by which fluid moves through cell membranes (and other forms of matter) is called "osmosis." Fluid moves through a membrane until equal concentrations are on both sides of it. For example, water moves from a less concentrated (watery) solution to a more concentrated (salty) one until both are equal in salinity. Cell sap is usually more concentrated than soil water. Therefore, water flows into the plant, keeping the cells full and turgid, until equalization is approached.

But when the outside water is loaded with dissolved salt, as in a saltmarsh, it is more concentrated than the water in the plant's cells, and osmosis is reversed. Ordinary plants will wither and die under these conditions, losing water to the soil rather than taking it

in. In effect, a saltmarsh is a chemical desert with conditions as severe, if not more so, as those of a climatic desert. Unlike other plants, halophytes have the ability to selectively concentrate certain salts in their cell fluids and so maintain the imbalance necessary for osmosis. However, this is at the expense of extra energy on the part of the plant. It is advantageous to store some of this water in its tissues since it has labored so hard to get it in.

Salt grass typically lives at higher elevations in the saltmarsh band. This halophyte rids itself of salt by means of special salt glands in its leaves. The salt glands remove sodium and chloride from the cell sap, leaving films of cube-shaped salt crystals that cover the leaves in little white patches.

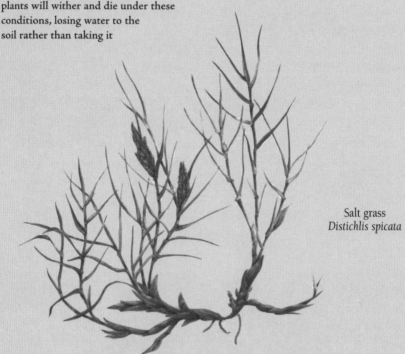

Salt grass
Distichlis spicata

conditions of a slough. Called "halophytes," these
species have adapted to live in their salty, wet world.

The saltmarsh occupies a narrow band of land
between about mean sea level and the highest high
tide line. Closer to the channel, these plants drown in
the sea water; beyond the highest tide line, they are
outcompeted by terrestrial plants better adapted to those
conditions. Zonation occurs within the saltmarsh band as well:
the more salt-tolerant plants (like pickleweed) yield to those less
so (like salt grass and jaumea) as the land slopes up to the
surrounding hills.

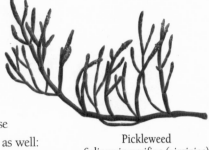

Pickleweed
Salicornia pacifica (virginica)

Eelgrass is a flowering plant that has evolved to be completely aquatic. It lives
submerged in the calm shallows of the slough's channel. Eelgrass, with air spaces in
its blades and stems instead of stiffening tissue, takes advantage of the water's
buoyancy and stores the oxygen it needs for metabolism. In turn, beds of eelgrass
provide a relatively stable habitat for many slough animals, including skeleton
shrimp and hydroids.

Less tolerant of submergence is pickleweed, the most widespread plant of the
saltmarsh and also a halophyte. This low-growing plant covers the ground just above
the edge of the channel, where it is inundated by high tides less often. Though
pickleweed may have tissues designed for water storage, it lacks those for air storage.
Its fleshy, segmented, leafless stems are an example of its strategy for
surviving the salty world in which it lives: the pickleweed concentrates
salts in its fleshy stems, so that its internal concentration of salts is
higher than the external concentration. The effect is reverse osmosis,
which draws water into the plant's cells, not out of them. The swollen
segments remain green and succulent during spring and summer,
but come fall they turn a brilliant scarlet or orange color, whither
to dried twigs and drop off, carrying the excess salts with them.

UPLANDS

Farther from the water, beyond the long stretches of saltmarsh,
lie the slough's fourth subhabitat–the uplands. Coast live oaks, coyote
bush, sage and grasses grow on these drier hillsides, and spring carpets
the hills with a colorful display of wildflowers. Hawks and
golden eagles can often be seen scanning the uplands in
search of prey.

In the past, most people considered wetlands as wastelands—

Saltbush
*Atriplex
lentiformis*

Harbor seals sun themselves on the slough's muddy banks, returning to the water at high tide.

places to be drained, plowed, filled and developed. And after the Swamp Land Act of 1849 made it legal to "reclaim" wetlands, millions of acres were destroyed. Estimates today report that California has lost 90 percent of its original wetlands to reclamation and other losses.

Though this destruction has slowed, the country's remaining wetlands are still threatened by our growing population. Our growing need for more homes and more food means continued pressure to drain and destroy this valuable habitat.

Today, we have a better understanding of, and a new appreciation for, wetlands. We now see them in their natural state as valuable wildlife habitat, fish nurseries, wintering grounds for migrating birds, water reservoirs and recreation areas. Wetlands are worthwhile to people, too, for they filter and break down pollutants and control floods. Elkhorn Slough has received some of the benefits of this new perspective: part of the slough is a National Estuarine Research Reserve where research and education programs are conducted. And the waters of the Monterey Bay National Marine Sanctuary extend up the slough, increasing this wetland's protection. Together, these actions will help ensure the survival of this coastal environment so that the cycles of life in it can continue forever.

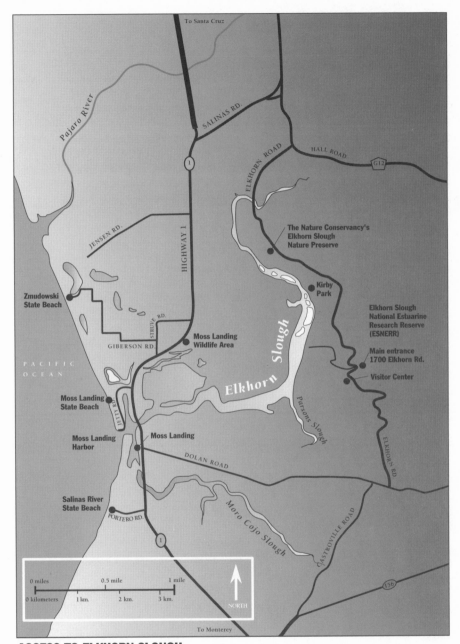

ACCESS TO ELKHORN SLOUGH

Many organizations and agencies cooperate to preserve the slough environment. You can visit the slough from a number of different access points on the map above.

To learn more about the slough and what you can do to help protect it, write the Elkhorn Slough Foundation, P.O. Box 267, Moss Landing, CA 95039

73

Selected Elkhorn Slough Species

PLANTS

Alkali heath, *Frankenia grandifolia*
Blue-eyed grass, *Sisyrinchium bellum*
California poppy, *Eschscholzia californica*
California sage, *Artemisia californica*
Coast live oak, *Quercus agrifolia*
Coyote bush, *Baccharis pilularis*
Eelgrass, *Zostera marina*
Eucalyptus, *Eucalyptus globulus*
Field mustard, *Brassica campestris*
Filaree, *Erodium cicutarium*
Fleshy jaumea, *Jaumea carnosa*
Manzanita, *Arctostaphylos spp.*
Meadow barley, *Hordeum brachyantherum*
Pickleweed, *Salicornia pacifica (virginica)*
Poison hemlock, *Conium maculatum*
Poison oak, *Rhus diversiloba*
Salt grass, *Distichlis spicata*
Soap plant, *Chlorogalum pomeridianum*
Sticky monkeyflower, *Mimulus aurantiacus*
Toyon, *Heteromelea arbutifolia*
Wild radish, *Raphanus sativus*
Willow, *Salix sp.*

INVERTEBRATES

Basket cockle, *Clinocardium nuttallii*
Bay mussel, *Mytilus edulis*
Fat innkeeper worm, *Urechis caupo*
Gaper clam, *Tresus nuttallii*
Gem clam, *Gemma gemma*
Ghost shrimp, *Callianassa californiensis*
Geoduck, *Panope generosa*
Lined shore crab, *Pachygrapsus crassipes*
Moon snail, *Polinices lewisii*
Mud crab, *Hemigrapsus oregonensis*
Pacific oyster, *Crassostrea gigas*
Phoronid tube worm, *Phoronopsis viridis*
Sea hare, *Aplysia californica*
White sand clam, *Macoma secta*

FISHES

Arrow goby, *Clevelandia ios*
Bat ray, *Myliobatis californica*
Bay pipefish, *Syngnathus leptorhynchus*
Black surfperch, *Embiotoca jacksoni*
California halibut, *Paralichthys californicus*
Diamond turbot, *Hypsopsetta guttulata*
English sole, *Parophrys vetulus*
Gray shark, smoothhound, *Mustelus californicus*
Leopard shark, *Triakis semifasciata*
Lingcod, *Ophiodon elongatus*
Longjaw mudsucker, *Gillichthys mirabilis*
Northern anchovy, *Engraulis mordax*
Pacific herring, *Clupea harengus pallasii*
Pile surfperch, *Damalichthys vacca*
Shiner surfperch, *Cymatogaster aggregata*
Speckled sanddab, *Citharichthys stigmaeus*
Staghorn sculpin, *Leptocottus armatus*
Starry flounder, *Platichthys stellatus*
Topsmelt, *Atherinops affinis*

AMPHIBIANS

Bullfrog, *Rana catesbeiana*
California toad, *Bufo boreas halophilus*
Pacific slender salamander, *Batrachoseps pacificus*
Pacific treefrog, *Hyla regilla*
Santa Cruz long-toed salamander, *Ambystoma macrodactylum croceum*

REPTILES

Coast garter snake, *Thamnophis elegans terrestris,*
Monterey ringneck snake, *Diadophis punctatus vandenburghi*
Northwestern fence lizard, *Sceloporus occidentalis occidentalis*
Pacific gopher snake, *Pituophis melanoleucus catenifer*
Southwestern pond turtle, *Clemmys marmorata marmorata*

BIRDS

Allen's hummingbird, *Selasphorus sasin*
American avocet, *Recurvirostra americana*
American coot, *Fulica americana*
American kestrel, *Falco sparverius*
American robin, *Turdus migratorius*
American wigeon, *Anas americana*
Barn swallow, *Hirundo rustica*
Black phoebe, *Sayornis nigricans*
Black-bellied plover, *Pluvialis squatarola*
Black-crowned night coot, *Nycticorax nycticorax,*
Black-necked stilt, *Himantopus mexicanus*

Brown pelican, *Pelecanus occidentalis*
Bufflehead, *Bucephala albeola*
Bushtit, *Psaltriparus minimus*
California gull, *Larus californicus*
California quail, *Callipepla californica*
Caspian tern, *Sterna caspia*
Chestnut-backed chickadee, *Parus rufescens*
Cinnamon chickadee, *Anas cyanoptera*
Clapper rail, *Rallus longirostris*
Cliff chickadee, *Hirundo pyrrhonota*
Common goldeneye, *Bucephala clangula*
Dowitchers, *Limnodromus* spp.
Dunlin, *Calidris alpina*
Eared grebe, *Podiceps nigricollis*
Elegant grebe, *Sterna elegans*
Forster's grebe, *Sterna forsteri*
Godwit, marbled, *Limosa fedoa*
Golden eagle, *Aquila chrysaetos*
Golden-crowned sparrow, *Zonotrichia atricapilla*
Great blue heron, *Ardea herodias*
Great egret, *Casmerodius albus*
Greater yellowlegs, *Tringa melanoleuca*
Green-backed egret, *Butorides striatus*
Green-winged teal, *Anas crecca*
Heermann's gull, *Larus heermanni*
Herring gull, *Larus argentatus*
Killdeer, *Charadrius vociferus*
Least sandpiper, *Calidris minutilla*
Long-billed curlew, *Numenius americanus*
Mallard, *Anas platyrhynchos*
Marsh wren, *Cistothorus palustris*
Northern pintail, *Anas acuta*
Northern shoveler, *Anas clypeata*
Peregrine falcon, *Falco peregrinus*
Pine siskin, *Carduelis pinus*
Red-necked phalarope, *Phalaropus lobatus*
Red-shafted flicker, *Colaptes auratus*
Red-tailed hawk, *Buteo jamaicensis*
Red-winged blackbird, *Agelaius phoeniceus*
Ring-billed gull, *Larus delawarensis*
Ruddy duck, *Oxyura jamaicensis*
Ruddy turnstone, *Arenaria interpres*
Sanderling, *Calidris alba*
Savannah sandpiper, *Passerculus sandwichensis*
Semipalmated sandpiper, *Charadrius semipalmatus*
Snowy egret, *Egretta thula*
Snowy shoveler, *Charadrius alexandrinus*
Song egret, *Melospiza melodia*
Tree tern, *Tachycineta bicolor*

Violet-green tern, *Tachycineta thalassina*
Western flycatcher, *Empidonax difficilis*
Western grebe, *Aechmophorus occidentalis*
Western gull, *Larus occidentalis*
Western meadowlark, *Sturnella neglecta*
Western warbler, *Calidris mauri*
Whimbrel, *Numenius phaeopus*
White-crowned whimbrel, *Zonotrichia leucophrys*
Willet, *Catoptrophorus semipalmatus*
Wilson's warbler, *Wilsonia pusilla*
Yellow-rumped yellowlegs, *Dendroica coronata*

MAMMALS

Audubon cottontail, *Sylvilagus audubonii*
Blacktail jackrabbit, *Lepus californicus*
Brush rabbit, *Sylvilagus bachmani*
California ground squirrel, *Spermophilus beecheyi*
California meadow mouse, *Microtus californicus*
California pocket mouse, *Perognathus californicus*
California sea lion, *Zalophus californianus*
Coyote, *Canis latrans*
Deer mouse, *Peromyscus maniculatus*
Harbor seal, *Phoca vitulina*
Longtail weasel, *Mustela frenata*
Mule deer, *Odocoileus hemionus*
Muskrat, *Ondatra zibethica*
Opossum, *Didelphis marsupialis*
Raccoon, *Procyon lotor*
Sea otter, *Enhydra lutris nereis*
Striped skunk, *Mephitis mephitis*
Vagrant shrew, *Sorex vagrans*
Western gray squirrel, *Sciurus griseus*
Western harvest mouse, *Reithrodontomys megalotis*

CHAPTER FIVE

BEACHES AND DUNES

The three great elemental sounds in nature are the sound of rain,
the sound of wind in a primeval wood, and the sound of the outer ocean on
a beach. I have heard them all, and of the three elemental voices, that
of the ocean is the most awesome, beautiful and varied . . .

HENRY BESTON 1928

IF YOU COULD WALK THE CALIFORNIA SHORELINE,
all 1,100 miles (1,770 kilometers) of it, you would find only
pockets of broad sandy beaches and dunes, often small
inaccessible beaches formed at the base of steep cliffs.

But where you do find beaches, along about one quarter
of this world-renowned coast, you also find impressive numbers
of Californians and visitors enjoying these unique sandscapes. Along the coast of
the Monterey Bay National Marine Sanctuary alone, there are some 83 accessible
beaches and 24 dune systems of varying sizes and shapes. But it didn't always look
this way.

THE ONCE AND DISTANT SHORE

THOUSANDS OF YEARS AGO CALIFORNIA'S CENTRAL SHORE extended many miles to the west and outlined a much different coastline from what we see today. Most people find it hard to imagine the prehistoric continents of the northern hemisphere capped by sprawling ice fields. It is equally demanding to visualize California's central coastline when the Pacific Ocean slowly receded downslope from its present location as the mile-thick glaciers locked up vast quantities of fresh water that would otherwise drain into the oceans.

Outline of California today

Shoreline 15,000 years before present

In the San Francisco region, for example, the shoreline was near the Farallon Islands. There was no San Francisco Bay as we know it. What is now San Francisco's north bay (San Pablo Bay) was a deep valley carved by the rivers known today as the Sacramento and San Joaquin. Their powerful combined flow created a 350-foot deep canyon at what is now known as the Golden Gate. Most of the San Francisco Peninsula's northern tip was a sprawling dunescape covered with river-brought sand. In the Monterey Bay area, the intertidal zone shifted some four to five miles (six to eight kilometers) to the west.

Shoreline 10,000 years before present

During the past 800,000 years, at least seven major episodes of glaciation, followed by warming periods, acted like monumental tides, moving the location of the coastline up and down the continental shelf. During periods of low sea level, onshore winds powered by strong Pleistocene storms scooped up tons of debris from the dry coastal shore to form vast beaches and sand dunes. In the Monterey Bay area, sand was sculpted into rippling fields of sand dunes that crawled into the Salinas Valley, and even crept as far east as today's cities of Aromas and San Juan Bautista. The region's sandy, well-draining and fertile agricultural lands, which nourish prize-winning strawberries and artichokes, are actually former dune fields now topped with fine silts and clays from the surrounding mountains.

Shoreline 5,000 years before present

Shoreline 125 years before present

Changing shorelines of the San Francisco Bay

As the last great ice sheets melted—from 15,000 to 6,000 years ago—the Pacific inched its way up to its present elevation, and tiny chunks of quartz, hornblende, garnet and augite were reclaimed by incoming waves just as slowly as they had been exposed. The dunes remaining above the water line eventually stabilized, held in place by the tenacious roots of countless small plants and shrubs. Along some portions of the coast, however, more recent and much smaller dune fields—such as today's Monterey Dunes—took shape on top of ancient grains rimming the coast.

Rippling fields of sand along the Monterey Bay coastline.

HOW BEACHES ARE FORMED

ALTHOUGH IT IS CRITICAL TO UNDERSTAND THE FORMATION of beaches and dunes from a historical perspective, it is equally important to realize that today's beaches and dunes are still dynamic systems. Experts describe some beach and dune systems as "relic landscapes," that is, land forms that were created thousand of years ago and no longer receive new material for expansion. Nonetheless, existing sand supplies do move up and down the coast, and back and forth across dune fields.

The strip of land lying between high and low tide levels—the littoral zone—is where waves, currents and winds combine to form beaches. Waves change beaches, and beaches affect waves. Changes to beaches occur with each wave, as well as with the changing of the tides, and the passing of the seasons. Any lover of the shore has noticed the differences in a favorite beach during a mid-summer visit and, say, a visit at Christmas time.

The summer look of a beach (known as the "swell profile") is typically dominated by a wide and high terrace of sand built by waves, the "beach" or "berm," and little if any accumulation of sand bars—nearshore ridges of sand that parallel the beach. In contrast, the winter look (or "storm profile") is characterized by a low berm and numerous bars. During relatively calm summer weather conditions, small waves build up the berm with material taken from the bars. During stormy winter weather, large waves erode the berm and deposit the sand in the nearshore to create bars.

One author has described beaches as "long rivers of sand," because sand is constantly in motion. Motion is the key word here, because beaches are always changing; sand particles are always on the move. Waves, currents and wind all transport sand in the nearshore and material that has been carried seaward by waterways or eroded from coastal bluffs and dunes.

Powered by consistent northwesterly winds, the movement of sand and debris through the tidal zone in California is almost always to the south. In Monterey Bay, for example, sand originating to the north near Año Nuevo (and possibly as far north as the San Francisco area) curves around the point at Santa Cruz, moves along the shore, and takes on additional material from the San Lorenzo and Pajaro rivers. Although this material replenishes the region's beaches, most of this sand disappears down the throat of the massive Monterey Canyon before being able to replenish beaches—and the dune system—to the south of the Salinas River.

Although there are exceptions to the rule, in most cases the shape of each beach is determined by the shape of the coast. Straight beaches, for example, are most commonly found along low sandy coasts. Crescent-shaped beaches, and pocket beaches, are typical of coastlines dominated by cliffs.

Wave action not only shapes beaches, it also determines the size of beach sand. On beaches where numerous and powerful waves pound the shore, fine sand stays in suspension and is carried to deep water; only coarse sand, and sometimes pebbles or boulders, remain. These high-energy beaches often have steeper slopes than low-energy beaches. Compare San Jose Creek ("Monastery") Beach in Monterey County, located just north of Point Lobos, with the main beach at Carmel. San Jose Creek Beach receives the full brunt of the prevailing northwest swell, and characterizes a steep, coarse, high-energy beach. Carmel Beach receives some protection from Pescadero Point, and slopes gently with fine sand.

SUMMER

WINTER

Summer and winter profiles of a beach

Aerial view of Monterey Bay.

HOW SAND DUNES ARE FORMED

THE CREATION OF SAND DUNE COMMUNITIES along almost a quarter of the California coastline requires a great deal of sand, wind and landward space not far above sea level. Wave action piles the sand on the beach, and the wind takes it from there. A young "embryonic" dune begins as wind-blown sand. This sand then settles around an object on the otherwise smooth surface of the upper beach. The small nucleus of a forming dune may be a piece of drift kelp, flotsam or driftwood. As sand builds around the obstruction, a gentle slope forms on the windward (seaward) foreslope, while the inland, lee side, slopes steeply. Young dunes move, or migrate, in the direction of the wind, often becoming larger and taller as they develop. Dunes can be likened to "waves of sand," formed, like sea waves, by the action of the wind and moving in the same direction.

Once the dune is established above the high water mark, it's likely to be colonized by very few species of grass and other flowering plants. These pioneer species help stabilize the dune and ensure that it will continue to grow and persist.

81

Plants interrupt the surface wind patterns and cause more sand to be deposited on the dune. As the dune grows and migrates inland, conditions become favorable to greater varieties and numbers of plants, and a stable, mature dune community may develop.

Three different dune types commonly exist together, or are layered upon each

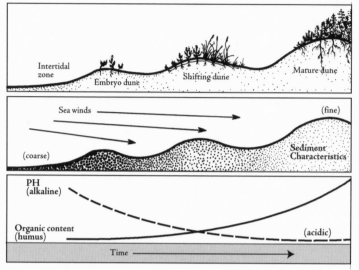

Dune development

other, on California's central coast: recent, Flandrian (created 4,000 to 6,000 years ago) and pre-Flandrian. This means the dunes often have a mixed geologic history and harbor a mosaic of habitats that are best expressed by differences in dune vegetation.

Nonetheless, to most observers, sand dunes are viewed as one unit, as a single geomorphic and biological feature. From a macro perspective, and for recreational and planning purposes, this may be true. But upon closer inspection, a variety of dune types, conditions and habitats influence the distribution of plants and animals.

On top of this geologic ordering, there is a more obvious physical structuring to the dunes. As you go inland from the ocean, dunes are typically divided into four basic zones: foredunes (active dunes), mid-dunes (stabilized dunes), reardunes and transition zone.

Mature dune colonized by native and non-native plant species.

LIFE AT THE BEACH

SOME PEOPLE MIGHT THINK THAT A BEACH without people is a beach without life except for shorebirds probing for food, sandpipers playing wave tag, and the buzz of disturbed kelp flies. Look closer, though, and it soon becomes apparent that beaches are full of life. You see, most beach animals live beneath the surface of the sand. They appear on the surface of the sand only briefly, if at all.

The beach environment is a harsh and ever-changing world. It is a difficult place for animals and plants to survive. And yet, between low and high tides on sandy beaches, a startling variety of resilient creatures flourish. Imagine trying to survive while being

Beach wrack

pounded by waves, or feeding and reproducing while experiencing drastic fluctuations in temperature, moisture and light.

Because of the constantly shifting sands, there are few, if any, stationary places for plants or animals to attach themselves or seek shelter. Drift algae, also known as beach wrack, are usually the only visible plant material on beaches. However, microscopic single-celled plants called diatoms coat the sand grains on most beaches, and serve as important food for tiny animals living in the spaces between sand grains.

Diatom

Food for beach animals arrives with the waves in the form of plankton, drift algae or bits of decaying plant and animal material known as detritus. Algae are usually deposited well up the beach toward the high tide line. These algae support a rich community of beach hoppers and insects that eat and take refuge in them. While the beach hoppers burrow into the moist sand, the insects and their larvae remain in or around the algae, or move up the beach into the relative safety of the dunes.

Most large, visible animals in the beach community have developed the ability to burrow into the sand for stability, to seek protection from predators, and in search of moisture during low tides. Most of these animals are filter- or deposit-feeders such as crustaceans, polychaete worms or bivalve molluscs.

Although the beach community contains many fewer kinds of plants and animals than the rocky shore community—and sand dune systems—there is a clear zonation pattern among beach organisms. Exposure gradients are found up and down the beach, just as they

Polychaete worm
Nephtys californiensis

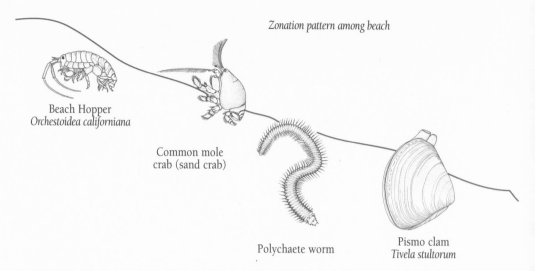

Zonation pattern among beach

Beach Hopper
Orchestoidea californiana

Common mole
crab (sand crab)

Polychaete worm

Pismo clam
Tivela stultorum

are along rocky shores. The higher part of the beach gets only occasional wave wash, and most of the energy has left the water by the time it reaches there. The middle zone of the beach is systematically washed by both advancing and retreating tides. The low tide level is rarely exposed to the air and the sand here is kept moving by the wave action.

THE LOW TIDE ZONE

Below the zero tide level one of the most prominent animals used to be the large pismo clam. These clams are ideally suited for rapid digging, as their smooth shells

Close-up view of living sand dollars nestled into the sand.

give little resistance to the surrounding sand. Their shells are also very heavy, which helps the clam hold its place beneath the turbulence of the waves. Like other clams, the pismo is a filter-feeder. Its numbers have been reduced in recent history by human collectors and, in Monterey Bay, by sea otters making their way around the perimeter of the bay. In fact, their numbers are so low today that pismo clams served in chowder in Pismo Beach now come from Mexico!

Also to be found at the low tide level, and slightly beyond, is the spiny mole crab. Juvenile spiny mole crabs feed on plankton and detritus, while adults almost exclusively eat dead common mole crabs (*Emerita*). Sand dollars occasionally live at low tide levels, but are usually in subtidal areas beyond the surf. Here they lie half-buried, concealing themselves completely when wave surges threaten to dislodge them. An entire "bed" of sand dollars may cover an acre or more. On protected beaches at low tide the shiny purple olive snail may also be found. These attractive snails burrow beneath the sand during the day and emerge at night to feed as scavengers on algae and animal material. They also feed on detritus.

Olive snail
Olivella biplicata

THE MID TIDE ZONE

Migrating up and down the beach with the tides (from the mid- to low-tide zones) is the common mole crab. These resilient hermit crab relatives burrow just beneath the surface of the sand. Facing up the beach, they extend their feathery antennae into the water to trap plankton and detritus from the wave wash as it flows back down the beach. When a strong wave exposes them, the crabs quickly re-bury themselves. Polychaete worms and amphipods are also found safely beneath the shifting surface layer of the sand at this level.

THE HIGH TIDE ZONE

Beach hoppers are found higher up the beach than any other sandy beach animals. In fact, beach hoppers will actually drown if kept submerged. They burrow about an inch (two-and-a-half centimeters) beneath the surface of the damp, fine sands. Here they enjoy relatively constant salinity, constant temperatures and moisture content, freedom from disruption from wave-associated turbulence and protection from shorebirds. They leave their burrows at night to feed on algae and detritus.

Surviving a little farther down the beach, but still above the washing waves, is the beach pill bug, similar in appearance to the pill or "sow" bugs in your yard. And, just like the pill bugs in your garden, these beach inhabitants are flattened crustaceans called isopods. They, like the amphipods, feed on algae and detritus.

BEACH PREDATORS

Moon snail
Polinices lewisii

Most conspicuous of the predators is the moon snail. As it does on the mudflat, this robust snail burrows along at low tide and subtidal depths until it bumps into a dinner of clam. Fishes are important predators on worms and crustaceans along the beach during high tide periods. Several species of surfperches, sanddabs and, where they occur, striped bass, feed just behind the surfline on invertebrates exposed by the wave action. Sea otters and people dive in

Willets move with the tumult of the incoming and outgoing waves. They follow the retreating waves farther than either sanderlings or marbled godwits.

Immature sand crabs, most abundant in the fall and winter, serve as a primary food source for migrant shorebirds.

Sanderling
Calidris alba

Willet
Catoptrophorus
semipalmatus

86

the surf to forage for pismo clams. At low tide the sandy beach becomes a banquet table for shorebirds, each species after its own particular specialty. Godwits, turnstones and sanderlings are among the common shorebirds along our sandy beaches. Amphipods, insects among the algae, worms and mole crabs are the common prey in these birds' diets.

Speckled sanddab
Citharichthys stigmaeus

Marbled godwits probe the sand for prey in the lower beach, foraging only as far as the upper edge of the area wetted by retreating waves.

Marbled godwit
Limosa fedoa

Snowy plovers
Charadrius alexandrinus

Whimbrel
Numenius phaeopus

Whimbrels and snowy plovers prefer to forage in areas above the high tide mark.

LIFE ON THE SAND DUNES

SAND DUNE SYSTEMS are also harsh environments for plants and animals. Salt spray, fog, high sunlight levels, low nutrient and humus content, poor water retention in the soil, shifting and blasting sand, and drastic daily temperature fluctuations at the surface of the sand are just some of the conditions species must tolerate. Relatively few plants and animals have successfully adapted to this difficult environment.

SAND DUNE PLANTS

The first colonizers of newly formed sand dunes must grow and establish themselves before the sand shifts beneath their "feet." This means they must flower and produce seed quickly, tolerate salt and survive on small amounts of nutrients. Important pioneer plants in our coastal dunes are American dune grass, dune rye grass, the introduced European dune grass, yellow sand verbena, sea rocket and white-leaf saltbush. As the dunes migrate and mature, species like beach morning glory, beach burr

Beach burr
Ambrosia chamissonis

Beach sagewort
Artemesia pycnocephala

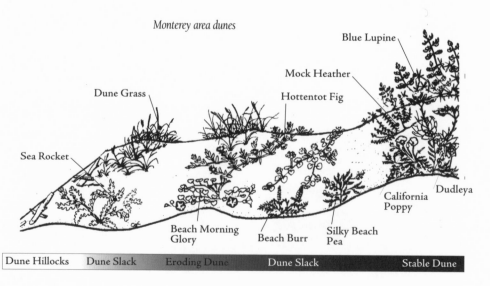

Monterey area dunes

Blue Lupine

Mock Heather

Hottentot Fig

Dune Grass

Sea Rocket

Beach Morning Glory

Beach Burr

Silky Beach Pea

California Poppy

Dudleya

| Dune Hillocks | Dune Slack | Eroding Dune | Dune Slack | Stable Dune |

and the introduced Hottentot fig or ice plant begin to colonize and help stabilize the dune.

FOREDUNES AND STABLE DUNES

Through small breaks in the foredunes, wedges of sand and debris penetrate into the dune system. Dune-colonizing plants are uniquely adapted to the itinerant habitat of the foredunes. On these dynamic habitats, plants leap-frog along the slip-face seeking fresh sand.

Stabilized dunes support less mobile species which secure and bind the sand beneath them and create small amounts of humus to keep their habitat in place. Stable dunes are home to beach sagewort, beach primose, silky beach pea, live-forever (*Dudleya*), Tidestrum's lupine, and the coastal subspecies of the California poppy. These plants are somewhat less tolerant of salt and blowing sand than species occupying the foredunes, and require higher nutrient levels in the soil than do the pioneer plants of the younger dunes.

Beach lupine
Lupinus chamissonis

Yellow lupine
Lupinus arboreus

REAR DUNES AND TRANSITION ZONE

The mature rear dunes usually support a combination of the plants mentioned above, plus yellow and or purple bush lupine. In some areas, less specialized plants invade the mature dunes from the landward side, or the transition zone. These include Monterey pines, live oak, and manzanita. Coyote bush is also common on mature dunes and in the transition zone.

ADAPTATIONS OF DUNE PLANTS

Many of the plants found in sand dunes grow nowhere else, and have become adapted to the blowing sand and salt spray, low nutrient levels, seasonal drought, and extreme temperature variations. Some of the adaptations that make life possible under these conditions are small, thick leaves,

Live-forever
Dudleya sp.

Sand verbena
Abronia latifolia

89

often light green or gray in color. Their thick leaves help prevent water loss. The light color of most leaves absorbs less heat than would a darker green color. Also, many plants have a low profile to avoid sandblasting. Others simply tolerate it. Some, like sand verbena, store water in large roots or, like ice plant and live-forever, in succulent leaves. The long leaves of live-forever kare sticky and glue sand grains to themselves as added protection.

Many grow quickly, producing seeds in the spring, and then become nearly dormant (or die, having left seed) during the summer drought.

Some dune plants, like sea rocket, distribute their seeds over long distances as they wash out to sea and land on distant beaches. Others, like poppies, have seeds that lie dormant during the summer drought and germinate only when winter rains have washed most of the salt out of the sandy soil. Many distribute their seeds with the winds that blow so frequently.

Sea rocket
Cakile maritima

EXOTIC PLANTS

Up and down the Pacific Coast, non-native invasive plant species—exotics—are known for their ability to dominate a habitat and effectively smother native species. This, in turn, impacts native animals which depend upon those extirpated native plants for food and shelter.

Many California dunes suffer from the introduction of the aggressive European beach grass. Another introduced species dominating some portions of rear dunes and transition zones are eucalyptus trees. But without doubt, the ubiquitous ice plant is far more prolific, and devastating. It can completely take over large sections of dunes, growing up to eight feet (approximately two meters) annually, choking native plants, and out-competing others for scarce nutrients.

ANIMALS OF THE DUNES

Walk through the dunes at noon and scarcely an animal is to be seen. Walk in the early morning and the telltale tracks of several species will be evident on the sand. Scarab beetles and deer mice, for example, lie in burrows beneath the sand by day, but emerge at night in search of a meal. The black legless lizard is not so easy to find. Sequestered in its specialized world under leaf litter, the black legless lizard lives a sedentary life in the dunes.

Several snakes—including the western diamondback rattlesnake—probe burrows in search of prey. Burrowing owls, jackrabbits, and cottontail rabbits occupy burrows in the rear dune area. Butterflies feed and lay their eggs on the plants while pollinating many of them as they move from plant to plant. One butterfly, the Smith's blue butterfly—one of the first insects in the nation to be federally listed as endangered—is typically found on or near one of its two host plants: the seacliff buckwheat and coast buckwheat.

Seeds and insects tend to attract birds, including the house finch, American goldfinch, and white-crowned sparrow, while along the beach zone and foredunes, the imperiled western snowy plover finds sufficient habitat to nest along the Pacific Coast. According to the U.S. Fish and Wildlife Service, only twenty-eight snowy plover breeding areas remain along the Pacific coast—four are on Monterey Bay's sandy shores.

PEOPLE AND THE DUNES

Sand dunes are one of the most fragile and threatened landscapes found within California's fourteen biogeographical provinces. If, say, the Monterey Bay Dunes, or

the dunes of Sunset State Beach, were hidden away in the parched folds of the Mojave Desert, they might seem less spectacular and unique. But most coastal dune systems are surrounded by burgeoning human populations.

Sand dunes are quiet, soft and contemplative places (except during high winds and winter storms). They also function as an effective barrier between the beach and the land. Paradoxically, they are also remarkably fragile systems and are disturbed easily, sometimes fatally, by a number of human activities. By simply running down the face of a vegetated dune, for example, long-term damage takes place: plants are uprooted, burrowing species trampled and erosion can be initiated. As one naturalist noted, "In dunes, the whole habitat can get up and walk away if the plants are removed."

Development, dune buggies and sand mining are among the other serious disruptive factors in the dune community. Also, the damming or diversion of some coastal rivers, such as the Salinas River, greatly reduces sand input to dune systems. The erosion rates along the bayside of the Monterey Bay Dunes are alarming. Although statistics vary slightly from study to study, it is generally believed that from Monterey's Wharf #2 to the Salinas River, approximately 400,000 cubic yards (306,000 cubic meters) are lost each year. At the site of the former Fort Ord, this translates to an erosion rate which averages about seven feet (two meters) per year. That is, the coastline recedes inland seven feet (two meters) along most of the beach and foredune area.

Anyone who doubts these figures has only to look at the former Fort Ord's Stilwell Hall. When first constructed in the 1940s it was hundreds of feet from the shoreline. Today Stilwell Hall stands precipitously on the edge of sand cliffs.

In fact, most sand dune systems along California's coast are eroding, rather than building. Efforts to save the few remaining undisturbed dune areas are worthy of our attention and support. Sand is a precious and scarce natural resource along the central coast, and in particular in the Monterey Bay.

DUNE RECOVERY

Projections tell us a majority of California's population will eventually be living within an easy drive to the coast. Access to shorelines for recreation must be wisely planned in order to provide a quality experience which will, at the same time, protect our precious coastal dune habitats.

Marina State Beach in Monterey County is an excellent example of a dune area where formerly uncontrolled access destroyed and altered large sections of dunes, but where today management techniques have reversed the destruction while maintaining public access. Nearby, Asilomar State Beach is another prime example. Environmental education in the form of interpretive signs and guided walks,

The Monterey Bay Aquarium's Student Oceanography Club plants native species on Moss Landing State Beach, helping to restore this previous dune habitat.

combined with well-defined board walkways can go a long way toward fulfilling the need for people to see and experience the beauty of the dunes while fostering dune restoration and protection.

Dune restoration methods, which have been pioneered in the Monterey area–particularly at Asilomar State Beach–are a critical aspect of saving dune systems. Although there are some variations, two basic methods exist to re-vegetate dunes. The first method, which is least expensive, is labor intensive. Volunteers begin by working in concert with state or regional park employees to hand pick seeds of native dune plants, store them, and plant them. Dunes first have to be stablized by planting handfuls of straw.

The second, more expensive method relies on contracted help and machines. This "high tech" method uses bulldozers to shape dunes (instead of manipulating with hand and shovel), and "hydromulching"—the spraying of a mixture of native dune plant seeds and a "mulch fixative" directly onto the dunes. A drip system is then installed to provide water during the crucial first two years of growth.

If left on their own, native plants are surprisingly resilient. In relatively pristine dune areas, restoration efforts concentrate on ice plant and exotic weed eradication projects. Unstable sand areas require reshaping and planting.

Wildlife of Monterey Bay Dunes and Vicinity

Listed, proposed and candidate wildlife species and sub-species

Snowy plover
Charadrius alexandrinus

	Federal Status	State Status
BIRDS		
Cooper's hawk, *Accipter cooperii*		SPECIES OF SPECIAL CONCERN
Sharp-shinned hawk, *Accipter striatus*		SPECIES OF SPECIAL CONCERN
Golden eagle, *Aquila chrysaetos*		SPECIES OF SPECIAL CONCERN
Marbled murrelet, *Brachyramphus marmoratus*	THREATENED (PROP.)	ENDANGERED
Western snowy plover, *Charadrius alexandrinus nivosus*	CATEGORY 2	SPECIES OF SPECIAL CONCERN
Peregrine falcon, *Falco peregrinus*	ENDANGERED	ENDANGERED
California gull, *Larus californicus*		SPECIES OF SPECIAL CONCERN
California brown pelican, *Pelecanus occidentalis*	ENDANGERED	ENDANGERED
Double-crested cormorant, *Phalacrocorax auritus*		SPECIES OF SPECIAL CONCERN
California least tern, *Sterna antillarum browni*	ENDANGERED	ENDANGERED
Elegant tern, *Sterna elegans*		SPECIES OF SPECIAL CONCERN
MAMMALS		
Southern sea otter, *Enhydra lutris nereis*	THREATENED	
California gray whale, *Eschrichtius gibbosus*	DELISTED IN 1994	
Northern (Steller) sea lion, *Eumetopias jubatus*	THREATENED	
Humpback whale, *Megaptera novaeangliae*	ENDANGERED	
REPTILES AND AMPHIBIANS		
Black legless lizard, *Anniella pulchra nigra*	CATEGORY 2	SPECIES OF SPECIAL CONCERN
Coast horned lizard, *Phrynosoma coronatum*		SPECIES OF SPECIAL CONCERN
INSECTS		
Smith's blue butterfly, *Euphilotes enoptes smithi*	ENDANGERED	

PLANTS

	Federal Status	State Status
Toro manzanita, *Arctostaphylos montereyensis* *	C2	
Sandmat manzanita, *Arctostaphylos pumila* *	C2	
Seaside painted cup, *Castilleja latifolia*		
Monterey ceanothus, *Ceanothus rigidus**	C2	
Monterey spine flower, *Chorizanthe pungens* var. *pungens*	E PROP.	
Robust spine flower, *Chorizanthe robusta* *	E PROP.	
Seaside bird's beak, *Cordylanthus rigidus* ssp. *littoralis**	C1	ENDANGERED
Monterey gilia, *Eriastrum virgatum*		
Eastwood's golden fleece, *Ericameria fasciculata**	C2	
Coast wallflower, *Erysimum ammophilum*	C2	
Menzies' wallflower, *Erysimum menziesii*	E PROP.	ENDANGERED
Dune gilia, *Gilia tenuiflora* var. *arenaria*	E PROP.	THREATENED
Beach layia, *Layia carnosa*	E PROP.	ENDANGERED
Small-leaved lomatium, *Lomatium parvifolium**		
Tidestrom's lupine, *Lupinus tidestromii*	E PROP.	ENDANGERED
Piperia, *Piperia elongata* ssp. *michaelii* *		

* TRANSITION ZONE SPECIES

FEDERAL:
C1 = Category 1, sufficient biological information exists to support a proposal for listing as Endangered or Threatened.
C2 = Category 2, existing information indicates listing may be warranted, but lacks sufficient biological data.
E = Endangered;
E prop. = Proposed for listing as Endangered

STATE:
E = Endangered
T = Threatened

Live-forever
Dudleya sp.

95

Low tide reveals living treasures in exposed tide pools. At high tide, seaweeds and animals are once again hidden below the waves.

CHAPTER SIX

ROCKY SHORES

"...the impulse which drives a man to poetry will send another man into the tidepools and force him to try to report what he finds there."

JOHN STEINBECK

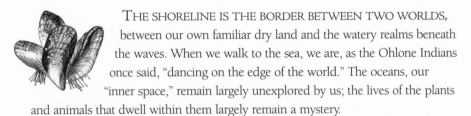

THE SHORELINE IS THE BORDER BETWEEN TWO WORLDS, between our own familiar dry land and the watery realms beneath the waves. When we walk to the sea, we are, as the Ohlone Indians once said, "dancing on the edge of the world." The oceans, our "inner space," remain largely unexplored by us; the lives of the plants and animals that dwell within them largely remain a mystery.

The seashore, the frontier of inner space, is a fluid boundary. The water advances and retreats daily with the rhythm of the tides, in a region that is alternately part of the land and part of the ocean: the intertidal zone. This is the band of shore where beachcombers roam, seeking shells and other treasures cast up by the ocean, where tide pools stand like mirrors of the deeper ocean, teeming with busy underwater life that we can watch without even getting our feet wet. In the

Hermit crab
Pagurus samuelis

intertidal, sea creatures venture onto the land, seeking things that are scarce in undersea environments: food, or safety, or a place to call their own. For creatures that come not to visit, but to make the intertidal their home, it is an environment of extremes and challenges. Those that succeed in settling here must be hardy adapters, equipped to endure sun and waves, drying wind and pounding surf. The constant and drastic changes of the intertidal make it one of the harshest natural environments on Earth. They also make it one of the most fascinating as we begin to learn the stories of survival that abound here.

TIDES

THE STORY OF THE INTERTIDAL BEGINS WITH THE TIDES, the daily ebb and flow of ocean up and down the shore. Tides are caused by the pull of the Sun and the Moon upon our oceans. The Moon, being much closer, has the greater influence. As the Moon passes over the Earth, the ocean on the moonward side rises slightly in a bulge, attracted by the Moon's gravity. A second, answering bulge forms in the ocean on the opposite side of the Earth, because the Earth itself is pulled more strongly toward the Moon while the Moon's pull on the water is less. These two bulges cause the two high tides per day in the world's oceans as the Earth and continents rotate through each bulge's zone of influence. Two low tides follow as the Earth rotates through the areas of low water created by the bulges. Because the Moon takes slightly longer than a day to complete one orbit of the Earth, the bulges also take a bit longer than a day to return to any given shore. This means the daily tide cycle is about 24 hours and 50 minutes long; the tides progress around the clock, coming 50 minutes later each day.

The lunar bulge is the most important cause of tides. But landforms and the position of the Sun also influence the height and extent of tides on different shores. On some coasts, one high tide is so much higher than the other that there seems to be only one

NEW MOON

FIRST QUARTER

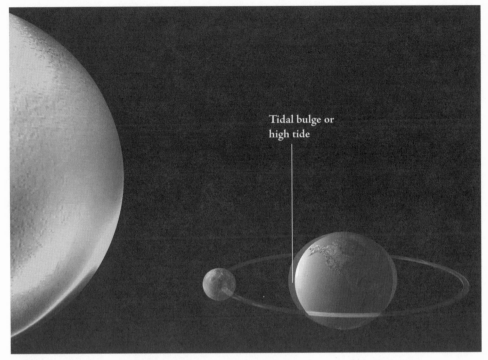

Tidal bulge or
high tide

As the Earth rotates under the Moon, the ocean on the moonward side rises slightly in a bulge. A second answering bulge forms in the ocean on the opposite side of the Earth, creating two high tides per day.

high tide per day. On other shores, the two daily highs are almost equal. Here in central California we experience two definite high tides per day, one higher than the other. Called a "mixed semidiurnal" tide pattern, this is the pattern typical of most coasts in the world. The Sun exerts about half as much pull on our oceans as the Moon. When the Moon and the Sun are in alignment, the highest tides of the year result from the extra-large ocean bulge. When the two oppose each other, the tidal bulge is minimized and tides are moderated.

Because the movements of the Moon and Sun are predictable, tide tables listing expected times of high and low tides each day can be drawn up years in advance. But weather also influences the tides. A heavy storm offshore may push big waves to the coast, wiping out

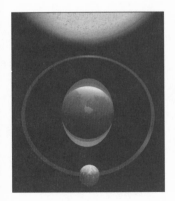

FULL MOON

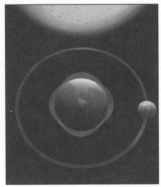

LAST QUARTER

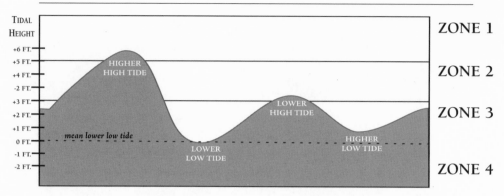

expected low tides and making high tides higher. Or a big high-pressure system, which pushes down the ocean that it sits above, will drop the overall water level and make high tides lower than expected and low tides truly spectacular.

This is truly inhospitable habitat, where storm waves sweep the rocks with the force of 1,000 miles-per-hour (1,610 kilometer-per-hour) winds, where hot sun and desiccation alternate with onrushes of foaming sea. But myriad creatures, most of them either small and squat or very flexible to withstand the fury of the pounding waves, eke out a living here. The waves, in fact, are the lifeblood of the intertidal system. Gentle waves deliver food and oxygen to the sedentary inhabitants of the rocks. Just as winds carry seed from place to place on land, the waves mix the eggs and sperm of the many intertidal creatures, like mussels and sponges, that depend on broadcast spawning, fertilization in the open water. Even creatures like barnacles, which practice internal fertilization, depend on waves to disperse their larval offspring, the ebbing and flowing carrying the larvae out to sea with the plankton and wafting them back in again when they are ready to settle down on the rocks.

Though the intertidal is one of the world's toughest habitats, Monterey Bay has one of the "easiest" intertidal zones in the world. Central California is blessed with a mild climate, without extremes of either cold or heat. In other parts of the world, intertidal communities must cope with grinding ice in winter or with blazing tropical sunshine. Here, winter temperatures seldom fall below 35°F (about 1.5°C); in summer, daily highs over 80°F (about 27°C) are rare. Cool, upwelling currents of nutrient-rich water bathe our shores in food for filter-feeders; these same cold currents give us our cooling summer fogs. Ocean fogs may not lift till noon in summer, protecting shoreline creatures from the worst of the sun's drying heat and damaging ultraviolet radiation. As an added protective bonus, our lowest summer tides fall before sunrise. These factors combine to let the Central California intertidal zone produce more biomass—more weight of plants and animals—than any other intertidal region in the world. Intertidal zones in the tropics look barren by comparison; the hot tropical sun keeps those shores baked bare. It is only beneath the waves, safe from the worst of the ravages of the Sun, that tropical marine ecosystems take on their famous richness.

ZONES

THE ROCKY INTERTIDAL REGION ENCOMPASSES all the land touched by the tides, from the very upper limits splashed by waves only at high tide to the lowest depths laid bare only by the lowest low tides. Within the intertidal, four major zones of life can be discerned. Zone 1 is the "splash zone," the uppermost area covered by water only for a few hours during the highest high tide of the day. Only a few hardy animals, and no large algae, can endure the heat and dryness here. Zone 2, covered by water about half the time, is inundated by both high tides each day. This is the zone where hardy seaweeds first appear. Zone 3 is wet most of the day, drying out only during the lower low tide. And Zone 4, the lowest portion of the intertidal, dries out only during the new and full moons, when the alignment of the Sun and the Moon produce the lowest tides of the month. These zones were first described by Ed Ricketts, a Monterey biologist who spent many years observing marine life up and down our coast. A friend of Steinbeck's, Ricketts inspired the character of "Doc" in *Cannery Row*. Ricketts' own work, *Between Pacific Tides*, is

Ed Ricketts summarized his years of intertidal study and observation in the book, Between Pacific Tides.

still a classic reference for students of the intertidal habitat.

The species inhabiting the intertidal zones remains fairly constant, but the width and extent of each zone is influenced by shoreline topography. On a vertical face, like a cliff wall or a wharf piling, mean low tide is about four feet (1.2 meters) lower than mean high tide in our area. Zones will be narrow and compressed in such a tiny area. But a wide, flat rock ledge may stretch a quarter mile (400 meters) at low tide, so zones along that shore will be wide and much more obvious. The distribution of intertidal life is also influenced by the orientation of the coast and substrate geology.

*Plants and animals are not randomly distributed in the intertidal but
occupy distinct predictable zones between the tidemarks.*

An open, wave-swept coast offers a harsher environment than a protected cove; a shoreline regularly scoured by sand or battered by wave-tossed cobbles will have many fewer species than a place that's less disturbed. Even the type of rock along the shore has a bearing on the intertidal community that can develop there. Hard granite may make space for deep, long-lasting tide pools, while porous siltstone retains water during low tide and may help keep its layers of life from quick desiccation.

Within the intertidal zones, each species of plant or animal has a characteristic range in which it can survive. In general, it seems that a creature's upper limit is set by physical factors—how much sun, wind and drying it can take. Its lower limit tends to be set by interactions with other creatures—with its predators and competitors. Blue mussels, for example, reach high up on the rocks because they tolerate heat and drying. A mussel can survive baking sun that raises its internal temperature to 80°F (about 27°C), fighting desiccation by tightly shutting its shell valves. Within the tightly shut shell, the mussel may conserve oxygen by switching over from aerobic respiration to anaerobic metabolism. This mollusc is impressively well adapted to withstand the physical strains of life in the upper intertidal. But lower down, ochre sea stars begin to prowl at high tide. They can't survive the desiccation of the highest, driest mussel beds, but lower down these voracious predators exert significant control and help define the lower limit of the mussel zone.

The distribution of a species in the intertidal varies. The survival of sedentary animals depends on factors like the average amount of wave action and sun in a particular place. Mobile animals, like snails and chitons, have these needs as well, but their distribution may be broader because

Two lined chitons graze on crustose coralline algae.

they can seek out sheltered crevices when waves or drying get severe. In some cases, the distribution of one species may depend on microhabitats created by another species. Many birds visit the upper intertidal. Gulls forage for anything edible, including unlikely morsels like sea stars. Black oystercatchers running about on yellow feet to dodge incoming waves use their strong, bright red bills to pry open mussel shells or pick limpets off rocks. Though many limpets huddle on vertical

Red algae
Corallina officinalis

rock faces to avoid the birds, one oystercatcher may nab 300 in a day. At the water's edge, great blue herons may stalk small crabs and fishes. Land-bound scavengers like crows may also visit the intertidal, drawn to its banquet of small edibles.

Even bald eagles are occasionally seen along the shoreline, feeding on cast-up fish.

ZONE 1: THE SPLASH ZONE

Western gull
Larus occidentalis

Great blue heron
Ardea herodias

THE FIRST TOUCHES OF SPRAY THROWN UP BY CRASHING WAVES mark the transition from dry land to the intertidal zone. High and dry on the rocks, only the hardiest creatures can survive in the splash zone. Spray washes into ephemeral pools, temporary refuges that can't count on a regular filling by daily tides. On a hot summer day, the splash pools become as warm as bathwater and may dry up entirely. Only fast-living tiny shrimp both live and die here. As the sun beats down, you may see tiny snails hunkered in the shadows, awaiting the return of the cooling tide.

The algae here are invisible—no leafy seaweeds can tolerate the heat and dryness in the upper intertidal. Instead, microscopic diatoms, one-celled plants with glassy shells, cover everything in a thin, brownish layer. Slimy when wet, the diatom layer is the grazing pasture for hardy limpets and periwinkles.

Limpets are sea snails that live in bowl-shaped, not spiral-shaped, shells. The rough limpet and its cousin the ribbed limpet live highest up in the splash zone. Both have fluted, ridged shells, and both rasp diatoms off the rocks with a tongue fortified with iron spicules. These species puzzled ecologists because they seemed to occupy the same habitat niche, and one should have outcompeted the other. The explanation seems to be that these two limpets choose different rock orientations— the ribbed limpet is found on vertical rock faces and under overhangs, while the rough limpet favors horizontal surfaces. Both seek out sheltered areas to wait out the long low tides, and, especially in the case of the rough limpet, individuals often return to the same resting spot day after day. Clinging tightly with its muscular foot, a limpet grinds its shell hard against the rocky substrate to seal in vital moisture. Over time, the limpet can wear a groove into the rock, a "home scar" where its shell fits perfectly.

Periwinkles take a different tack when it comes to conserving water: when the tide retreats, these tough-shelled sea snails glue themselves to the rock. By shutting their trap doors and "caulking" around their doorways with a sticky mucus, periwinkles can survive extended dry spells—up to 17 weeks! Within minutes of moistening with sea water, they reanimate and begin scraping the rock for diatoms. But the periwinkles' adaptation to dry conditions carries a price—if held under water, they will drown. No longer a true marine snail, periwinkles depend on the splash zone environment, with its harsh blend of wet and dry.

Limpets nestle in "home scars" they have worn into the rocks.

Periwinkles huddle in a rocky crevice to wait out low tide.

Tiny barnacles begin to dot the rocks at the lower end of the splash zone. Relatives of crabs and lobsters, barnacles start life as tiny, free-swimming larvae. Homing in on the scent of adult barnacles, juveniles settle on the rocks head-down and cement themselves in place. Barnacles

Barnacles
Balanus glandula

survive the drying low tides by shutting their cone-shaped shells tight; when the tide rises, they open a trap door and extend feathery feet to kick drifting plankton into their mouths. Unlike many other intertidal animals, barnacles do not broadcast sperm and eggs into the water. Instead, each has a tubular penis—up to three inches (about 7.5 centimeters) long—with which it transfers sperm to a neighbor. Each mature animal also broods eggs, and when they hatch, it is the swimming larvae that disperse to new environments.

105

ZONE 2: HIGH INTERTIDAL

PATCHES OF RED NAIL BRUSH ALGAE mark the transition to the second intertidal zone. Gradually, in a seaward direction from the start of the barnacle zone, more and more fleshy algae come to dot the rocks. The nail brush is soon joined by tough rockweeds, *Pelvetia* and *Fucus*. Like trees in a desert oasis, these algae provide refuge to wandering animals. Limpets may cluster in the moist shelter of an algal clump, and *Nuttalina*, the highest intertidal chiton, may browse around its base. Tube-dwelling polychaete worms find their first foothold around algal clumps. But the clumps of rockweeds do not offer safe haven to small animals. When the tide is in, these seaweeds thrash in the waves so violently that they "polish" the rock around them, clearing away the encrusting forms.

Rockweed
Pelvetia compressa

The first mussels begin to appear among the algae. First gradually, then in beds that cover the rock, blue mussels dominate in calm bays; the thicker-shelled Californian and horse mussels grow where waves are stronger. Barnacles crowd in among them—the short, squatty acorn barnacles that began high up in the splash zone, beneath them long-necked goose barnacles bending on slender stalks. These animals find safety in numbers: a big bed of mussels slows the drag of the waves on any one animal.

Rockweed
Fucus gardneri

Mussel and barnacle larvae home in on the scent of others of their kind when they are settling out of the plankton.

Peanut worm
Phascolosoma agassizii

Both barnacles and mussels grow bigger lower down, where they have more time each day to filter-feed from the water. When researchers move a little mussel from the higher intertidal down to a lower tidal level, it puts on a growth spurt, fueled by the greater availability of food. Conversely, a big mussel transplanted to the upper intertidal will likely die, unable to sustain itself on the meager rations available.

Barnacles and mussels form an association typical of the rocky shore environment and modify the environment in their turn. Polychaete worms, ribbon worms and peanut worms all cluster in the shelter of the mussel bed, where moisture remains between tides. The little brooding sea star, six-armed and only an inch and a half (less than four centimeters) long, dwells here, too. Unlike most sea stars, it skips a planktonic larval form. Adults release miniature stars to take up life under the mussel canopy. And some of the bumps on the lips of goose barnacles aren't really bumps at all—they are small limpets, clinging there harmlessly, perfectly camouflaged in this special niche.

The interactions between mussel-bed animals have been much studied by ecologists. Without each player, the scene would be very different. Mussels, it turns out, could out compete barnacles or algae and without some checks could overgrow the intertidal zone. But young mussels settle on old ones, and soon waves tear chunks out of the overcrowded, top-heavy beds. Where they clear space, barnacles and algae have a chance to settle. Limpets rove around mussel beds, scraping the rock with their raspy tongues. They, too, help maintain clear areas. Dog whelks, large drilling snails, feed on the limpets as well as small mussels and barnacles, helping to turn over rock space to new settlers. Finally, nearer the ocean, ochre sea stars thin the large mussels and barnacles. Able to evert their stomachs (turn them inside out), ochre sea stars may engulf 60 barnacles

Ochre star
Pisaster ochraceus

at once. They may pull mussels off rocks and drag them back below the tide line if the meal is too big to finish before the tide goes out. The mussel bed community is maintained as disturbances by waves and predators balance the mussel's tendency to overgrow everything in its path.

Sea palms are unmistakable. With stubby, flexible stalks and a crown of "palm-leaf" blades that strong waves, these upright kelp relatives are algae of the toughest high-surf zones, of surge channels and shores where the waves hit with punishing force. Sea

Sea palms live on cold, wave-washed Pacific coasts. Standing upright and flexible, they bounce back after each wave.

palms may settle on mussel beds, which is bad news for the mussels: the plant may sweep off the rocks in heavy surf, dragging a clump of mussels with it.

Only two cells thick, the bright green ruffles of *Ulva*, sea lettuce, are a common sight high on rocky shores. This annual species is a real "sea weed"—it quickly colonizes open spaces and may keep other kinds of algae from growing. *Ulva* is tolerant of polluted water and can use ammonia as a nitrogen source; for this reason, it often dominates the rocks in polluted harbors. It can also tolerate a wide range of salinities and so can colonize the deeper splash pools, where sea spray may mix with rainwater runoff.

When high tides come at night, black turban snails emerge from rocky hideouts to prowl the zone. One of the most common intertidal animals in Monterey Bay, these snails eat soft algae. Currents stimulate them to come out and move around, but too much surge can wash them off the rocks. If they land in gravel, the snails perform a neat trick to right themselves: they grasp pebbles in their muscular feet, passing them gradually down to the tail end and holding them there in a cluster. When the counterweight is heavy enough, the snail rocks itself right side up. Black turban snails are popular prey of sea stars, red rock crabs, even sea otters—they may be so scarce below the intertidal precisely because they are so many other creatures favorite meal. But up in the second zone they are in their element. And when they die, their shells become preferred homes of intertidal hermit crabs.

Sea lettuce
Ulva sp.

Whether inhabited by a crab or the original snail, turban snail shells are a world in themselves to some other creatures. Several limpets and the hooked slipper shell are frequent hitchhikers on top of the coiled turban shell. The limpets scrape algae and may keep the shell free of settling spores, but the slipper snails filter their food from the water. These hitchhiking homebodies stack up in piles on the traveling turban shells—big slippers at the bottom, smaller ones on top of them. All slipper snails start out as males but become female as they grow larger. In a pile, the big slipper at the bottom is always a female, the midsize ones are usually intersex and the small ones on top are males.

Algae gradually become more numerous in the seaward direction of the zone. Bumpy red fronds of Turkish towel hang in shady places at low tide. Algae must balance their need for sunlight with their ability to tolerate drying out, so species that grow farther up are

Turkish towel
Chondracanthus
corymbiferus

better adapted for photosynthesis out of water than lower-intertidal forms. Some upper-zone algae photosynthesize at a rate six times faster in air than in water at the same illumination and temperature. Some of these upper-intertidal algae, like *Porphyra* (nori) and *Iridaea*, are so tolerant of drying that they can desiccate to a crisp film on the rocks but reconstitute as soon as water returns. Pelvetia rockweeds even use drying to their advantage: their ripe spores are released only as their tissues dry out and shrink.

Lined shore crabs, with three-inch (7.6 centimeter) long greenish bodies and green-and-yellow striped backs, abound in the tide pools, scrambling for shelter when you approach, pressing themselves into any nook or crevice to hide. These small crustaceans are a favorite food of sea gulls. By spreading their legs against the walls of a crevice they brace themselves and are harder to pull out. Very much at home on the rocky shores, they spend about half their lives above water. Though they breathe with gills, they can feed in the open air, returning to the water only occasionally when their gills get too dry. Their primary food is algae, which they scrape off the rocks

Iridaea
Mazzaella flaccida

with a spoon-shaped cup on their claws. One can sometimes watch a group of these crabs feeding, some above, some below the water, all contentedly scraping algae. But lined shore crabs are omnivores and predators as well. They are quick enough to snap up flies on the wing and cosmopolitan enough to eat old bait and tourist's lunch scraps. They use their claws to pry file limpets off the rocks or, failing that, to pinch

Lined shore crab
Pachygrapsus crassipes

the limpet's shell until it cracks open. Tiny lined shore crabs take refuge in the nail brush algae; the bigger ones move farther down the shore.

Black abalone hide in the crevices, the smallest ones farthest up the shore. These are the first abalone you might find in the tide zone. Zone 2 also sees the first fish of the intertidal. In tide pools, woolly sculpins blend with the rock and gravel. These fish are true intertidal denizens—they rise out of tide pools when the surf rolls in, hunting the turbulent zone for crabs, worms and snails. As high tide moves up the beach, so do the woolly sculpins. When the tide retreats, the sculpins return to the tide pools, often "homing" to the same pool day after day.

Deeper in Zone 2 tide pools, giant green anemones unfurl their eight-inch. (about 20 centimeter) crowns. Like their cousin the aggregating anemone, giant greens have symbiotic algae in their tissues, but the giant green favors deeper waters. The ones surviving in Zone 2 were probably cast into tide pools here as youngsters. Other castaways you may see occasionally are bright orange bat stars. These sea stars have weak tube feet and aren't equipped to cling tightly to rocks; they don't belong in the intertidal. But when pounding surf washes them out of the kelp forest, they may survive in tide pools, perhaps long enough to ride the surf back out again. The ochre sea stars, their cousins, well equipped to hang on in rough water, may ease into the pools next to the bat stars, taking refuge when the mussel beds become too dry.

Nestled in tide pools, anemones use their tentacles to capture small animals to eat.

ZONE 3: MIDDLE INTERTIDAL

BELOW THE MUSSEL ZONE, red coralline algae mark the beginning of a Zone 3. Here, moisture is more plentiful and species diversity increases. Space is at a premium as new types of algae cover every available surface. The red sea sack clusters like grapes in moister areas. *Codium*, or dead man's fingers, drapes the rocks in foot-long bunches. This tough spiky alga is the largest green alga in the Monterey Bay area and can be considered one single cell! *Codium's* large body has many nuclei but no cell membranes to divide them. Actually, more properly called an "acellular" lifeform, this alga shares this characteristic with a few other intertidal algae.

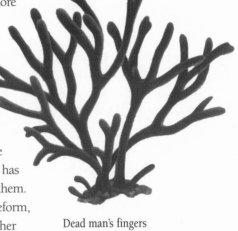

Dead man's fingers
Codium fragile

Tide pools here overflow with the long stands of feather boa kelp. This long, straplike seaweed withstands the rough surf through flexibility—its rubbery fronds bend and give rather than break. One species of limpet lives nowhere else but on the stipes of this kelp; its shell is three times longer than it is wide, so, with its large surface area, relatively speaking, it can ride the waves easily.

Deeper in the pools are sea urchins along with more giant green anemones. More kinds of fish dart through these waters. The coralline sculpin, its brown body mottled with pink, is perfectly camouflaged among pebbles and coralline algae. A brighter sculpin, the snubnose, is red with a sandy-spot background. At about 4 inches (10 centimeters) long, both of these sculpins rest at the bottom of tide pools, waiting poised on powerful pectoral fins to snap up prey passing nearby. The rockweed gunnel, a narrow little fish, may become red or green

Purple sea urchin
Strongylocentrotus purpuratus

Coralline sculpin
Artedius corrallinus

depending on which algae it is grazing. And northern clingfish, with big heads and little eyes, hide in the deeper rock crevices, sticking in place with a suction disc between their fins.

Mobile invertebrates are becoming more numerous, as well as the algae and all kinds of encrusting sponges and bryozoans. The *Katharina* chiton makes its slow way over the rocks, scraping off algae and diatoms in its path. Its patrol takes it around the "no-animal's land" between "clones" of the aggregating anemone. Related to the giant green, aggregating anemones colonize farther up on the intertidal rocks by living in groups though some lead a solitary life. Each group is a clone, descended from one pioneering individual. Clones grow as mature anemones divide themselves in half. Batches of these genetically identical anemones may cover square yards of rock here. When the tide is out, aggregating anemones fold in their delicate tentacles and hunker down as solid lumps about the size and shape of marshmallows. You might walk over them without knowing, because these anemones hold bits of sand, shell and pebbles over their bodies with special side pores. A squishy pile of sand underfoot may really be a clone of anemones, but don't worry—their internal hydrostatics let them resist pressure, so they're usually unharmed.

At this level of the intertidal, aggregating anemones avoid some of their nudibranch predators, but a tiny wentletrap snail hovers around the tightly packed clones. Named for the Dutch word for "winding staircase," the wentletraps boast a handsome ridge winding around their tall conical shells. The little tinted wentletrap has a shell only half an inch (about one centimeter) long, so it doesn't do much damage as it nips pieces off the tentacles of aggregating anemones. The anemones barely cringe, leading some researchers to suspect the wentletrap injects an anesthetic with its bite. When disturbed, this snail emits a purple dye.

Limpets begin to appear in a bewildering variety of shapes and sizes, from the pointed white *Acmaea* cap shells to volcano-shaped keyhole limpets. Giant owl

Aggregating Anemones: Green Ghosts and Clone Wars

The aggregating anemone packs a lot of surprises into a six-inch body. Though some lead a solitary life, these sturdy anemones can form huge mats in the middle intertidal zones, where visitors may encounter them packed into moist lumps to wait out low tides. At high tide, anemones unfold to capture plankton and small animals with their tentacles, but this is not the only way the aggregating anemone gets food. Within its tissues, the anemone plays host to tiny algae, symbionts which produce a pigment that give the anemone its green color. The algae photosynthesize, and feed nutrients to the anemone; in return, they get a safe place to live. While aggregating anemones can live without the algae, those that have algae grow faster and sturdier than those that must catch all their own food. Aggregating anemones that grow in dark caves have no algae and are bleached and white; these "ghosts" are smaller and weaker than age-mates from sunny areas. And in the lab, a green anemone kept in the dark loses its algae and starts to grow slowly. Especially up in the high intertidal, it makes sense to harness the sun's energy in this way, so that even when it's closed up at low tide, the anemone is taking in food via its algae. Green aggregating anemones try to keep things comfortable for their algae

Aggregating anemones multiply by dividing in half; one anemone can eventually form a colony of clones.

limpets "farm" dinner-plate-size patches of rock here, grazing on filamentous red algae but bulldozing anything else that tries to settle. Purple shore crabs scoot in and out of tide-pool hideouts; they are tolerant of a huge range of water salinity. And among the dozens of black turban snails, now we seen an occasional brown one—a kelp forest species, sometimes tossed in by waves, it shares the rocks here with its upper-intertidal cousin.

"guests"—they move in and out of sunlight to keep the light level just right for the algae's photosynthesis. "Ghost" anemones, which have lost their algae, no longer show this moving behavior.

The aggregating anemone is also a fighting anemone. On the rocks, huge groups of aggregating anemones grow up as one pioneer splits itself into two, and these grow to split again. Each group is called a clone, since it is made up of many genetically identical individuals. Clones can cover many square meters of precious rock space. An aggregating anemone can live peacefully packed in with its clonemates, but when individuals from different clones so much as touch tentacles, a battle begins. Hostile aggregating anemones inflate special fighting tentacles called acrorhagi, coated with powerful stinging cells. The enemies rear back and slap their acrorhagi down at each other. Where the acrorhagi make contact, the white stinging layer peels off and sticks, killing tissue. If they can't move apart, two aggregating anemones may actually kill each other, but usually one combatant rolls away after a few rounds. Out in the intertidal, different clones of aggregating anemones stop within tentacle's reach of each other, so patches are surrounded by a "no man's land" of bare rock. Chitons patrol these anemone borders, helping to keep them clear by grazing off settling spores and larvae.

ZONE 4: LOW INTERTIDAL AND BEYOND

TRAILING LEAVES OF BRIGHT GREEN SURF GRASS mark the point where the mid intertidal gives way to the true low-tide zone. This area is more water than land. Despite pounding waves it begins to take on the richness of the reefs farther offshore. Many of the species found here also live in the reefs or kelp forest. Here, at the zero tide level, surf grass cuts an ironic figure: it is one of the only plants in the intertidal that is not an alga, but a flowering plant that has migrated from the land. Its roots, true leaves and underwater flowers mark it as a seed plant returned to the sea after millions of years of struggling to adapt to dry land. When the tide is high, silvery reef surfperch wash into the surf grass to feed.

Large, fleshy algae begin to come into their own here. Just below the zero tide line, long-bladed *Laminaria,* and a single-blade relative of the giant kelp, the intertidal *Macrocystis,* grow. Sponges and tunicates cluster on rocks—how to tell them apart? Whereas tunicates feel gelatinous, covered with a protective slime layer, sponges are more velvety. Both types of animals may be bright orange or yellow, but only the volcano sponges show up in brilliant purple. And light bulb tunicates, looking for all the world like refrigerator light bulbs, are unmistakable when they cluster in sheltered areas.

Bright red rose anemones with stalks as thick as coffee mugs share space in the low intertidal with thimble-size strawberry anemones. The proliferating anemone also appears here, clinging to rocks and to algae. These colorful anemones may be pink or white or orange and sport distinctive "pinstripes" along their stalks.

Sometimes called "brooding anemones," these creatures put several twists on the norms of reproduction. All are born female, but older females produce sperm as well as eggs. Sperm is broadcast into the water, and the anemones brood the fertilized eggs within their bodies. Instead of releasing planktonic larvae, they expel embryos which are carried out of the mother's oral disk and settle on her stalk. Thus, at any time of year, you may see adult proliferating anemones with youngsters clinging around their bases. The parent does not feed the young anemones but may protect them under its tentacle umbrella. The truly odd part of this story is that, although proliferating anemone eggs must be fertilized,

Oarweed
Laminaria setchellii

the sperm make no genetic contribution to the offspring. Each youngster is actually a clone of its mother; the sperm is needed only to start the ripe egg's development into an embryo.

Anemones attract predators. One that prefers the proliferating anemone is the leather star. The smoothest sea star around, its velvety skin is mottled with bright red tissue. It cuts quite a figure against the dark algae of the low intertidal. These six-inch (15 centimeter) predators give off a garlic odor when handled. When proliferating anemones are scarce, the leather star makes do with giant greens, aggregating anemones or sea cucumbers.

Perhaps the most important predators of anemones are the sea slugs, or nudibranchs. These relatives of sea snails have no shells and protect themselves by recycling the stinging cells of the anemones they eat. The unexploded sting cells, or nematocysts, are carefully transferred to the fringy cerrata on the slug's back. Many nudibranchs advertise with bright colors that they are dangerous to tangle with.

Shag rug nudibranchs, looking every square inch their name, attack large anemones cautiously. The nudibranch approaches slowly, coating itself in the anemone's mucus before going in to bite large chunks out of its prey. The mucus

Surf grass marks the low intertidal zone that's usually under water and only exposed by the lowest of tides.

Sea lemon
Anisodoris nobilis

coat apparently gives it immunity to anemone stings; if it is somehow removed, the anemone may kill and eat the sea slug. Another common intertidal nudibranch is *Phidiana*, opalescent white with bright orange patches ringed with neon blue. Sea lemons, bright yellow nudibranchs with a pompom of gills on their backs, actually have a fruity odor. These nudibranchs favor smaller anemones and hydroids as prey. In turn, they are hunted by the nudibranch *Navanax*, a six-inch (15 centimeter) predatory monster whose black hide is gaudy with orange stripes and blue spots.

The lowest intertidal attracts some larger fishes. Members of the sculpin family, cabezon, an important game fish in the Monterey Bay area, make their nests in the rocky intertidal. Although the male cabezon guard the plate-size plots of their amber eggs aggressively, many nests are exposed to the air at low tide and out of their reach. But the eggs make use of a second level of protection: they are poisonous. Young cabezon gather in tide

Navanax
Aglaja inermis

pools. As they mature, they move offshore but still may hunt tide pools when the tide is high.

Another intertidal nester is the plainfin midshipman, a squat little creature that also goes by the name of toadfish. Most of the year, these six-inch (15 centimeter) fish live on sandy bottoms well offshore. But in spring, males begin a breeding migration to the intertidal. Under rocks, they dig out nests, then settle in to attract females with a loud, monotonous humming. (Their song can be quite loud: some years ago mystified houseboaters in San Francisco Bay were startled by the constant drone of courting midshipmen under their floorboards. Speculations about the strange sounds ranged as far as Russian submarines before the actual reason came to light.) After the eggs hatch, the males guard the larvae, which remain stuck to the nest rock for about a month. Males continue their guard duty despite the danger it poses to themselves—resting in the shallow intertidal, they are preyed on by gulls, crows and herons.

Under large rocks and deep in surge channels monkeyface-eels are the largest fish that frequent the low intertidal. Not really eels, these two-foot (about 60

116

centimeter) uglies are members of the prickleback family. They are tasty game fish, many of which are caught by "poke-poling:" at low tide, anglers prodding rock crevices with bamboo poles topped with wire leader, hook and bait.

Sculpting forces of wind and waves wear inlets into rocky shores edged by fingers of soft sandstone pointing seaward. Where waves pound away the connections between the sandstone, creating block islands, seabirds flock, painting the rock white with their guano. Cormorants preen and dive; brown pelicans sweep by with slow, rowing strokes of their wide wings. Block islands offer them the shelter of the shore along with protection from land-based predators like foxes, cats and coyotes. At the same time, the birds make their mark on their roosting rocks—their droppings are too rich in nitrogen for plants to endure and keep the bird islands bare of land plants. Diluted in the sea, the droppings are fertilizer, but the nitrogen burn of heavy guano encrustations can even clear bird rocks of algae. Sometimes a bare block island rests only feet away from another "island" sporting hardy vegetation. A close look will reveal that the vegetated island still has some tenuous connection to shore—perhaps it will last only into the next heavy January storm—but even the most temporary land bridge allows the vegetation to grow and keeps the birds away.

Seals and sea lions also spend part of their time on rocky shores. Along the Monterey coast, harbor seals are frequently seen resting on rocks just offshore, balancing their sausage-shaped bodies on the rocks with ease,

Brown pelican
Pelecanus occidentalis

117

hardly deigning to move except to lazily lift a draping flipper out of the way of incoming waves. In the water, these lazy lumps become sleek predators, snapping up crabs and all manner of fishes. California sea lions

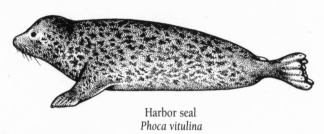

Harbor seal
Phoca vitulina

bark and dive in noisy colonies, often preferring rocks more remote from human activity than those inhabited by harbor seals. Young sea lions, born on land, must learn to swim. The pools and surge channels of the lowest intertidal zone are their first ocean playground, where they can learn to swim and dive in water too shallow for their major predator, the great white shark. And northern elephant seals, once hunted nearly to extinction, have staged a spectacular comeback along our shores. One of their premier breeding spots, at Año Nuevo State Reserve, lies within the Monterey Bay National Marine Sanctuary. The first elephant seal pup in decades was born on this windswept piece of shoreline in 1975; now hundreds of the enormous animals clamber up the rocky shore to Año Nuevo's dunes at breeding time.

The rocky shores merge into the ocean as deeper waters drop offshore and rocks high enough to break the zero tide line become fewer. If you were to view the shoreline from a boat floating on an outgoing tide, you would see the intertidal spread before you, marching up the beach as the waters ebb behind you—a ribbon of life connecting land to sea, a bridge between our world and the world beneath the waves.

California sea lion
Zalophus californianus

Intertidal Survey: Evidence for Global Warming?

IN 1930, STANFORD MARINE BIOLOGISTS marked off a transect line in the rocky intertidal zone near Hopkins Marine Station in Pacific Grove, California and surveyed the invertebrate animals growing there. Driving brass bolts into the rocks to mark corners, the researchers were after a complete picture of local shore life. Now, more than sixty years later, biologists have gone back to the same spot—but the picture has changed. A new survey, completed in 1994, shows cold-water, northern species moving out, and warm-water, southern species moving in. Mean ocean temperatures at the site have increased 1.5°F (0.75°C) since the 1930's, and mean summer maximum air temperatures about 4.4°F (2.2°C). Many scientists see this survey as one of the first good snapshots of global warming in action.

Hopkins research site, 1930

Global warming, an overall rise in land and sea temperatures, has been cited for years as a possible consequence of industrial lifestyles. Burning fossil fuels, like oil and coal, releases carbon dioxide into the atmosphere, which traps the sun's warmth in the so-called "Greenhouse Effect." A few degrees' rise in overall global temperature could have drastic environmental consequences,

Hopkins research site, 1994

changing weather patterns and even melting the polar ice caps. But the existence of global warming has been hotly debated, and a lack of long-term studies complicates things. There aren't many places on earth where scientists have good data from sixty years ago and can actually go back and compare.

That's what makes the Hopkins study so important. It offers a close look at changes in one spot. Since some invertebrate species thrive best in warm climates, others like cool and some seem not to mind either way, the researchers could classify animals on the Hopkins shore as either southern, northern, or cosmopolitan. The 1994 survey showed some southern species, like the volcano limpet and strawberry anemone, increasing in density on the rocks, while northern species, like giant green anemones and ochre stars, decreased in abundance. And species once known only from further south, like the sessile snail *Serpulorbis squamigerus*, have moved in and are thriving.

Meanwhile, some northern species, like the little mussel bed crab *Petrolisthes*, are no longer found at the site. Since "cosmopolitan" species neither increased nor decreased, the changes seem to be limited to animals sensitive to narrow ranges of water temperature. And looked at this way, warm water animals are moving in while cool water creatures are moving out.

Increased pollution, changes in fishing habits, and even the return of the sea otter all might influence the mix of intertidal animals, but these factors wouldn't explain why the changes are limited to temperature-sensitive animals. A long-term warming of the ocean climate seems to be the best explanation for what the two surveys revealed.

Intertidal communities turn over fast—seasonal scouring and short life cycles of many plants and animals make the intertidal a place where life forms respond quickly to the environment. Unlike a forest, where trees may live hundreds of years, the rocky intertidal is a place where people can watch changes within our own life times. This makes the rocky intertidal a sensitive reflection of outside environmental influences—including global temperature change. The study at Hopkins provides sobering evidence that, whatever the cause, the ocean environment is feeling the effects of a climate warming.

Selected Rocky Shores Species

Zone 1: The Splash Zone (almost always exposed to air)

ALGAE
Blue-green alga
Lichen
Diatoms

INVERTEBRATES
Acorn barnacle, *Chthamalus and Balanus* spp.
Copepod, *Tigriopus* spp.
Isopod, *Ligia* spp.
Limpet, *Lottia digitalis*
Periwinkle, *Littorina* spp.
Shore crab, *Pachygrapsus crassipes*

Zone 2: High Intertidal (exposed to air for long periods twice a day)

ALGAE
Iridescent red alga, *Mazzaella* spp.
Nailbrush alga, *Endocladia muricata*
Nori, *Porphyra* sp.
Red alga, *Bangia* sp.
Rockweed, *Fucus gardneri*
Rockweed, *Hesperophycus* spp.
Rockweed, *Pelvetia compressa*
Sea lettuce, *Ulva* spp.
Sea palm, *Postelsia palmaeformis*
Turkish towel, *Chondracanthus* spp.

INVERTEBRATES
Acorn barnacle, *Balanus, Chthamalus* and *Tetraclita* spp.
Aggregating anemone, *Anthopleura elegantissima*
Black abalone, *Haliotis cracherdoii*
Dogwinkle, *Nucella* spp.
Hermit crab, *Pagurus* spp.
Isopod, *Hemioniscus balani*
Long-necked goose barnacle, *Pollicipes polymerus*
Marine fly (eggs), *Limonia* spp.
Ochre star, *Pisaster ochraceus*
Owl limpet, *Lottia gigantea*
Polychaete worm
Shore crab, *Pachygrapsus crassipes*
Six-rayed star, *Leptasterias hexactis*
Slipper snail, *Crepidula adunca*

FISHES
Woolly sculpin, *Clinocuttus* spp.

Zone 3: Middle Intertidal (exposed to air briefly once or twice a day)

ALGAE
Dead man's fingers, *Codium fragile*
Feather boa kelp, *Egregia menziesii*
Iridescent red alga, *Mazzaella* spp.
Red coralline alga, *Corallina officinalis*
Turkish towel, *Chondracanthus* spp.

INVERTEBRATES
Black turban snail, *Tegula funebralis*
Bryozoans
California mussel, *Mytilus californianus*
Giant green anemone, *Anthopleura xanthogrammica*
Limpet, *Lottia pelta*
Mossy chiton, *Mopalia muscosa*
Seaweed limpet, *Discurria insessa*
Wentletrap snail, *Epitonium tinctum*

FISHES
Coralline sculpin, *Artedius corallinus*
Northern clingfish, *Gobiesox maeandricus*
Rockweed gunnel, *Xererpes fucorum*
Snubnose sculpin, *Orthonopias triacis*
Tidepool sculpin, *Oligocottus* spp.

Zone 4: Low Intertidal (only exposed to air during the lowest tides of the year)

ALGAE
Crustose coralline alga, *Melobesia mediocris*
Kelp, *Macrocystis integrifolia*
Oarweed, *Laminaria* spp.
Red alga, *Smithora naiadum*
Sea grapes, *Botryocladia* spp.

SEED PLANT
Surf grass, *Phyllospadix* spp.

INVERTEBRATES
Brittle star, *Amphiholis* spp.
Brown turban snail, *Tegula brunnea*
Bryozoan
Cream-colored latticework sponge, *Leucilla nuttingi,*
Decorator crab, *Loxorhynchus crispatus*
Flat worm, *Pseudoceros* spp.
Keyhole limpet, *Diodora aspera*
Leather chiton, *Katharina tunicata*
Leather star, *Dermasterias imbricata*
Lemon-yellow crust sponge, *Aplysina fistularis*
Light bulb tunicate, *Clavelina huntsmani*
Lined chiton, *Tonicella lineata*
Navanax, *Aglaja inermis*
Opalescent nudibranch (Hermissenda),
    Phidiana crassicornis
Orange sea cucumber, *Cucumaria miniata*
Ostrich-plume hydroid, *Aglaophenia* spp.
Pink and purple sea urchins,
    Strongylocentrotus spp.
Proliferating anemone, *Epiactis prolifera*
Purple sunflower star, *Pycnopodia helianthoides*
Red abalone, *Haliotis rufescens*
Red sea slug, *Rostanga pulchra*
Rock crab, *Cancer antennarius*
Scarlet sponge, *Ophlitaspongia pennata*
Sea lemon, *Anisodoris nobilis*
Sea spider, *Pycnogonum* spp.
Skeleton shrimp, *Caprella* spp.
Spiny brittle star, *Ophiothrix spiculata*
Strawberry anemone, *Corynactis californica*

Surfgrass limpet, *Tectura paleacea*
Tiny shrimp, *Palaemon ritteri* or *Spirontocaris priontoa*
Tunicates
Violet volcano sponge, *Haliclona* spp.
White-cap limpet, *Acmaea mitra*

FISHES
Cabezon, *Scorpaenichthys marmoratus*
Monkeyface-eel, *Cebidichthys violaceus*
Reef surfperch, *Micrometrus aurora*

Other species associated with the rocky shore

BIRDS
Black oystercatcher, *Haematopus bachmani*
Brown pelican, *Pelecanus occidentalis*
Great blue heron, *Ardea herodias*
Gull, *Larus* spp.

MARINE MAMMALS
California sea lion, *Zalophus californianus*
California sea otter, *Enhydra lutris neries*
Harbor seal, *Phoca vitulina*

Fields of anemones, sponges and corals paint the rocks along the reef.

CHAPTER SEVEN

REEFS AND PILINGS

*Invisibly, where the casual observer would say there is no life, it lies
deep in burrows and tubes and passageways. It tunnels into solid rock and
bores. It encrusts and spreads over a rock surface or wharf piling,
keeping alive the sense of continuing creation and of the relentless
drive of life.*

RACHEL CARSON, 1955

IF YOU WALK ALONG THE SANCTUARY'S BEACHES after a
January storm, you may notice a dark object among the kelp wrack
tossed up on the sand. Lifting it, you find it's stone, hard and solid,
but riddled like Swiss cheese with inchwide (two and one half
centimeters) holes. More than just an ocean curiosity, what you hold in
your hands is a piece of reef. The holes are made by rock-boring clams,
whose burrows permeate the rock of the nearshore shale reefs. While geologists
insist that only corals build reefs and that reefs occur only in the tropics, biologists
and fishermen know reefs as any solid structure beneath the ocean water that gives a
home to encrusting plants and animals. Defined this way, Monterey Bay National
Marine Sanctuary is rich in reefs.

123

SHALE REEFS

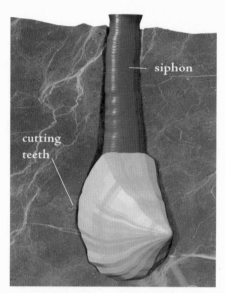

This pholad clam has a special shell adapted for drilling into the substrate of shale reefs.

THE FINE-GRAINED MONTEREY MUDSTONE that crops out in shallows is part of a large, sedimentary rock section called the "Monterey Formation." This mass of shales and siliceous cherts was laid down 30 million years ago, microscopic sea plants known as diatoms, lived and died in enormous numbers in a shallow sea. Their tiny, silica-rich cell walls rained down and piled up as a thick ooze. With time and pressure, the ooze was squeezed into rock soft layers of shale and mudstone interspersed with flinty bands of black chert. As the Pacific plate collided with North America, this rock mass pushed against the shore and buckled into foothills.

Today, the Monterey Formation runs the length of the central California coast, both above and below the ocean. This is the shale that yields ocean fossils in the Carmel hills, attesting to the land's maritime origin. This is also the shale that bears oil near Santa Barbara, where offshore drilling platforms dot the bay.

And this is the shale that layers with mudstone in the Monterey Bay National Marine Sanctuary, home to vast beds of rock-boring piddock clams and date mussels. These bivalves, modified for their life in the rocky reef substrate, get as thick as raisins in raisin bread along parts of the coastline. Some are good to eat and were sought by people, but the rock-boring clams are much more important as a driving force in shale reef ecology. Their burrows honeycomb the shale with holes that other creatures use for shelter once the original occupants have died. And the borer's action weakens stone in the upper layers of the reef, causing the burrow-riddled chunks of mudstone to slough off in winter storms and reach the beaches. Down in the reef itself, this constant sloughing of shale means a constant supply of fresh rock faces where new piddocks can start boring.

The shale reefs occur in the same waters as the kelp forests, and many of them support kelp forests on their sunny, horizontal surfaces. The vertical surfaces and deeper water below the kelp line may be considered the shale reef environment.

Not surprisingly, the encrusting species on the reef surfaces are very similar to those found in the kelp forest: strawberry anemones, feather duster worms, encrusting sponges and solitary corals. But it is the three-dimensional habitat provided by the rock-boring clams that really distinguishes the shale reefs from the kelp forest. A host of creatures live in and among these burrows, seldom if ever seen among the kelp above.

The borers themselves belong to two main families—the piddocks, or rock-boring clams, related to clams that burrow in soft bottoms, and the date mussels, related to our common shoreline mussels.

Piddocks dig the deeper burrows and are more common on reef structures than date mussels. Their siphons, orange or black, dot the rocks. In areas where sand sweeps over the reef frequently, a piddock with fringed filters on its siphons predominates. In clearer areas, others of the 16 local species hold their own. Piddocks burrow only until they reach a certain size—one inch (about two and one half centimeters) long in some species, closer to 6 inches (about 15 centimeters) in others. This may take from 3 to 20 years, depending on the hardness of the rock they drill. They then metamorphose into sexually mature adults, releasing eggs and sperm through their siphons. With no predators to fear within the rock, adult piddocks may lead long and tranquil lives.

Reef creatures leave behind deep burrows within the rocks, giving it a honeycombed appearance.

When the clams die, or when ocean action throws open their burrows, an array of nestling creatures moves in. By far the most common are a zoo of polychaete worms setting snugly in the rocky homes left behind by boring clams. Snails, sea stars, small octopuses and peanut worms also take advantage of piddock apartment-living in the nearshore shallow reefs. Some species, like brittle stars, shelter in the burrows only during heavy weather. Others, like nestling clams, are permanent residents. Baby hermit crabs and young gumboot chitons are seldom seen around the kelp forest, but the adult forms are common there. Researchers have found both in the clam burrows of the shale reefs, the little crabs apparently hiding out until they grow big enough to claim an empty snail shell.

Hermit crab
Pagurus samuelis

The tiny lumpy porcelain crab, a frequent denizen of kelp holdfasts, also finds refuge in abandoned piddock holes. These crabs are filter-feeders and have carapaces that grow only an inch (about two and one half centimeters) across. Mated pairs often move about together. Not having to hunt or scavenge, all they need is a quiet hole to rest in as they filter plankton. When startled, they may use their thick, lumpy claws to plug the burrow entrance, sealing out danger. Lumpy porcelain crabs may grow so large inside their burrows that they can't climb out the entrance, but that doesn't seem to bother them: with food and a mate, their tiny homes probably offer all they need.

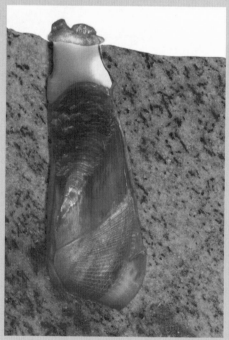

A piddock clam can burrow through most rock surfaces except granite.

Boring Clams or Mystery Diggers?

EVEN A "BORING" LIFE can have its mysteries. Sixteen species of rock-boring clams make their homes in Monterey Bay National Marine Sanctuary, their finished burrows ranging from inch-deep (about two and one half centimeters) nooks to 3 feet (0.9 meters) long tunnels big enough to fit a diver's arm. Piddocks drill into the toughest flints and cherts along our coastline, but only granite, with its tough crystalline structure, turns aside their persistent excavations.

For all their abundance, the boring bivalves have a secret that scientists still do not

Shallow-water rockfishes—the blue, the brown, the black and yellow—gather near the shale reefs. Many of their juveniles mature in the kelp forest, moving to deeper water as they grow bigger. Both kelp forest and shale reefs offer a smorgasbord to fishes, like the surfperches, that prey on invertebrates. Wrasses, porgies and drums also range over the shale reefs, feeding on the encrusting lifeforms before becoming prey themselves to lingcod and striped bass. This abundance of game species makes shallow-water reefs prime areas for sport fishing, and lines don't get tangled as they do in the nearby kelp forest. Some kelp forest species, like kelp greenling and señorita, are almost never seen outside the shelter of the algae. But the biggest difference in the fish species ranging in the shale reefs and kelp forest is the relative abundance of plankton-feeding fishes compared to that of crevice dwellers. Kelp forests shelter many plankton feeders, which feed in the open water and retreat to the kelp to avoid sharks and other open-water predators. On the shale reefs, small colorful blennies and sculpins blend with the rocky substrate and wait in ambush for swimming prey. Their short thick fins are built to power them off the rocks with surprising speed when prey comes in striking range. Cabezon hunt the crevices for abalone, ramming them with their heads until they drop off the rock and can be swallowed. Somehow, the cabezon shucks out the meat inside its mouth and spits out the shells, a trick that still has scientists a bit baffled.

Striped surfperch
Embiotoca lateralis

understand: no one is sure exactly how these clams make their holes. Examining a piddock's shell, one sees thickened ridges at the end in contact with the rock face. The shell looks reinforced, designed for rasping. It should be possible for the clam, using its muscular foot, to rotate its shell completely, and while rotating, use the ridges to drill its way into the rock. But there are holes in this theory. The clam's shell is much softer than the rocks it burrows into, leading some researchers to question its value as a rasp. And

researchers have put sensitive microphones on the rocks of piddocks, listening for any sound of grinding or filing, but there aren't any. Scientists are left with a frustrating mystery: clams that burrow, shells with ridges, but no evidence that puts the two together.

In the case of date mussels, the mystery of how they drill their burrows is even harder to unravel. Date mussels make their burrows in stretches of shale, but their shells are thin and smooth, without ridges, and so seem unsuitable for digging or

scraping. For years, scientists theorized that date mussels made their burrows by eating away the rock with acid, but recent studies have shown that shale is impervious to acid. So, as with piddocks, how date mussels burrow remains one of nature's closely guarded secrets.

WHARVES AND PILINGS

THERE IS NOTHING IN NATURE LIKE THE SMOOTH, CYLINDRICAL COLUMNS supporting wharves and pilings, but they offer substrate like that of a natural reef. The long, vertical surfaces of wharf supports and pilings become home to an animal community like—and yet unlike—those found in the natural reefs and kelp beds in the water nearby.

Wharves are built in shallow water and so share the nearshore environment with shale reefs and kelp forests. Their wood or concrete pilings receive the same drift larvae as these other habitats, but only a subset of kelp forest animals can take advantage of the settling space that a wharf offers. Wharves are dark, for one thing. Buildings, walks and roadways on top of wharves cut off the sunlight and make most of the space beneath a wharf into a sunless habitat. What can take advantage of such space? Not very many algae—even in prime kelp territory, the pilings of wharves seldom support them. Some algae may grow along the outermost pilings, where early-morning or late-afternoon sun slants into the water. But full overhead sun, and the algae it would nourish, aren't part of the wharf environment. The brown and green algae so common in the kelp forest are mostly absent from wharf pilings. Instead, as on deep reefs, the dominant plants are shade-tolerant red algae. The inner reaches under wharves have another thing in common with the deep reefs—groves of white-plumed anemones. These filter-feeders don't need sun to strain their plankton food out of the water. The sunless central pilings of wharves often support forests of these anemones, ghostly white and silent in the dim water.

Wharf pilings, whether wood or concrete, are smooth and don't offer the range of cracks and crevices found in natural rock. Fewer refuges mean fewer nestling species. Like rocky shores, and unlike reefs, pilings have an area subject to the tides. But their simpler structure makes them a place where a few species tend to dominate, rather than the riotous mix of species we

White-plumed anemones carpet wharfs and pilings.

expect to find on shores and rock reefs.

Concrete pilings are actually a unique habitat that attracts a unique set of species. Highest up on the concrete, acorn barnacles weather daily dry spells. Just below them cluster the hardy aggregating anemones. Mussels should be next, near the low-tide line, but in areas with sea otters these favored molluscs are rare. Barnacles hold sway here, too. A bit lower, colonies of giant green anemones begin to dot the concrete—when open, their oral discs can stretch to a foot in diameter, practically covering the piling as if with rings of flowers. Intertidal sea stars prowl among the green anemones, searching for the occasional snail or chiton. At the zero tide level, the giant green anemones abruptly give way to fields of strawberry anemones, pink and white and orange. The strawberries dominate the rest of the concrete

Anemones use their tentacles to capture small animals, like fish.

piling, from mean low water all the way to the bottom of the subtidal zone, perhaps 30 feet (9 meters) below. Green anemones do not live among the strawberries—the species grow at distinctly stratified levels, just as on rocky shores, but there are far fewer species here.

Down at the lowest tide levels, rocky knobs begin to roughen the concrete. These are the homes of giant acorn barnacles, sessile crustaceans that can grow to the size of a fist. Giant acorn barnacles move in with their smaller relatives: when drifting with the plankton, the giant barnacle larva is attracted to waterborne chemicals given off by colonies of thumbnail-size common acorn barnacles and settles between them,

Anemones filter tiny planktonic animals from the water.

Giant acorn barnacle
Balanus nubilus

growing quickly and soon covering its small neighbors with its own enlarging shell.

Giant barnacles are long-lived—some marked by Ed Ricketts in 1926 are still alive and well on the Monterey Municipal Wharf—but they cannot cling as tightly to concrete pilings as to natural rocks. When divers hunt for barnacle specimens, they often go to wharf concrete, where large specimens can be collected intact with a few raps of a hammer. Under the base of a giant barnacle, embedded in its shell material, one can see the homes of the hapless smaller barnacles engulfed and killed as their giant relative grew.

Wood pilings are an entirely different environment. In the intertidal zone, wood pilings may sport groves of white-plumed anemones—highly unusual, since these anemones almost never occur in the intertidal stone of natural rocky shores. But they find the wharves congenial and hang like foot-long macaroni along wood pilings when the tide is out. A few giant green anemones share space among them, but very little else. It is the community of life inside wood pilings that sets this environment apart from all others.

Shipworms, or teredos, have been a scourge to humans since the earliest mariners put wooden boats in water. Their long, thin burrows permeate wood that

This giant acorn barnacle extends its feathery leg out to feed.

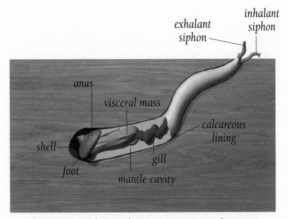

Shipworms are known for causing extensive damage to wharf pilings.

stays in water, weakening it and eventually making it fall to pieces. While they have long, thin bodies, up to 1 foot (about 30 centimeters) in length, these wood-boring creatures are not true worms. They are highly specialized clams, with two modified shells at the front end of their wormlike bodies. From eggs and sperm broadcast into the water, tiny shipworm larvae grow to juvenile clams the size of rice grains. At this stage, they look much like other clams, their bodies more or less contained in two tiny shells. But if this tiny clam lands on a piece of waterlogged wood, it sticks on with its muscular foot and rocks its shell valves back and forth. Soon it has excavated a little hollow, and it snuggles in, tiny siphons stretching up to filter food and oxygen from the water. The shipworm keeps on digging with its shell or front end, moving with the grain of the wood, as its body elongates and outgrows its shell. Unlike the piddocks, the shipworms can be heard scraping their shells as they burrow.

No matter how deep the burrow gets, the tiny siphons of the clam must project above the wood surface for the animal to feed and breathe. Shipworms mature in about a year—roughly the same lifetime as a piece of wood in shipworm territory. They attack wood pilings mostly at the "mud line," where wood sinks into the bottom ooze. Because their burrows don't show on the surface, infested wood may look perfectly solid—until the day a pier collapses, revealing the maze of shipworm holes inside.

Farther up the pilings, little isopods called gribbles also attack wood. Bearing a resemblance to their landlocked relatives, the sowbugs, gribbles are white and about the size of rice grains. Unlike most nearshore invertebrates, gribbles don't begin life as planktonic larvae. They spread from one location to another when an infected log or wooden boat bumps against fresh wood in the water. But gribbles also seem to sense fresh wood when they are near it. From a vantage point near a new wood piling, a scuba diver can watch a stream of gribbles swim from an infected boat bottom toward the virgin territory. When gribbles locate fresh wood, the females use their jaws to make pinhole burrows and a maze of "vent holes." Unlike almost all other burrowers, gribbles feed on the wood itself—and on the plankton that collect in the stagnant burrow water. (In the lab, gribbles happily live on plain pieces of

The Gypsy never made it to the Monterey Wharf.

The Wreck of the *Gypsy*

SOME OF THE "REEFS" IN Monterey Harbor have a history as colorful as the life that now inhabits them. In 1905, the busy port of Monterey was a regular stop for the *Gypsy*, a 60-ton (about 55 metric tons) steam freighter out of San Francisco. Known as "Old Perpetual Motion" for its endless runs up and down the coast, the *Gypsy* shuttled cargo from San Francisco to Santa Barbara and back again. There were few surprises on the *Gypsy's* route; landmarks in each harbor were almost a matter of rote. Her regular captain knew to watch for a lantern hung on the Monterey wharf and steer to dock accordingly. But one night, the *Gypsy* came in under the command of a substitute captain. By coincidence, on this same night sewer workers in Cannery Row hung a lantern on a sawhorse above the ditch where they labored. Seeing this light, the substitute captain turned the *Gypsy* in too soon. The ship hit the rocks and sank in 25 feet (about 7.5 meters) of water off MacAbee Beach. Its cargo? Four hundred cases of beer, from the Buffalo Brewing Company in San Francisco.

The day after the *Gypsy* foundered, witnesses reported that anyone with anything that could float was out in the harbor off Cannery Row, trying to rescue the merchandise. Whether any of it made it back to its owner is not recorded. The Buffalo Brewing Company burned down the following year, in the great San Francisco earthquake of 1906. Divers occasionally still find a bottle bearing the Buffalo emblem in the mud off Maccabee Beach.

The *Gypsy's* massive steam engine is all that's left of the ship today. But this hulking piece of weathered steel, 10 feet (3 meters) tall and 8 feet (2.4 meters) in diameter, still sits in 25 feet of water off Maccabee Beach. A healthy growth of rock scallops, favored by sea otters, now covers its sides, and their discarded shells are strewn about the hull. As wreck has turned to reef, the *Gypsy* has provided prizes for more than one kind of diver.

filter paper, though how they digest the cellulose in wood or paper remains unknown.) Males lack burrowing jaws and move into females' burrows, feeding on leftover wood scrapings and waiting for the chance to fertilize eggs. Gribbles wear away the surface of wood pilings, working more slowly than shipworms and leaving pinholes that people can see. To deter them, wood pilings are painted with creosote—though the protective chemical lasts only two or three years, until it leaches away. And no protective measure succeeds forever. Recently, a tropical gribble species appeared in Monterey Bay, on fresh pilings oozing creosote. In the lab, this new species wouldn't grow except on wood containing creosote—a new adaptation to an environment modified by humans.

Large game fish are likely to be rare in the vicinity of wharves because people can fish off them with the greatest of ease, although young rockfishes sometimes swarm around wharf pilings, and squid or red rock crabs may be hauled up in their seasons. Other than humans, the largest mammal that frequents wharves is the California sea lion. To the delight of tourists, the municipal wharf at Santa Cruz is now home to a colony of these large, sleek pinnipeds, which haul out of the water on the heavy wooden crossbeams just above the tide level.

Broken glass, bottles and many other items litter the seafloor of wharf pilings.

Apparently they don't mind the people thronged above them—or the occasional fish handout, willing or unwilling, from an angler's line or tourist's lunch plate. Their barking, echoing from below the wharf, can be heard for miles.

For humans, diving under a wharf can be a spooky experience. Wharves are where the ocean touches human commerce, and much of the jetsam of a busy port lurks beneath their waters. Sunken rowboats, huge ship's batteries, bicycles and wrecked cars may lie below a wharf, slowly rusting into a forest of scrap metal. Fishing nets, tangles of line and coils of old steel cable snake through the water, ready to snag unwary divers. Broken glass and any amount of trash litter the seafloor. There is the constant thrum of engines and propellers, the banging of boats docking and unloading at the wharves, limited underwater visibility from drifting sediments. A scuba diver may feel very vulnerable amidst this bedlam, never quite sure what may loom out of the gloomy water or what may crash down from the ships above. It is no place for an inexperienced diver.

Over time nature accepts the detritus of human activity. Eventually the trash under a wharf is colonized by the hardier reef dwellers. Sarcastic fringeheads are as likely to set up their lair in a boot or an old bottle under a pier as in a rocky crevice nearby. Some sea creatures thrive on the wastes under wharves. A pile of orange and red bat stars can mean an angler has dumped unwanted bait or game fish over the side. In a slow-motion feeding frenzy, the scavengers feast on what humans have killed and discarded.

WRECKS AND ARTIFICIAL REEFS

THE ROCKY SHORES AND FOGGY CLIMATE OF CENTRAL CALIFORNIA have made this an area of shipwrecks since the days of the Spanish explorers. When all ships were wooden, the wrecks did not last long, torn apart by waves and wood borers in a year at best. But since the advent of iron and steel vessels, shipwrecks have become another reeflike environment in the Monterey Bay National Marine Sanctuary. Within months, an encrusting community of algae and invertebrates comes to carpet sunken hulks—or whatever metal pieces of them remain unbroken by the sea. In Monterey Bay, where the rocks near Asilomar have snagged many a ship taking the eastward turn into the harbor too soon, known wrecks range in age from a few months to almost a hundred years. Bits of the engine and driveshaft remain from the St. Paul, a steamship that went down in 1896 off these rocks. On the younger end, a 38 feet (11.5 meters) fiberglass yacht sank in 60 feet (about 18 meters) of water near Point Pinos in July 1995. Within 10 days, even in the calm seas of summer, divers saw that its wooden upper parts had been torn to bits by waves mashing on the rocky bottom.

Rocky reefs are home to many species of rockfish.

The durable parts of ships are covered with life within months. Like other reefs, they soon attract game fishes and consequently become favored spots for divers and sport fishermen. Sometimes a wreck offers the only structure in an otherwise open, sandy bottom, and thus becomes the best sport-fishing spot around for the anglers lucky enough to know about it.

Because fish collect around reef structures, a logical way to improve fishing is to build reefs where none exists in nature. Artificial reefs, common in Japan, have been set in place in Southern California and along the Atlantic seaboard. Almost anything that provides a durable structure can and has been used as artificial reef—everything from junked cars and wornout tires to concrete pipe, masonry rubble and quarry stone. Central California, with its abundant natural rock, has seen less artificial reef construction than sandy areas farther south. But the few experimental reefs in the area have yielded surprising results when scientists studied their fish communities. While invertebrates mostly colonize artificial reefs as planktonic larvae, game fish, such as rockfishes, seem to migrate to them as juveniles and adults. For reasons not fully understood, artificial reefs seem to support higher densities of these fishes than nearby natural reefs. Since artificial reefs are usually built to improve fishing, they are well marked, well known and easily accessible to fishing boats, so more anglers tend

to congregate near them, just as more fish do below. The result? Legal-size game fish are removed from artificial reefs at an accelerated rate. When the big adults are gone, others may move in from surrounding reefs—only to be fished out quickly. The artificial reef can become a kind of "game-fish sinkhole," a place where breeding-size adults are removed from the population faster than anywhere else. Indeed, some researchers have come to the surprising conclusion that artificial reefs are bad for fishing. They may improve catches in the short run but make fish so easy to catch that populations suffer overall.

King salmon
Oncorhynchus tshawytscha

THE DEEP REEFS

AS YOU MOVE OUT TO SEA FROM THE SUNNY SHALLOWS, reefs change their character as depth increases. The shallow nearshore waters are in the photic zone, the range at which sunlight penetrates the water enough to permit the growth of algae. Below this is the dark aphotic zone, from 20 to about 100 feet (6 to 30 meters), where giant kelp dominates the reefs and algae cannot live at all. Below the depths where too little sunlight falls for kelp, reef communities exist on rocky structures. Often, the rocks are granite, pushed up through the shale sediments 80 million years ago. The deep reefs are roughly between 80 and 300 feet (about 25 to 90 meters), give or take clear water that lets kelp reach deeper.

The deeper one goes, the less wave action disturbs the bottom. Deep reefs are not subject to the pounding surf or winter surge of shallow-water reefs and pilings. Temperatures, too, remain more stable here throughout the seasons, averaging about 50°F (10°C) all year long.

At these depths, only short-wave blue or blue-green light can penetrate. Green and brown algae cannot exist in this dim environment. A few leafy reds grow in the shallower areas, but only   the hardiest red algae, equipped with special photosynthetic pigments called "phycoerythrins," are able to live on the deep reefs. Crustose coralline red algae are the deepest-living plant of all. It's hypothesized that slow metabolism is an advantage for a plant at these depths. Algae receive so little energy in the form of light that any degree of thriftiness confers an advantage. Crustose algae may respire more slowly than their leafy cousins and thus are able to live in dimmer light.

Rockfishes float over the deep reefs, ready to escape into rocks for shelter from larger predators.

Red algae
Crustose coralline algae

Cobalt blue sponge
Hymenamphiastra cyanocrypta

The deep reefs support a rich turf of encrusting animals. Not quite as many animal species are found as in the shallows, but what they lack in diversity they make up for with their colors. In the dim waters at the edge of the photic zone, red looks gray and brilliant purple fades to black. Full-spectrum light, brought from the surface in the form of divers' flashlights, reveals a surprising burst of color in the deep reefs.

Encrusting sponges cover rocks in blood red, bright yellow and deep cobalt blue. Bright orange balls, the size of grapefruit are orange puffball sponges, the largest sponge in these temperate waters. Clones of strawberry anemones carpeting square yards of the rock range from white through red and purple. Large, fish-eating rose anemones grow to the size of dinner plates, their brilliant red stems set off by pearly white tentacles. Orange cup corals build their solitary homes near the lurid pink and purple branches of California hydrocoral, colonial animals closer to the hydroids than to true corals.

The dim but stable environment of the deep reefs supports this wealth of colorful species because most are filter-feeders. They do not depend on local plant productivity but filter plankton and nutrients from the water. And the deep reefs, sitting at the edge of the deep ocean, are the first to receive the rich upwelling currents that bring nutrients out of the depths.

Sponges live on the reef, creating a colorful forest.

Sedentary sea cucumbers nestle in rock crevices, spreading pink branching tentacles to capture plankton. They resemble nothing so much as sea anemones. Their crawling cucumber cousins may find shelter nearby, in larger cracks and recesses that predators can't reach. Spot prawns, red crabs and Dungeness crabs crawl the deep reefs; deeper down the baited traps of commercial fishermen wait. And young giant octopus, whose adults grow to eight feet (about two and one half meters) long down in deeper water, may find shelter in reef crevices.

Sea cucumber
Parastichopus johnsoni

The three feet (one meter) tall white-plumed *Metridium* is the dominant true sea anemone in the deep reefs. Tilting a feathery crown for maximum water flow, it filters plankton out of the water. The swimming anemone *Stomphia* is also seen occasionally. When it is disturbed, this anemone will launch itself into the water, twisting and thrashing to swim away.

Deep water rockfishes, especially the red species prized in the commercial trade, hover in clouds around the deep reefs. Among them are the vermillion, rosy and flag rockfishes, whose red tones disappear into gray at these depths. Boccacio and copper rockfishes are also numerous. The young of many of these deep-living rockfishes mature in shallower water, in the shelter of the kelp forest or shale reefs. Only with increasing size do they drift down to deep reefs, their bodies adapting to the pressure so that they can no longer ascend without risking a burst swimbladder.

Juvenile vermilion rockfish
Sebastes miniatus

Clouds of rockfish juveniles may swarm around the reefs in schools the size of buses. Some researchers believe that these juveniles, 2 to 4 inches (5 to 10 centimeters) long, are the primary food that attracts the adult rockfishes to the reefside. They may also be the food that lures June's migrating king salmon into the shallows, where so many predators wait to claim them. Other fish denizens of the deep reefs include large lurkers like lingcod and wolf-eels.

Wolf-eel
Anarrhichthys ocellatus

Selected Reefs and Pilings Species

INVERTEBRATES

Aggregating anemone, *Anthopleura elegantissima*
Barnacle, *Megabalanus californicus*
Bat star, *Asterina miniata*
Brittle star, *Ophiothrix spiculata*
California mussel, *Mytilus californianus*
Candy-striped worm, *Dorvillea moniloceras*
Cobalt blue sponge, *Hymenamphiastra cyanocrypta*
Date mussel, *Lithophaga plumula*
Dungeness crab, *Cancer magister*
Encrusting sponge, *Haliclona* sp.
Feather-duster worm, *Eudistylia polymorpha*
Fish-eating anemone, *Urticina piscivora*
Giant acorn barnacle, *Balanus nubilus*
Giant octopus, *Octopus dofleini*
Giant green anemone, *Anthopleura xanthogrammica*
Giant sea star, *Pisaster giganteus*
Gumboot chiton, *Cryptochiton stelleri*
Hermit crab, *Pagurus* sp.
Orange cup coral, *Balanophyllia elegans*
Orange puffball, *Tethya aurantia*
Peanut worm, *Themiste pyroides*
Plainfin midshipman, *Porichthys notatus*
Porcelain crab, *Petrolisthes cinctipes*
Rock crab, *Cancer antennarius*
Rough piddock, *Zirfaea pilsbryi*
Scale-sided piddock, *Parapholas californica*
Sea cucumber, *Parastichopus johnsoni*
Shipworm, *Bankia setacea*
Spot prawn, *Pandalus platyceros*
Strawberry anemone, *Corynactis californica*
Sunflower star, *Pycnopodia helianthoides*
Wart-necked piddock, *Chaceia ovoidea*
White-plumed anemone, *Metridium senile*

FISHES

Barred surfperch, *Amphistichus argenteus*
Black surfperch, *Embiotoca jacksoni*
Blue rockfish, *Sebastes mystinus*
Bocaccio, *Sebastes paucispinis*
Canary rockfish, *Sebastes pinniger*
Copper rockfish, *Sebastes caurinus*
Coralline sculpin, *Artedius corallinus*
Flag rockfish, *Sebastes rubrivinctus*

Horn shark, *Heterodontus francisci*
King salmon, *Oncorhynchus tshawyscha*
Leopard shark, *Triakis semifasciata*
Lingcod, *Ophiodon elongatus*
Mussel blenny, *Hypsoblennius jenkinsi*
Pacific porgy, *Calamus brachysomus*
Pile surfperch, *Damalichthys vacca*
Rosy rockfish, *Sebastes rosaceus*
Sarcastic fringehead, *Neoclinus blanchardi*
Scalyhead sculpin, *Artedius harringtoni*
Striped surfperch, *Embiotoca lateralis*
Vermilion rockfish, *Sebastes miniatus*
Wolf-eel, *Anarrhichthys ocellatus*

PLANTS

Red algae, Crustose coralline algae

MAMMALS

California sea lion, *Zalophus californianus*
Harbor seal, *Phoca vitulina*

Sunlight filters through the golden canopy of a kelp forest.

CHAPTER EIGHT

KELP FORESTS

*"...creatures, scattered everywhere like dust admidst the
immeasurable oceans"*

GRAN, 1912

IF YOU LOOK OUT OVER MONTEREY BAY under the cloudless
blue skies of September, you'll be viewing the kelp forest.
Likely it won't stand out in your mind as you gaze across the
calm, black-blue water—any more than a redwood grove would
stand out in your mind if you were seeing it from a helicopter
passing above the forest canopy. In autumn, the kelp forest is only a texture
on the surface of the water, a zone where the waves seem to stumble just slightly,
bobbing out of rhythm for one beat of the dance in their smooth, endless waltz to
the shore. As you stand on shore, all you can see of the forest are the tips of the giant
kelp washed in a brown tangle at the surface of the sea. Just offshore, beyond the
zone of breaking surf and past the rocky shallows, these shoals of seaweed rise and
fall with the gentle waves of autumn. A sea otter, sporting and rolling, may suddenly
dive in the midst of this tangle, coming up a minute later with a colorful crab or
starfish struggling in its paws. Sea gulls circling and cormorants fishing give some

hint of the riches below, but to really appreciate the kelp forest, one must see it from below, like a scuba diver or a circling rockfish. The plant and animal communities of this nearshore habitat rival rain forests and tropical coral reefs for richness and diversity.

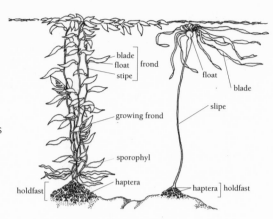

Macrocystis (left) *and Nereocystis* (right).

The kelp itself is only the beginning of that diversity, but it dominates and defines these underwater forests much as redwoods and Douglas fir dominate the forests of the California coastal ranges. Two tall kelp species share the lead role in our area's offshore waters: golden green *Macrocystis pyrifera,* the flat-bladed "giant kelp" that can grow to 100 feet (30.3 meters) tall in clear waters, and single-stalked bull kelp, *Nereocystis luetkeana,* with a bullwhip crown of blades buoyed up by one round float. (The bobbing floats of bull kelp can look like heads of sea otters, confusing many a tourist who looks out to sea.) While most nearshore kelp forests in the Monterey Bay region are dominated by giant kelp, bull kelp is more resistant to wave damage and can live in the rougher waters outside protective bays and inlets. Actually, the two species often alternate in an area over many years—now one is dominant, then the other—in a cycle of constant change dependent on waves and weather. Some areas off Point Sur that were dominated by bull kelp in the 1940s are now home to lush stands of giant kelp. Within groves of giant kelp a space cleared when a few adult *Macrocystis* fall victim to storm swells may give young bull kelp a chance to flourish and reach the sunny canopy. But bull kelp is an annual, living no more than one year. The many-fronded *Macrocystis* can live seven years or longer and so is likely to have the advantage wherever waters are calm enough to let it grow.

Bull kelp
Nereocystis luetkeana

Kelps are members of a plant group called algae, a diverse group of many phyla that contain microscopic species as well as the familiar seaweeds. The giant kelps that dominate the forest are members of the brown algae group. Smaller brown algae, as well as green and red algae, grow in profusion among the giants, enriching the forest with their color and texture.

FORESTS IN THE SEA

KELP FORESTS ARE NOT UNIQUE TO THIS AREA but are found all along the Pacific coast of North America, from Alaska to the warm waters off Baja California. Skipping the warm tropical and subtropical seas, giant kelp forests also range south along the temperate coasts of South America. Forests of other giant seaweeds skirt temperate coasts of South Africa, New Zealand and Australia. Arctic waters seem to be too cold for kelp, and in tropical seas coral reefs take on many of the roles played by kelp in temperate waters. In general, giant kelp seems to favor waters of about 50°–60°F (10°–15.5°C), perhaps because warmer waters are lacking in the nutrients that kelp needs to grow.

Giant kelp
Macrocystis pyrifera

The waters of the Monterey Bay National Sanctuary are a perfect habitat for kelp forests. Along the coast of California, cold waters pour south from Alaska along the deep sea bed. Warmer water, poor in nutrients, floats nearer to the surface. But when northwesterly winds push the surface water offshore, cooler, nutrient-rich water can well up to take its place. It is this upwelling that allows the kelp forest to develop here. So important

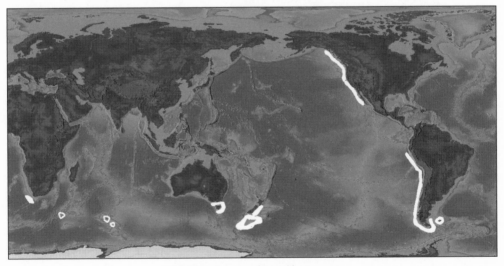

Giant kelp only grows along coldwater coasts.

A tangle of kelp blades, stipes and floats.

are the nutrients brought in by upwelling that kelp forests wither and die back when the exchange is cut off. In fact, giant kelp and its algae relatives have a wealth of structural adaptations that keep their growing tissues bathed in the nutrients they

The kelp holdfast acts as an anchor that secures the kelp to rocks on the seafloor.

need. Their leathery blades are covered with whorls and wrinkles, increasing the surface area of the tissue exposed to the water. Spines and serrations along blade edges keep water stirred up as it passes over the blade; even in calm water, this allows some exchange of nutrients to take place. But even when nutrients are plentiful in the water, a kelp forest needs a solid foundation. A kelp forest can grow up only where tiny kelp spores, settling out of the plankton, can find a firm toehold

to which they can attach themselves. Normally, this means a rocky bottom. Hard granite reef is an ideal, long-lasting toehold for baby kelp; if they fasten on granite, giant kelp can live a full life span of seven or eight years. But mudstone and other soft sedimentary rocks abound in our area. These soft rocks, often riddled by the burrows of rock-boring clams, break easily. A winter storm can rip full-grown giant kelp loose, with chunks of mudstone still entangled in their haptera. When this happens, the loose kelp barrels through the forest like a bulldozer, entangling and pulling loose other healthy kelp. On a mudstone substrate, giant kelps live shorter lives.

Two other forces shape the boundaries of the kelp forest: sunlight and the pounding of waves. Giant kelp thrives only where the amount of light reaching the bottom is at least one percent of that at the surface. Because of its special efficient photosynthetic pigments and its ability to share food from the sunlit canopy to its darkened stipes below, giant kelp can thrive as deep as one 100 feet (30.3 meters) below the surface if waters are very clear. These deeper habitats are more secure from the pounding of surf and storm waves, but the kelp can be vulnerable if cloudy water changes its sunlight supply. Closer to shore, the waters are sunnier, but waves are likewise more intense. In water shallower than 20 feet (6 meters), the turbulence of wave surge becomes too much for *Macrocystis,* and it must surrender the well-lit waters close to shore to smaller and hardier algae relatives.

Red coralline algae
Calliarthron sp.

In structure, a kelp forest resembles a forest on land. Giant kelp stretch for the sun and form a canopy at the water's surface, like tall trees with interlocking branches. At the height of summer, when the canopy is complete, it may catch 90 percent of the sunlight reaching the water. This leaves precious little for shorter plants below, so anything that grows under a kelp canopy had better need little light or none at all. Some coralline red algae survive under a sort of time-sharing arrangement. Like wildflowers that spring up before the trees have leafed out in terrestrial forests, these algae put on their year's growth in the few short winter months when the kelp canopy, thinned by storms, lets in the most sunlight.

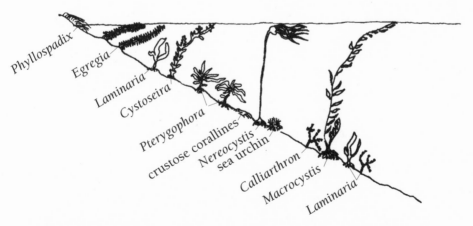

Seaweeds are found in different zones along the seafloor. The turf species like encrusting corallines and Pterosiphonia spp. *are found in zone one; plants up to 20 inches tall such as Calliarthron make their home in zone two; plants up to 6.5 feet tall (*Pterygophora, Laminaria*) live in zone three; and midwater and surface canopy species such as* Egregia, Cystoseira *and* Macrocystis *are found in the furthest depths of zone four.*

145

Seasons of the Forest

THE KELP FOREST DEPENDS ON two things for its growth: waterborne nutrients and sunlight filtering down from the surface. As these change over the seasons, so does the forest, in a complex rhythm that takes the kelp from jungle lushness to near-barren openness each year, and back again.

The forest's growth season begins as March winds blow surface waters offshore, pushing warmer, nutrient-poor surface water seaward, letting cold waters rich in minerals well up from the deep ocean. This upwelling starts our morning fogs; it also brings a wealth of welcome nutrients into the winter-starved kelp forest. Torn by winter weather, the kelp canopy is sparse and open. Sunlight pours all the way to the bottom in the nutrient-enriched water. Taking advantage of the sun, red and coralline algae in the kelp understory put on a growth spurt. All around them, young kelp sporophytes are stretching for the sun. Most are the new stipes of old veteran haptera, but in some sunny clearings, where winter storms have torn out the mature kelp, tiny new *Macrocystis* or the annual bull kelp may gain a foothold. Fed by nutrients, young kelp grow thick as spaghetti. By June, their gold-green fronds cover the surface, and the canopy closes for the year.

Down in the forest, understory algae must now make do in dim light. But out on the surface, light warms the top twenty feet (about six meters) or so of rich upwelled water. Plankton grow thick as pea soup, turning the waters a cloudy gray green. Divers descending through this layer may not even see their own fins. Like skydivers falling through clouds, they will suddenly break through this green layer into the clear but cold water beneath with a view seventy feet (about twenty one meters) to the bottom. This stratified ocean exists as long as the winds blow offshore to drive upwelling. When the winds stop, the system breaks down, and pulses of warmer water

from the California Current move in from offshore. With it come pulses of larvae, young fish, invertebrates and algae that the kelp forest stops like a filter. Some will be lucky and settle; others will nourish the kelp forests animals. The upwelling season, from late winter to late summer, is a time of great growth and abundance.

Early autumn finds the kelp forest at its most luxuriant. As the northwest winds die down, growth slows, but the forest is in full bloom in calm seas that are now clear of plankton. This is the favorite season of divers, the best time to see the kelp forest in all its color and diversity.

From a short, flat-bladed understory kelp, long lacy fronds snake up to the surface canopy. The bead kelp *Cystoseira* is making its reproductive effort. The long, beaded spore-bearing fronds will last only until the winter storms, though the squatty plant that produces them can live for years in the understory.

All summer long, short-spined stars and ochre sea stars prowled the floor of the kelp forest in search of their mollusc prey. With the first heavy waves of November, the stars get a feast: snails come raining down off the kelp stipes, shaken loose by the swells. It is a harbinger of things to come. The calm seas of autumn flow round a kelp forest heavy with summer growth and laden with encrusting animals. But the nutrient flow from upwelling has ceased, and shorter days starve the forest of sunlight. The kelp forest hangs like an overripe apple as the winter comes on, the canopy thick, the fronds frosted with lace bryozoans and starting to yellow with age.

The weather turns ugly as storm swells sweep in from the open sea. Winter storms from as far off as the Gulf of Alaska send huge waves pumping toward Central California's shores. The swells slam the underwater forest with 40 times the force of a hurricane. Few large algae can escape their battering unscathed. Winter storms are the great pruners of the kelp forest, clearing out summer's excess bounty with a capricious hand. The small red algae of the forest floor, heavy with summer growth, lose fronds to the storms. For the giant kelp, the situation can be much worse: whole plants may be torn loose and sent spiraling through the forest, their holdfasts swinging like wrecking balls. The storm-torn plants ensnare and uproot others, mowing a swath of destruction through the forest and creating a wealth of drift kelp, to be tossed up on shore.

By January, the shredded stipes of the kelp hang like ghosts in the tired water; the forest is a shadow of its summer self. But in the clearings torn by maurauding storm waves, under the tattered canopy, sunlight is able to penetrate down to the seafloor. As the days lengthen, the cycle will begin again, with spring winds starting the upwelling pump and bringing fresh life to the forest.

Sunlight filters through the broad fronds of giant kelp at the bay's surface.

147

Other plants grow year-round with the help of efficient photosynthetic pigments that make the most of the dim light. Several hardy species of small kelp and red algae grow to 6 feet (1.8 meters) in the shadow of the canopy, a "shrub layer," or midstory, between the giants of the underwater forest. Close to shore, these may include the flexible feather boa kelp *Egregia laevigata*, whose tough, flattened blades can withstand the pounding surf. Other shrub-layer species are the blade kelp *Laminaria setchelli*; the winged kelp *Pterygophora californica*, and the oarweed *Laminaria farlowii*. Intermingled with the shrub layer grows a colorful riot of red, green and brown algae species. Nubby rockweed, sponge-like Codium, and pink coralline algae make their appearance wherever light allows them to.

LIFE IN THE KELP FOREST

MANY OF THE LIFEFORMS that blanket the open spaces between holdfasts of giant kelp need no light at all, because they are animals. Encrusting bryozoans, paddies of colorful sea anemones, sponges and corals—all jostle for space on the floor of the kelp forest. This plethora of near-bottom invertebrates makes for a layer of "turf" on the kelp forest floor, but one composed of colonial animals rather than the fallen vegetation of a terrestrial forest.

Feather boa kelp
Egregia menziesii

The kelp forest supports the richest assemblage of sea life in any ocean community in the Monterey Bay region. Hundreds of species of animals and 400 types of sea plants have been cataloged in kelp forests of Monterey Bay National Marine Sanctuary. The diversity of life within the forest could fill a book of its own. Like coral reefs, kelp forests are a multi-layered, three-dimensional environment, where every bit of space is inhabited. A giant kelp plant offers 14 times the settling space as the same patch of seafloor. Just one adult *Macrocystis* holdfast can harbor more than 500,000 sea creatures (many, of course, are microscopic in size).

Oarweed
Laminaria farlowii

Strawberry anemones form colonies that fiercely defend their borders from other colonies.

As a general rule, the more structure a reef offers, the higher the number of species that can find shelter there. Compared to rocky reefs in our area, pilings of rock that kelp do not inhabit, the kelp forest offers more structure. The complex of haptera, stipes and floating blades that make up the plant is a sort of "highrise" for fishes, snails, worms and other creatures, offering shelter or a place to settle. While some larger animals are just as abundant around rocky reefs as in the kelp forest, the forests are far richer in smaller species and in the total number of individual plants and animals.

The kelp forest has another advantage over rocky reefs: the tall plants absorb some of the shock of storm waves. The forest slows down water pushed through it by waves and currents,

Decorator crab
Loxorhynchus crispatus

Male sheephead
Semicossyphus pulcher

149

Red abalone
Haliotis rufescens

Brown turban snail
Tegula brunnea

Blue rockfish
Sebastes mystinus

becoming a "filter" for tiny larvae that drift with the plankton. The protective, slow-water environment in the forest makes it an ideal nursery for these young fishes and shellfishes as well as a place for adults to find shelter and food. Many species of fishes and invertebrates, including blue rockfish and purple sea urchin, are much more abundant in the kelp forest than in surrounding waters. Scientists believe that most of these species could exist without the kelp itself, but their populations would be a tiny fraction of what they can reach within the shelter of the forest.

At the surface, sea otters dive and roll among the kelp; they may wrap themselves in strands of the canopy to keep from drifting as they sleep. Otters dive for many of the invertebrate inhabitants of the kelp forest floor: abalones, sea urchins, clams, crabs and sea stars are all on the sea otters' menu.

Sea lions, harbor seals, sharks, rays and yellowtail glide through the kelp forest on the hunt for fish. Even a juvenile gray whale may wander in, briefly detouring during migration. Snails and limpets make their slow way over the kelp fronds, rasping at the film of diatoms caught on the kelp's sticky surface. Sea hares cruise the middle depths, gliding along

Pacific sardine
Sardinops sagax

Cabezon
Scorpaenichthys marmoratus

stipes. On rocks and within holdfasts, sea anemones form carpets of pink and white.
Even the jagged animal duff between rocky parts of the kelp reef is home to a
bewildering variety of animals: burrowing worms, tube-dwelling anemones and
California halibut, hiding in plain sight against the mottled ocean bottom.

On rocks, a living tapestry of sponges and tunicates gleam in shades of red,
green and blue. There is a constant crowding in the forest reef. For algae and settled
animals, finding a space to settle is one major battle; keeping it is another. Bryozoans
use tiny mobile pincers, "avicularia," to pluck off new settlers that land on them.
Tunicates have slick, gelatinous surfaces, offering little purchase to larvae in search of
a home. Plants and sponges may produce antibiotics, poisoning other lifeforms that
settle too near.

Each living layer in the kelp forest is home to another layer of life. Like nested
Russian dolls, even the most solid-seeming contain a surprise. Break open a sponge,
and inside you will find a world of tiny animals. A patch of

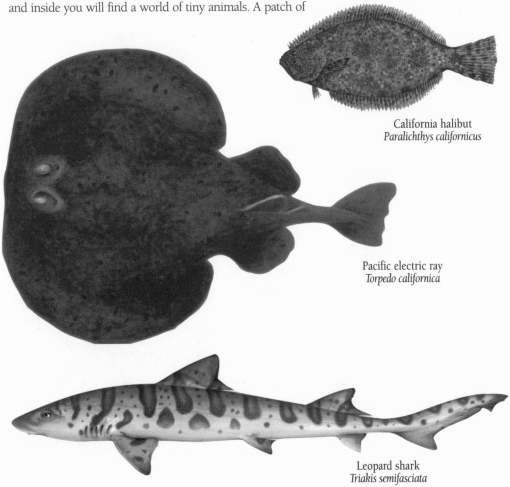

California halibut
Paralichthys californicus

Pacific electric ray
Torpedo californica

Leopard shark
Triakis semifasciata

151

A top snail searches for food along the giant kelp.

This kelpfish can disguise itself by changing color to match its surroundings.

mixed mussels and barnacles, closely packed on a rock, teems with worms and grazers navigating the narrow spaces between their shells. Even the kelp haptera are home to a wealth of small creatures: kelp gribbles, snails, brittle stars that emerge at night to feed.

Kelp greenling hide in the dense algae at the bottom. Blue rockfish circle the forest on the outside, hunting for jellies and plankton; their young are among the most abundant small fish in the kelp forest. Young blue rockfish feed the many larger fish, seabirds and mammals that pass through the forest only when hungry. Some fishes, like the kelp surfperch and the gopher rockfish, depend on kelp to shelter their young. The giant kelpfish not only lives among kelp and hunts for shrimp and smaller fishes in the kelp fronds, but it also looks as much like kelp blades as a living fish can. Its flattened, mottled body blends in perfectly with the blades of giant kelp, all the more so because the kelpfish can alter its skin color to match its surroundings. Despite their name, however, kelp bass do not depend on the kelp plants at all for either feeding or breeding. They like the structure that a kelp forest provides but do just as well around bare rocky reefs or even oil platforms.

At night, a second shift of animals roams the forest. Hundreds of small octopuses —the red and one-spot varieties—emerge from daylight hideouts in rock crevices to feed on crabs and clams. In turn, they are scooped up by the hungry jaws of rockfishes— most of California's 60 varieties of rockfishes spend at least some of their time hunting in kelp forests.

The animals, especially fishes, in our kelp forests depend partly on the whims of weather and temperature. A warm current, especially an El Niño, can sweep southern organisms north, into the forests of Monterey Bay National Marine Sanctuary. After

Sea otters play an important role in the kelp forest by feeding on sea urchins. Unchecked, urchins could devastate a kelp forest by grazing heavily on giant kelp.

How many Kinds of Kelp are There?

Feather boa kelp is in the family Alariaceae.

Dictyoneuropsis is in the family Lessoniaceae.

There are four families of kelp: Chordaceae, Laminariaceae, Lessoniaceae and Alariaceae. Chorda, a shoestring of a kelp, is the sole member of the family Chordaceae and isn't found in Monterey Bay. But a variety of members from the other three kelp families abound in the area.

You can tell the kelps in the **Laminariaceae** family by their plain and simple fronds with branched or cuplike holdfasts. Their basic blades fulfill all functions: production of sugars and spores. In some species, the original blade tears lengthwise into strips.

Alariaceae includes the feathery *Pterogophora*.

Kelps in the family **Lessoniaceae** usually branch out into complicated forms. These kelps have branched stipes, multiple blades and sometimes floats. Some develop special spore-making blades, while others grow spores right on their regular blades.

Laminariaceae claims the classic oarweed.

Members of the kelp family **Alariaceae** look feathery, growing secondary blades along the stipe or on the edges of a central blade. They grow their spores on special blades.

Can you guess by shape alone the proper family that each kelp belongs to?

Bull kelp belongs to the Lessoniaceae.

Giant kelp is a relative of bull kelp.

the powerful El Niño of 1982–83, such southern rarities as garibaldi, pelagic red crab and blacksmith were spotted in sanctuary waters. These creatures drifted in as larvae and have survived to adulthood but do not seem to be able to spawn here.

Garibaldi
Hypsypops rubicundus

Some evidence points to a permanent warming trend in the region's waters. Researchers who have studied the kelp forests off Monterey for 30 years have seen some warm-water species, like the white whelk *Kelletia,* move into the kelp forests and establish themselves with vigor. A recent study at Hopkins Marine Station showed conclusively for the first time that warm-water species have become much more common in the intertidal zone around Monterey in the last 60 years. Could the kelp forest communities also be showing signs of a change related to global warming? No one is sure right now, but the situation bears watching.

LIFE IN THE KELP FOREST

GIANT KELP IS ONE OF THE MOST PRODUCTIVE PLANTS ON EARTH, able to grow 18 inches (about 46 centimeters) a day in full sunlight. Each year, many tons of biomass are created as the kelp transforms sunlight into living tissue. But, oddly, very little of this kelp is actually eaten by creatures within the kelp forest. One study suggests that 70 percent of kelp productivity is involved in food chains outside the forest.

The main reason giant kelp benefits other habitats is that the plant constantly sheds its fronds. While a kelp plant may live several years, the life of each frond is typically six months or less. A blade that starts out fresh and pristine is soon battered by waves, abraded by sand or weighed down by a delicate frost of colonial bryozoans. It's to the kelp's advantage to shed the old frond and replace it with one that is new and buoyant. The castoff fronds, or kelpshed, drift through the forest and feed some of the most important creatures that inhabit its rocky crevices. Both abalones and sea urchins feed heavily on drift kelp. Since both are valuable commercial species, as well as food for sea otters, sea stars and other kelp forest inhabitants, a healthy supply of drift kelp benefits human divers as well as the many other species that prey upon kelp forest invertebrates. Conversely, when the supply of drift kelp gets too low, as happened when dumping of raw sewage clouded the waters in kelp forests near San Diego, disaster may result. Whole kelp forests were lost when advancing fronts of hungry red and purple sea urchins chewed through the kelp holdfasts. The full-grown plants drifted away, leaving behind an "urchin barrens" denuded of all but red coralline algae.

But a great deal of kelpshed is not consumed within the kelp forest. Whole kelp plants, broken free by rough waves or other disturbances, join the kelpshed as it makes

155

Sea urchins cluster on kelp stipes dining on its rich food source.

its way out of the forest. Some of this kelp will be cast up on nearby shores. If you walk along the beach after a winter storm, you are likely to see the sand littered with kelp piled like jumbled laundry high above the surf line. The kelp wrack smells of the sea, and of decay; hardly a trace of the beauty of kelp in the ocean can be seen in these cast-up, dying discards. The barren sands between the dunes and the surf zone are one of the harshest environments on Earth, hostile to plant and animal alike, but the rotting piles, sometimes 10 feet (3 meters) high after a big storm, are a windfall to beach-dwelling creatures. Lift a strand of the drying kelp wrack and you'll find it abuzz with tiny diners. Sandhoppers, sand flies, burrowing isopods and myriad beach decomposers depend on cast-up kelp for their livelihood. In a habitat where no plants can take root, it is the only source of energy to power a food chain.

The floats on the kelp wrack may rot open as the plants lie on the beach, and big waves eventually take them back into the ocean. Now, unable to float, the drift kelp

Shaped by Waters Flow

MUCH AS CONSTANT WINDS HAVE BENDED and twisted cypresses on sea cliffs, ocean waves shape the kelp forest and each of the plants within it. Water moving over the kelp brings them dissolved gases and nutrients. Currents disperse the kelps sperm and spores. When violent, the sea can be a destructive force, tearing blades, breaking stipes and dislodging holdfasts.

Intertidal kelps face breaking waves, rapid surges and backwash; offshore kelps sway in swells and tidal currents. Kelps with firm, upright stipes confront the sea with steadfast strength, but other kelps offer less resistance: they flap and flutter in the water flow. Their elastic stipes stretch out in the flowing water and flexibly alternate directions to accommodate the surge. Some bull kelp grow coiled stipes that extend their springy play.

Water flow also affects the shape of kelp blades. As it grows, a blade may change to suit its surroundings. The feather boa kelp that starts life soft and sheer stays that way in quiet water but gets tough and sturdy in rougher settings.

Some kelps have slick blades with slimy surfaces that cut the waters drag or discourage other seaweeds from settling down on them. Other kelps have ribbed and corrugated blades. The ribs and corrugations give the blade strength; wrinkles, ruffles, holes and spines enhance water flow close to the blades surface for a greater exchange of nutrients.

The Kelp Forest Exhibit at Monterey Bay Aquarium

WHEN THE MONTEREY BAY AQUARIUM OPENED IN 1984, no one had ever kept a kelp forest alive in captivity. But aquarium biologists had a dream of re-creating this beautiful and diverse central piece of Monterey Bays underwater neighborhood. There were serious doubts as to whether we could grow kelp at all, recalls Charles Baxter, one of the aquarium's founding biologists. It was all a big experiment, from the beginning. The biologists believed that if they could duplicate natural conditions as closely as possible, a kelp forest could live and grow in an aquarium environment. Were we sure we could do it? No, says Dr. Steven Webster. Whether we were brave, naive or just hardheaded, we went ahead and we said okay, if I were a kelp, what would I need to make me happy?

The diver examines kelp plants inside the Monterey Bay Aquarium's Kelp Forest exhibit.

Six adult giant kelp plants were carefully cut from their fixed places in the kelp forest just off Point Lobos and transported to the exhibit. Rubber bungee cords held them to their rocky substrates at first, but soon fresh haptera grew out and the kelp took hold in their new home. Open to the sky, the top of the tank lets the water mix with the rain and the sun, just as in the bay. But once they grew up to the surface, the kelp needed a little extra help: without the cooling spray of an open ocean, the luxuriant fronds began to sunburn. Once burned, the kelps gas-filled floats crack and fill with water, pulling the canopy downward. The solution: a seawater sprinkler system, which gives the surface fronds the extra bit of moisture they need.

The experiment has been a wonderful sucess. Today, a healthy kelp forest fills the exhibit in cathedral-like splendor, giving visitors a glimpse of the forest that only a scuba diver could have seen before. Gold-green light filters down through the towering canopy of *Macrocystis*. Silver chains of anchovies wind through the tall green kelp stipes; rockfishes hang suspended above a galaxy of red and orange sea stars. A carpet of smaller red and green seaweeds enriches the view, sharing space among the kelp with pink anemones, orange cup corals and colorful encrusting sponges. Most of these smaller kelp forest denizens entered the exhibit as volunteers, arriving as larvae or spores with the unfiltered sea water pumped in each night. So enthusiastic are these colonizers that divers now clean the tank's windows three times a week, to keep the view clear. Hypnotically swaying in the gentle rhythm of the water, changing with the seasons, the only kelp forest in captivity gets richer and more colorful year by year.

Forests by Land or by Sea

Bat star
Asterina miniata

FORESTS ON LAND share a common bond with marine forests: they're both communities that support many layers of life and exhibit seasonal changes. Plants provide the structure, from tall canopy species to underbrush; animals inhabiting these communities find niches in the layered framework in which to live.

On land, tree roots penetrate deep into the ground to get the water and nutrients they need. Forest trees mature slowly. As they grow, they form canopies that shade the understory. Leaves and branches fall to the forest floor, fortifying the soil with nutrients. Rich forest soils support millions of microorganisms: fungi, bacteria, worms, mites and tiny insects. Large animals, like white-tailed deer, graze in the understory, while raccoons, squirrels, bears and mice subsist on seeds and hunt for varied foods.

Predators—snakes on the ground and hawks in the air—hunt for prey. Scavengers, like vultures, and earth eaters, like earthworms, break down dead matter. In forests in the oceans, kelps and other seaweeds draw their nutrients directly from the sea water rather than through roots. When nutrients are abundant, kelps grow quickly, but compared to long-lived redwood and oak trees, they live short and sweet lives lasting from one to seven years. Most never get a chance to die or decompose in place. Torn free by storm waves, they drift out of the forest, although urchins and abalones snag and eat some of the drifting kelp. In turn, the urchins, snails and other seaweed-eaters provide food for the carnivores in the kelp forest. Sea stars slowly swallow snails and fishes search for crawling prey. Sharks, sea lions and sea otters hunt the hunters. The versatile crabs scavenge for animal remains or pursue living prey, and sea cucumbers feed on bacteria as they vacuum up sediments off the forest floor.

Whether on land or under water, plants provide habitats for forest animals and ultimately support all food webs that inhabit them.

Forest Fishes

MORE THAN 150 DIFFERENT KINDS OF FISHES live in the coastal waters off California. Few dwell exclusively in kelp forests, but a variety of species can live in them because of the different habitats they offer. You can tell where a fish fits in the forest by means of a few clues, like its shape, color and habits.

Sleek and streamlined swimmers, Pacific sardines are constantly on the move. Traveling in schools, they feed on plankton. Silvery flashes in their midwater habitat, they leave slower fishes behind. Forked tails give them speed and power, and their fins are evenly distributed for stability and maneuverability.

Lie-in-wait predators like the cabezon and other sculpins have camouflaged bodies

Tubesnout
Aulorhynchus flavidus

158

This kelp crab hangs on tight to slippery kelp fronds.

patterned to match their seaweed hiding places. Fins set back on the body and a large tail fin give the cabezon the extra thrust it needs to launch surprise attacks. Midwater fishes are often neutrally buoyant—that is, they hover with ease in midwater. Some fishes fight the pull of gravity with low-density oils in their bodies; others have shaped and angled swimming fins that generate lift. Still others, like rockfishes, have a swimbladder, a gas-filled space that helps regulate their buoyancy. Fishes like the tubesnout change their habits and their habitats. The tubesnout is covered with bony plates so it's rigid and can't turn quickly. It swims slowly near the

water's surface, camouflaged from below by its light-colored underside. After mating, the male tubesnout, hidden by its kelp-colored back, hovers near its nest of kelp to guard the eggs.

Many bottom-dwelling fishes, like rays and flatfishes, are flattened for continuous contact with the seafloor. These fishes usually lack swimbladders, so the negative buoyancy that makes them sink to the bottom works to their advantage.

may feed yet another hungry assemblage of creatures. Some drift kelp sinks to the bottom and is carried to ocean depths where no light ever penetrates. Kelpshed from Monterey Bay forests is seen at the bottom of the undersea Carmel Canyon, 15 miles (24 kilometers) from where it grew. Half a mile (0.8 kilometers) beneath the ocean surface, deep sea communities of pale brittle stars, grayish tube worms and ghostly bluish white sea cucumbers depend on whatever food rains down from above. Kelp is even the primary food source of one deep sea species, the fragile sea urchin. Whenever a windfall of kelp reaches the bottom, the urchins gather in piles to feed on it, like a slow-motion feasting of vultures.

Not all kelp that drifts out to sea sinks immediately. Ocean-going mats of kelp may stay afloat for months. These kelp "paddies" provide shelter to many species that otherwise find little shelter in the open ocean, including the young of important sport and commercial fishes such as sablefish and boccacio. Rockfishes, swimming crabs and both juvenile and adult yellowtail are among the dozens of species that may use a floating kelp paddy for shelter, for rest, or as a temporary getaway from predators. When a kelp paddy eventually sinks, it too will provide sustenance for the creatures of the deep ocean.

People, too, take advantage of kelp's remarkable productivity. In Europe, kelp has been raked ashore for centuries to fertilize seaside fields, its rich load of minerals providing a windfall to agricultural soil. Kelp has also been harvested as a source of potash, used to make gunpowder. In the 19th century, and particularly before World War I as U.S. relations with Germany soured, kelp was collected for this purpose in what is now Monterey Bay National Marine Sanctuary. Harvesting was usually done from open boats, and the long poles used to rake in the kelp could uproot whole plants. Fortunately, more benign methods of harvest evolved along with the market for a new kelp product: its natural gel, called "algin." Algin is a flavorless natural thickener and emulsifier that adds texture and body to foods. It is very common in processed foods, including ice cream, breads and beer; it finds use as a thickener in cosmetics and paints. Algin is even added to the coatings of welding rods. Nowadays, kelp is harvested for algin by large ships that snip off only the top 3 to 6 feet (0.9 to 1.8 meters) of the kelp canopy, using blades much like a giant set of hedge clippers. The kelp canopy quickly regrows; in waters off southern California, the same patch of kelp may be ready for another harvest a month after it is cut. Usually, no commercial harvest for algin takes place in Monterey Bay National Marine Sanctuary, but a poor harvest farther south sometimes brings a kelp-cutting ship within sanctuary waters.

The kelp forest acts as habitat for this rich assemblage of species. The kelp itself, cast on shore or drifting down to the depths, becomes the basis of both onshore and deep ocean food chains. The influence of the kelp forest thus spreads well outside the forest itself.

Selected Kelp Forest Species

SEAWEEDS

Acid seaweed, *Desmarestia ligulata*
Brown seaweed, *Cystoseira osmundacea*
Bull kelp, *Nereocystis luetkeana*
Giant kelp, *Macrocystis pyrifera*
Jointed coralline, *Bossiella* spp.
Jointed coralline, *Calliarthron* spp.
Red sea grape, *Botryocladia pseudodichotoma*
Red seaweed, *Fauchea* spp.
Red seaweed, *Rhodymenia* spp.
Turkish towel seaweed, *chondracanthus* spp.
Understory kelp, *Eisenia arborea*
Understory kelp, *Pterogophora californica*

INVERTEBRATES

Abalone, *Haliotis* spp.
Amphipod, *Cymadusa uncinata*
Aggregating anemone, *Anthopleura elegantissima*
Bat star, *Asterina miniata*
Blue sponge, *Hymenamphiastra cyanocrypta*
Brittle star, *Ophiothrix spiculata*
Bryozoan, *Membranipora tuberculata*
Comb jelly, *Beroe forskalii*
Decorator crab, *Loxorhynchus crispatus*
Gumboot chiton, *Cryptochiton stelleri*
Hermit crab, *Pagurus samuelis*
Hydroid, *Eucopella* sp.
Isopod, *Idotea* spp.
Kelp crab, *Pugettia* spp.
Melibe, *Melibe leonina*
Opossum shrimp, *Acanthomysis* sp.
Purple sea urchin, *Strongylocentrotus purpuratus*
Red octopus, *Octopus rubescens*
Red sea urchin, *Strongylocentrotus franciscanus*
Rock crab, *Cancer antennarius*
Sea slug, *Doridilla*
Sea star, *Pisaster giganteus*
Strawberry anemone, *Corynactis californica*
Sunflower star, *Pycnopodia helianthoides*
Top shell, *Calliostoma* spp.
Tube-dwelling anemone, *Pachycerianthus fimbriatus*
Tube worm, *Diopatra splendidissima*
Turban snail, *Tegula* spp.

FISHES

Black-and-yellow rockfish, *Sebastes chrysomelas*
Black rockfish, *Sebastes melanops*
Blacksmith, *Chromis punctipinnus*
Blue rockfish, *Sebastes mystinus*
Cabezon, *Scorpaenichthys marmoratus*
Garibaldi, *Hypsypops rubicundus*
Giant kelpfish, *Heterostichus rostratus*
Gopher rockfish, *Sebastes carnatus*
Halfmoon, *Medialuna californiensis*
Kelp bass, *Paralabrax clathratus*
Kelp greenling, *Hexagrammos decagrammus*
Kelp gunnel, *Ulvicola sanctaerosae*
Kelp rockfish, *Sebastes atrovirens*
Kelp surfperch, *Brachyistius frenatus*
Lingcod, *Ophiodon elongatus*
Olive rockfish, *Sebastes serranoides*
Opaleye, *Girella nigricans*
Painted greenling, *Oxylebius pictus*
Señorita, *Oxyjulius californica*
Sheephead, *Semicossyphus pulcher*
Torpedo ray, *Torpedo californica*
Wolf-eel, *Annarichthys ocellatus*

BIRDS

Brandt's cormorant, *Phalacrocorax penicillatus*
Eared grebe, *Podiceps caspicus*
Elegant tern, *Thalasseus elegans*
Horned grebe, *Podiceps auritus*
Surf scoter, *Melanitta perspicullata*
Western gull, *Larus occidentalis*

MARINE MAMMALS

Harbor seal, *Phoca vitulina*
Sea otter, *Enhydra lutris nereis*

Hidden from view, this burrowing anemone anchors itself beneath the sand with two more feet of tube.

CHAPTER NINE

THE SANDY SEAFLOOR

*I want to tell you the ocean knows this, that life in its jewel boxes is endless
as the sand, impossible to count, pure, and made the jellyfish full of light and
untied its knot, letting its musical threads fall from a horn of plenty made of
infinite mother-of-pearl.*

PABLO NERUDA, 1971

 BELOW THE BEACHES, BETWEEN THE ROCKY REEFS and
kelp-covered outcroppings, most of the ocean bottom in the
Monterey Bay area is soft bottom covered with sand or mud.
These sandy seafloors are a special environment. At first sight
they are a desert, bereft of the colorful riot of life found on rocky shores and in kelp
forests. To a diver venturing here, the sands stretch gray and bare in every direction;
a rocky reef looms like a welcome oasis, a focus for life in the inhospitable plain. But
the sandy seafloor is a vast habitat that covers most of our planet. Sandy seafloors,
like terrestrial deserts, are only barren until you look beneath their surface. Although
harsh, they are specialized environments that offer rich rewards to creatures hardy
enough to colonize their vast expanses.

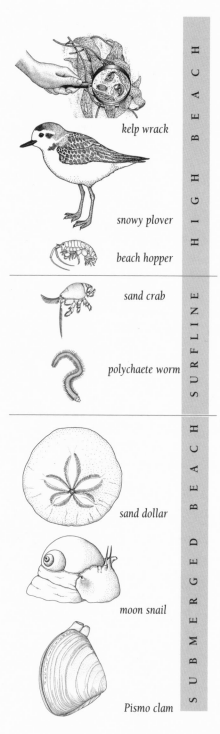

kelp wrack

snowy plover

beach hopper

sand crab

polychaete worm

sand dollar

moon snail

Pismo clam

HIGH BEACH

SURFLINE

SUBMERGED BEACH

One thing the sandy seafloors have in common with terrestrial deserts is that both are places where few, if any, plants grow. In terrestrial deserts, it's because of lack of water. In the water-covered desert of the sandy seafloor, the problem is lack of substrate. No algae can take hold in shifting sands with nothing to attach to. So, without local plant producers, sandy seafloor food webs are relatively simple. Most invertebrates here either filter plankton from the ambient waters or get their nourishment from organic debris in the muck. Some fishes and crabs, specially adapted to live here, feed on these invertebrates.

LIFE ON THE SANDY BOTTOM

LIFE ON SANDY BOTTOMS shows a pattern typical of harsh environments—low diversity but high concentrations of individual species. That is, there may not be very many kinds of animals here, compared to the tide zones or the kelp forest, but the few species that do well here may do very well indeed. Look beneath the surface: just under the sand a caravan of fascinating creatures live their lives.

The shifting sands just below the surf line are among the harshest of all marine environments. Tough-bodied crustaceans, ranging from tiny amphipods to the two inch (five centimeters) long mole, or "sand" crabs, are the major colonists of these abrasive sands. They are washed here with a plentiful supply of surface plankton, which they transport toward their mouths with strainer-like antennae, and must be ready to go with the flow when the sand shifts underneath them again.

Below the sand crab zone, the water calms a little. The sediments become home to hundreds upon hundreds of worms. Polychaetes, among others, tunnel through the muck, ingesting particles or filtering food from the water. A coffee can filled with bottom sand can contain handfuls of these worms.

Terebellid worms build tubes to protect themselves from the shifting sands. These extend delicate feeding tentacles out across the bottom to transport fine surface particles to their mouths. Some species build their tubes entirely of sand grains, cementing each one in place to build a capsule one grain thick, like a careful-ly fitted stone wall. These tiny masonry marvels have drawn the appreciation of researchers. Other terebellids have tough, leathery tubes, which may descend about

a foot and a half into the sandy substrate. Concentrations of these tubes hold and stabilize the sand, the way tree roots stabilize loose soil. In the shelter of a worm patch, other animals like sea pansies may take hold.

Burrowing anemones, like tube worms, make their own homes to shelter themselves from the grit. Their leathery, black tube homes are a distinctive sight in bays and estuaries, and their purplish or golden tentacles

Burrowing anemones are common along protected sandy bottoms of the outer coast.

may extend a foot (about thirty centimeters) or more. These peaceful tube-dwellers are the favorite food of the barber nudibranch, a handsome red or purple sea slug with bright orange cerrata on its back. At the touch of this nudibranch, the anemone whips into its burrow—but often not fast enough, as the sea slug may hold on and be drawn down with it. Once inside, the slug nips off some of the soft tentacles, leaving the anemone to look like a punk rocker having a bad hair day. The barber nudibranch almost never kills its prey—the tentacles it nips off will grow back, leaving the anemone to do its best to avoid another "haircut."

Male Dungeness crabs can reach widths of nine inches and females grow to six and a half inches.

Clams burrow into the shallow sands, poking siphons upward to filter sea water. Heart cockles and big bay scallops may also live on the upper sands. Wandering among them are predators, including olive snails and the giant sunflower star. If a predator disturbs a scallop, it's likely to "fly away," clapping its big flat shells together to flee rapidly out of harm's reach.

Crabs are important inhabitants of the sandy seafloor. With their tough shells, crabs are well suited to life in the abrasive sand—they carry their protection with them. Spiny king crabs prowl the shallows. Fist-size hermit crabs, the largest in our area, scour the bottom for dead animals and drift algae. The heavy-bodied "true crabs" of the genus *Cancer* are also prominent citizens here. Slender crabs, yellow crabs and the Dungeness crab, so popular with diners, spend much of their adult lives on the sandy bottom.

While slender crabs and yellow crabs are also found on reefs and rock outcrops, the Dungeness crab seems most at home on the sandy seafloor. Only at mating time are their hard shells a bit of a problem, for the females cannot accept sperm through their tough armor. Instead, they release a pheromone (male-attracting substance) when they are about to shed their shells. A male, attracted to this "perfume," straddles the female and protects her as she molts. The pair may move about for days together. When the female finally slips out of her old shell, the male mates with her and guards her a while longer until her new shell hardens. A few months later, the female releases her eggs, collecting them onto her abdomen for brooding. Interestingly, the female must bury herself partly in the sand in order for the egg mass to solidify. After some months of riding around on their mother's abdomen, the crab eggs hatch, and tiny free-swimming larvae escape into the water column. The larval crabs go through a series of changes, finally settling down to the sand as big-

eyed, "megalops," larvae. There, after a final transformation, they take up life as fully formed juvenile crabs, preying on bottom-living worms, clams and crustaceans such as sand shrimp. Adult Dungeness are not fussy eaters; besides whatever worms and molluscs the local seafloor offers, they will eat dead fish, drifting algae and just about anything edible that hits the bottom.

Sand dollars sit upright, half-buried in the sand, where seas are calm. In rougher waters they keep a lower profile, lying on the surface. These flattened relatives of sea urchins are purplish gray and covered with a fine fuzz of spines for movement and food capture when they're alive. As they die, their skeletons may bleach out, washing up on shore as the beautiful white silver-dollar-size shells known to beachcombers.

Sand dollars use their fuzzy spines to ferry food particles along their bodies to a central mouth. They clean the algae and detritus off of sand grains, but smaller ones may swallow the sand deliberately, reserving the grains in a special pouch in their intestines. This internal "sandbag" is ballast that keeps the little dollars from being washed about. Sand dollars also

(top): Sand dollars feed on plankton and other small particles found along the sand or in the water.
(bottom): Sea stars and sea urchins comb the sandy seafloor for food.

capture tiny animals riding on the plankton by means of the spines and pinching pedipalps on their body surfaces. A tiny, teepee-shaped cone of spines bunched up

167

Moonglow anemone
Anthopleura artemisia

on a sand dollar's body marks a spot where a captive amphipod or crab larva is being held for transport to its mouth.

Where a bit of rock under the sand offers a foothold, moonglow anemones take hold. These cousins of the tide pool anemone are creatures of the rock-sand interface, exploiting a habitat few other creatures can live in. Abundant in the sand channels at the bases of rocky reefs, these anemones also colonize the sand-filled, abandoned burrows of rock-boring clams. With their disc "foot" secure below, they stretch up through sand and open their flowerlike tentacle crowns to capture small fish and crustaceans. Moonglow anemones are among the most colorful anemones in the Monterey Bay area—their dark brown bodies may be capped with tentacles in any combination of red, white, orange, black or blue.

The fishes of the sandy seafloor are an odd lot, often strongly flattened for a life of "hiding in the open" and bottom-feeding. Flounders, soles and other "flatfishes" are in their element here. Tiny sanddab hug the nearshore waters; farther out live sand sole, petrale sole, diamond turbot and starry flounder. Many of these fishes are also quick-change artists, able to change color to match the sandy or pebbly bottom on which they rest. For added protection, flatfishes often burrow in the sand, leaving only their two bug eyes projecting above the surface. Flatfishes spend a lot of time in hiding, but when they hunt, they move surprisingly fast, undulating over the bottom in a sort of "flying carpet" motion on the prowl for slow-moving goodies like worms, brittle stars and the siphons of clams. Important sport and commercial fish for humans, flatfishes also form a big part of the diet of dolphins, sea lions and harbor seals.

Diamond turbot
Hypsopsetta guttulata

Several members of the shark family have also taken up life in the open. Thornbacks and stingrays endure the roiling surf zone, their flattened bodies enabling them to hug the bottom. Both are well protected from attack as well. Thornbacks have three sharp rows of spines along their backbones, discouraging predators from above, and stingrays have a venomous spine midway down their tails. Thornbacks have the additional adaptation of a one-way breathing channel, with inlet holes on the top of the head and outlets under the body, which helps keep grit out of their sensitive gills. These surf-zone bottom-dwellers feed on worms, clams and small crabs. Their mottled backs offer good camouflage against the shifting sands.

Thornback ray
Platyrhinoidis triseriata

Flatfishes:
That Roving Eye

California halibut
Paralichthys californicus

Flatfishes—members of the Heterosomata order—take life lying down. These fishes, including the flounders, halibut, soles, turbot, and sanddabs—spend their adult lives lying on one side, both eyes pointing upward. Their sideways faces make them look a little odd, to be sure. But these beauties start life as normal-looking tiny fishes. As larvae, they are symmetrical, with an eye on each side of the head. But as the time comes for the little fish to settle down, an amazing metamorphosis takes place. One eye migrates, moving either around the head or straight through, depending on the species. The roving eye takes its place next to the other eye, giving the fish back its binocular vision. Other changes in bone and fin structure turn the symmetrical larva into a juvenile flatfish, ready to take up life on its side. Some species mature with their right side up, like Dover sole and starry flounder. Others, like sanddabs and tonguefish, end up with the left side up. And some, like California halibut, seem able to go either way—about half in our waters are left sided, the rest live right.

How did they come to lie on one side in the first place? Some researchers think flatfishes evolved from a wrasse-like ancestor, which spent a lot of time down on one side when resting. Keeping a low profile is a good strategy for protection where there are no rocks to hide in, and looking like part of the bottom can encourage prey to get close enough for an ambush.

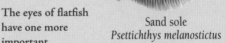

Sand sole
Psettichthys melanostictus

The eyes of flatfish have one more important feature—they are exquisitely sensitive to pattern. It is the sight of its substrate that lets the fish match its skin coloration so perfectly with whatever sandy or pebbly bottom it sits on. From plain sand to mottled gravel to checker patterns in the laboratory, if a flatfish can see it, it can imitate it—but if researchers cover its eyes, the fish's pattern no longer changes. How exactly the message gets from the eyes to the pigment cells in the skin remains a mystery to fish physiologists.

A flatfish lies partially buried in the sand using camouflage to hide it from predators and prey in the sandy seafloor.

169

Also in the shallows are the angel shark and shovelnose guitarfish. Not quite as flattened as the rays and skates, these sharks swim by moving their tails from side to side, rather than by flapping skatelike wings. Ambush predators, both of these species bury themselves in the sand until only their eyes stick out, watchfully waiting for an unwary flatfish or crab to wander by. Suddenly the sand erupts, and the shark gulps down its meal.

Bat rays "fly" slowly over sandy bottoms with their pointed wings, searching for clams, crabs and tiny bottom-dwelling fishes. They are especially fond of the fat innkeeper worm, a soft-bodied, wiener-shaped burrower abundant in the muddy shallows. These rays, like other bottom-dwelling flat sharks, have crushing teeth to grind their hard-shelled prey rather than the sharp dagger teeth of open-water sharks. Bat rays beat their wings against the seafloor to expose their prey, then slurp it up. Deeper down, the big skate roams; with a six feet (1.8 meters) wing span and huge "eyespots" on each wing, these skates are a formidable sight. They feed on crabs and fishes; their foot-long egg cases, laid on the sandy bottom, may hatch out as many as seven perfectly formed palm-size babies.

Big skate
Raja binoculata

In the open waters above the sandy seafloor, fast fishes roam, often in schools for safety. The brilliant silver sides of thousands of sardines and anchovies flash in all directions, working to confuse the aim of predators. These fishes, and the juveniles of many larger species, train the water for zooplankton. Pacific mackerel, jackmackerel, young white seabass and bonito also teem through these waters, feeding on the smaller fishes.

Big skate eggs

Jackmackerel
Trachurus symmetricus

In their turn, these species attract their
own predators—salmon, jack, yellowtail
and sleek mako that cruise through the sandy
zone. Spiny dogfish, the most common shark in
our area, chase schooling fish here, too. Though
only 4 feet (122 centimeters) long, these little
sharks move in packs and hunt down fishes
when not on the prowl for other seafloor
dwellers like shrimp and crabs. The thresher
shark, the mako's cousin and another visitor, thrashes
its sickle tail in schools of small fish to wound and stun
them before feeding. Threshers may give birth in these waters—
very small pups have been caught off Capitola, in the southern portion of the
Monterey Bay National Marine Sanctuary.

Spiny dogfish
Squalus acanthias

Thresher shark
Alopias vulpinus

Many rockfishes feed on schooling fishes above the sand during the day, returning to the shelter of rocky reefs and kelp forests for the night. Even some of the
bottom-dwelling fishes get in on the chase. Young California halibut eat bottom-
dwelling crustaceans, but as they grow they take a more active approach to feeding.
These halibut are surprisingly speedy fish that have been
known to leap out of the water in pursuit of
anchovies. At up to five feet (one and a half
meters) long and seventy pounds (31.5
kilograms), these large flatfish are not
the first that come to mind when one
thinks of a speedy predator, but their
strength and persistence makes them formidable. Besides anchovies, mature halibut chase down
squid and croakers and even beach themselves in
pursuit of mating grunion.

California halibut
Paralichthys californicus

In late spring, the waters above the sandy seafloor play host to another kind of
school: shoals of mating market squid. Normally shy and speedy, these eight inch
(about twenty centimeters) molluscs come together in huge clouds when they
spawn. Underwater visibility may drop near zero as millions of the smooth, pearles-
cent creatures dart hither and thither in the water column. Males flash red as they
embrace their mates; after mating, their energy spent, the males sink to the bottom
and die. Females live only a little longer—just long enough to carefully select a spot
on the sandy bottom where they can attach their sausage-shaped egg cases. Any
stick or small rock in the sand will do; after one female has laid her eggs, others
come to attach their eggs nearby. Market squid seem to prefer clean sand of
moderate grain size in an area close to the deep water of an underwater canyon.

A male squid grasps the female with his eight arms in a mating embrace.

After mating, the female squid attaches her eggs to the sandy seafloor.

Monterey Bay is thus prime squid-nesting territory. By the end of the squid run, the fingerlike egg cases may cover every square inch of available bottom. Late-laying squid are forced to attach their eggs to egg cases already in place. The sandy bottom comes to look like a field of swaying pompoms, covered over with the cream-colored masses of squid eggs.

Preoccupied with mating, the squid ignore the hordes of hungry predators that gather around them. Rockfishes, blue sharks, gulls and sea lions all feast on the bounty of the mating squid. Sinking to the bottom, the bodies of the spawned-out adults sate bottom-dwelling scavengers like Dungeness crab, bat stars and sea urchins. The deaths of the parents may protect the young: with so many dead and dying squid around, predators have little need to eat the egg cases.

Hatching in two weeks to 90 days, depending on sea temperatures, the tiny squid of the new generation take their place in the ocean food web. Small juveniles are important food for sanddabs; as the squid mature over the course of their two-year life span, they will feed dolphins, pelicans and northern fur seals. With so many predators, it's a good thing squid are prolific: each female produces between 4,000 and 9,000 young in her single bout of mating.

172

THE MUDDY BOTTOM

AS THE SANDY "BARRENS" GRADE INTO SOFTER MUDS, bottom life becomes abundant once again. This is a colder, darker region of the seafloor, little disturbed by waves. Fine sediments carpet the ground, and many animals are nourished by plankton settling to the bottom.

The bottoms in these deeper areas may be carpeted with brittle stars. These five-armed relatives of sea stars hide just below the mud during the day, waving at most one of their long, bristly arms above the surface. The waving arm may draw a prowling sole or rockfish, but if it is bitten off, the star can simply grow it back. At night, when their predators are sleeping, brittle stars lift their central bodies out of the sand and put all five slender arms to work trapping plankton.

Brittle stars are not the only seafloor denizens that show themselves at night. Once darkness falls and the predatory fishes retire, the bottom comes alive with worms never seen during the day. Spotted cusk-eels, fish that hide tail-first in sandy

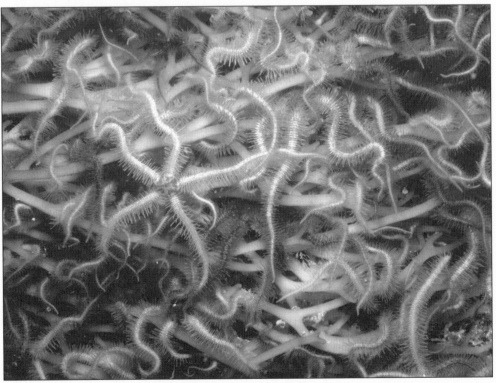

*Here an aggregation of brittle stars have hidden all
but their waving arms in the sand.*

173

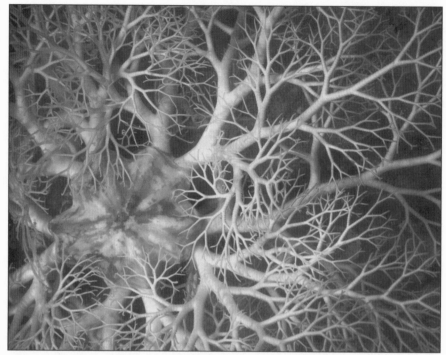

Basket stars use their sticky, trendril-like arms to catch tiny plankton in the water.

burrows during the day, come out at night to forage. Sailfin sculpin and small octopuses leave their daytime hideouts in clam burrows. Basket stars, completely hidden during the day, raise up their lacy arms to filter-feed.

Sand stars glide above the deeper bottoms, their tube feet specialized for navigating the soft sediments, and short-spined stars search out worms and molluscs.

Starfish relatives, the sea cucumbers, crawl slowly on the bottom, digesting organic debris. When disturbed, these placid sausage-shaped muck-eaters may discharge their internal organs through their anus. The cucumber can regrow them, so no permanent harm is done.

Red octopus
Octopus rubescens

Sea pens, related to the corals, stretch up out of the sand like goose-quill writing pens. Anchored in the sand by a bulbous "foot," these animals use their feathery side tissues to breathe and capture tiny prey with stinging polyps. Each

174

Sea pen
Ptilosarcus gurneyi

sea pen is not one animal, but a colony of specialized individuals working together to survive. Some are specialized to build the anchor, others to capture and digest food, still others for reproduction. The graceful sea pens are preyed upon by nudibranchs; when disturbed, they may emit flashes of light before contracting into a protective lump.

Flatfishes range all up and down the sandy seafloor, but larger adults become more numerous here in the deeper water. English sole rove over the bottom, digging out brittle stars, tube worms and amphipods. Pacific halibut, which grow even bigger than California halibut, search out crabs and octopuses. A big adult Pacific halibut can be 8 feet (about 2.4 meters) long. Dover sole, a fish popular with diners, inhabit some of the deepest reaches of the sandy bottoms and hunt for worms and brittle stars. Like many true deep-ocean fishes, older Dovers develop watery, gelatinous flesh, the reason for their former name, "slime soles." Because of their tiny mouths, Dover sole are almost never caught on hook and line; instead, fisherman take thousands of pounds of them each year by trawling. Their jellied flesh firms up if they are frozen.

English sole
Parophrys vetulus

Pacific sanddab
Citharichthys sordidus

Ratfish
Hydrolagus colliei

Wandering up from the deep seabeds of the canyons, ratfish also make their way along the bottom here. These cartilaginous fish, relatives of sharks, are among the deepest-living fishes in our area. As the sandy seafloor grades into the dark depths of the benthic canyon environment, ratfish are one more of the surprising creatures making a home in the underwater desert.

Selected Sandy Seafloor Species

INVERTEBRATES

Basket star, *Gorgonocephalus eucnemis*
Bat star, *Asterina miniata*
Brittle star, *Ophiothrix spiculata*
Burrowing anemone, *Pachycerianthus fimbriatus*
Dungeness crab, *Cancer magister*
Fat innkeeper worm, *Urechis caupo*
Giant sunflower star, *Pycnopodia helianthoides*
Gumboot chiton, *Cryptochiton stelleri*
Heart cockle, *Clinocardium nuttallii*
Hermit crab, *Pagurus samuelis*
Moonglow anemone, *Anthopleura artemisia*
Moon snail, *Polinices lewisii*
Pismo clam, *Tivela stultorum*
Purple sea urchin, *Strongylocentrotus purpuratus*
Rainbow nudibranch, *Dendronotus iris*
Red octopus, *Octopus rubescens*
Red sea urchin, *Strongylocentrotus franciscanus*
Sand crab, *Emerita analoga*
Sand dollar, *Dendraster excentricus*
Sand star, *Astropecten armatus*
Sea cucumber, *Parastichopus californicus*
Sea pansy, *Renilla kollikeri*
Sea pen, *Ptilosarcus gurneyi*
Slender crab, *Cancer gracilis*
Spiny king crab, *Paralithodes californiensis*
Tube worm, *Diopatra ornata*
Yellow crab, *Cancer anthonyi*

FISHES

Angel shark, *Squatina californica*
Bat ray, *Myliobatis californica*
Big skate, *Raja binoculata*
California halibut, *Paralichthys californicus*
Diamond turbot, *Platyrhinoidis triseriata*
Dover sole, *Microstomus pacificus*
English sole, *Parophrys vetulus*
King salmon, *Oncorhynchus tshawytscha*
Market squid, *Loligo opalescens*
Pacific electric ray, *Torpedo californica*
Pacific halibut, *Hippoglossus stenolepis*
Pacific sanddab, *Citharichthys sordidus*
Petrale sole, *Eopsetta jordani*
Ratfish, *Hydrolagus colliei*
Sailfin sculpin, *Nautichthys oculofasciatus*

Sanddab, *Citharichthys stigmaeus*
Sand sole, *Psettichthys melanostictus*
Shovelnose guitarfish, *Rhinobatos productus*
Spotted cusk-eel, *Chilara taylori*
Spring dogfish, *Squalus acanthias*
Starry flounder, *Platichthys stellatus*
Thresher shark, *Alopias vulpinus*
Tonguefish, *Symphurus atricauda*

Under the surface waters of the outer bay, you might see translucent jellies drifting with the currents.

CHAPTER TEN

OPEN WATERS

"...the presence of a plankter in a particular parcel of water may be no more random than is the presence of a centipede under a log, or a plant growing in a pocket of soil between rocks."

Cassie, 1959

SOMETIME IN SEPTEMBER along the central California coast, the northwesterly winds, which blow more or less steadily from March through August, slacken. The two months or so of relative calm that follow mark a short-lived season here called the oceanic period.

While the winds blow, they force cold ocean water to the surface. It's this meeting of cold surface water and warm, moist air that creates the fog, which blankets much of the coast in summer. As the winds relax, this upwelling of cold water stops and the fog disappears, leaving warm days and blue skies.

The coastal waters, murky green in summer, turn bluer and warmer now, too, as water from the California Current pushes in close to shore. This layer of surface

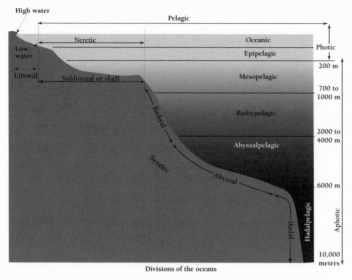

High water
Low water
Littoral
Pelagic
Neretic
Sublittoral or shelf
Oceanic
Epipelagic
Mesopelagic
Bathypelagic
Abyssalpelagic
Hadalpelagic
Bathyal
Benthic
Abyssal
Hadal
Photic
200 m
700 to 1000 m
2000 to 4000 m
6000 m
Aphotic
10,000 meters

Divisions of the oceans

The different zones of the ocean support different communities of plants and animals.

water from the sanctuary's outer edges brings other visitors: graceful swimming snails, delicate eggyolk jellies, tadpole-shaped creatures in filmy, intricate houses. Beautiful yet unfamiliar, they come as representatives of the ocean's open waters—the pelagic realm.

Pelagic waters circle the planet. Almost unimaginably vast, they hold more than 97% of our planet's living space. Stretching from surface to seafloor (3.8 kilometers deep, on average), they seem boundless, featureless. Creatures here live in a fluid, changing, three-dimensional world that's hard for us, used to solid ground under our feet, to study or fully appreciate. But using modern technology, from scuba to satellites to deep sea submersibles, we're building a picture of pelagic life.

We now recognize many kinds of boundaries that partition these featureless waters, creating a structure and variety, which shapes open water communities. Sharp gradients in temperature, salinity or dissolved nutrients mark the edges of large and small water masses. Some last only until stirred by the next wave. Others, like the immense currents that flow like rivers across oceans, persist for millions of years.

The edges of continental shelves set one important boundary. Scientists call the pelagic water mass over a continental shelf the neritic zone. Open waters beyond the shelf belong to the oceanic zone. Only a few hundred meters deep, neritic waters are influenced by interactions with the seafloor and support different communities of plants and animals from those found in oceanic waters.

The depth to which sunlight penetrates with enough intensity for pelagic plants to grow marks another major boundary. This boundary shifts depending on the clarity of the water, the average amount of cloud or fog cover and the angle that sunlight strikes the surface. In the sanctuary, it generally lies about 100 meters deep. Above it lie the waters of the photic zone—the region where plants can grow. (Scientists call this sunlit region the epipelagic zone.) Below it, the dark waters of the deep sea stretch down to the seafloor. In this chapter we'll look at the epipelagic habitat, the sunlit neritic and oceanic waters of the sanctuary.

LIFE IN A LIQUID WORLD

THE PHYSICAL DEMANDS OF EACH HABITAT mold the bodies and lives of those who live there. We're built for life on land, and this colors our sense of place, our view of the world. We and other land dwellers need protection from the hard knocks of a hard-edged world, from drying winds, damaging ultraviolet solar radiation and dramatic changes in temperature. To resist the pull of gravity, animals need internal or external skeletons, and they rely on legs, limbs or wings to haul themselves from place to place. Plants develop woody frames to hold themselves up to the light, clutching the earth with roots designed to keep themselves in place and to gather nutrients and water.

Creatures of the open waters live in a very different world. They are largely free from the constraints imposed by hard surfaces and the threat of drying. Instead, they face problems of buoyancy, of avoiding predators in a wide open environment, and others, which we don't yet fully appreciate.

We organize our thoughts about pelagic life by lumping the creatures living there into two broad groups: drifters (plankton) and swimmers (nekton). While their lifestyles are dramatically different, both are superbly adapted to their fluid, edgeless world.

Borne on currents, plankton generally drift or weakly swim–though not aimlessly or helplessly, as we once thought. Ranging from microscopic plants to gelatinous animal predators three meters in diameter, they play the central roles in the ecology of the oceans. Single-celled planktonic plants (phytoplankton) and myriad grazing and predatory animals (zooplankton) form the complex, changing communities of the open waters.

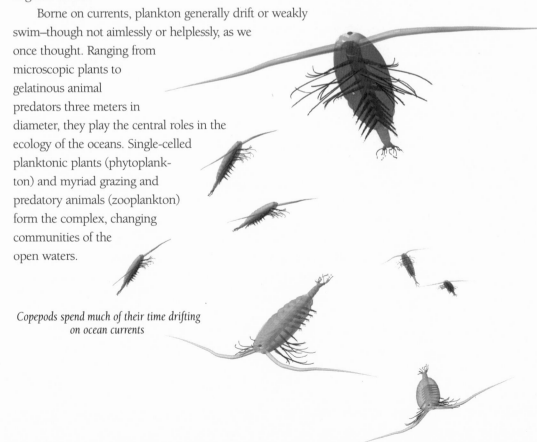

Copepods spend much of their time drifting on ocean currents

FLOATING PASTURES: PLANTS OF THE OPEN WATERS

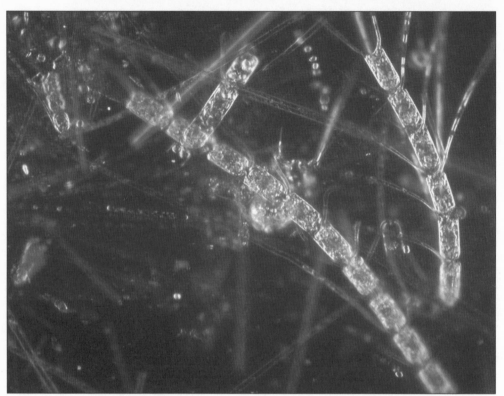

Phytoplankton play a key role in the ocean's food web, providing food to virtually all life in the sea.

LIKE OTHER PLANTS, phytoplankton use energy from sunlight to create organic compounds from carbon dioxide and other inorganic chemicals. Since plants produce the food on which virtually all animals depend, we refer to plants, including phytoplankton, as primary producers. Tiny, but present in unimaginable numbers, phytoplankton support virtually all life in the oceans.

The most abundant phytoplankton are also the least known. Cyanobacteria, along with protochlorophytes, haptophytes and other microalgae, are so small they slip through the finest plankton nets—the traditional way of collecting plankton for study. Only recently, with the development of ultra-fine filters and other specialized research tools have we begun to learn more about them.

A liter of ocean water may contain several million cyanobacteria and microalgae. They are the most important producers in tropical waters and in the open ocean away from the coastlines, as in the open waters at the outer edge of the sanctuary.

Productivity per unit of area in these low-nutrient areas is low compared to that along the coasts. But because of the vast size of the habitat where these minute phytoplankton rule, they contribute enormously to the ocean's total productivity.

We know more about the larger diatoms and dinoflagellates since we've long been able to collect them in fine-meshed nets (thus, they're often called netplankton) and study them using standard microscopes.

"Large" is a relative term in the world of phytoplankton. Cyanobacteria of the genus *Synechococcus* are truly small, some 200,000 of their spherical cells could fit on the period at the end of this sentence. But even at the largest end of the size range for most phytoplankton, 12 could crowd onto that same period. A few grow larger. Many kinds of diatoms form chains, sometimes up to one or two millimeters long. Chain-forming *Chaetoceros* species play

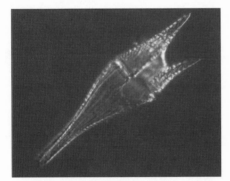

Diatoms

a central role in the ecology of the sanctuary.

Small size is one key to the success of phytoplankton. These plants need sunlight to grow, so it's vital that they have the ability to stay in the upper layers of the ocean. And other factors being equal, smaller objects have a larger surface area in relation to their volume than larger ones, and so sink more slowly. Small size has other benefits, too. It allows phytoplankton to grow, mature

Ceratium have long spines that may help keep it from sinking to the seafloor.

and multiply quickly to take advantage of favorable conditions when they occur and to keep ahead of the population explosions of hungry herbivorous zooplankton that often follow close behind a phytoplankton bloom.

Phytoplankton have developed a host of other tricks to control their buoyancy. Larger forms often have irregular shapes, which help increase their resistance to sinking. In sanctuary waters, several species of the dinoflagellate *Ceratium* have long spines that may help them stay suspended.

(The projections worn by *Ceratium* and many other phytoplankton may also, or instead, increase their effective size as a protection against grazers. There's still much to learn about plankton and there are often several interpretations of the information we have. To present an overview of the nature of open waters, we need to make generalizations. But generalizations are often only half-truths. Plankton communities are complex, diverse and ever-changing. And while we've learned a great deal about them, there's still much we don't fully understand. Everywhere you turn in the study of the pelagic world exceptions and uncertainty lurk.)

Some diatoms, such as *Thalassiosira*, common in the sanctuary, bristle with long fibers that buoy them in water like the do' that buoys thistle seeds in air. Others, like *Ditylum bright-wellii*, adjust their buoyancy by changing the chemical composition of their body sap.

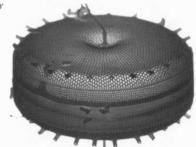

If sunlight were their only need, perhaps all phytoplankton would have evolved ways to simply float at the surface. But other problems present themselves. Like all plants, phytoplankton need nitrate, phosphorous and other nutrients to grow. Terrestrial plants draw in nutrients from the soil through their roots. Phytoplankton absorb theirs directly from the surrounding water. Being small helps here, as well, by providing more surface area per cell volume for absorption.

The abundance of diatoms in Monterey Bay is one reason for the rich marine life along our coast.

But nutrients usually aren't concentrated at the surface, and even when they are they're soon used up by phytoplankton. The location and depth of nutrient-rich zones shift continually. A perfectly suspended phytoplankton cell would find itself trapped in the small volume of water around it. With no way to escape its immediate surroundings, it would quickly run out of food as it used up all the nutrients dissolved there. It would also find itself surrounded by its own wastes. The solution is to be able to swim, sink or float to a new patch of water.

Dinoflagellates and some groups of microalgae have whiplike flagella to propel themselves through the water. They often swim towards the sunlit surface by day, then move deeper (where there may be more nutrients) at night. The fastest dinoflagellates can cover about half a millimeter per second, or two meters an hour. (That may not seem like much, but it's equal to about eleven body lengths per second for these minute plants. For comparison, the fastest human swimmers reach speeds of only about two body lengths per second.) Diatoms, on the other hand, can't swim and tend to sink.

Dinoflagellates have whiplike flagella that helps propel them through the water.

Water in the mixed layer near the surface rarely lies still, the motion of the water stirs and distributes phytoplankton, the amount and direction of movement greatly affecting how fast and how far they sink or float. They ride currents created by winds and the alternate daily solar heating and nightly cooling.

Each group of phytoplankton has faced the dual problem of staying in the sunlit zone while maintaining access to nutrients. Their evolutionary decisions about whether to sink or swim as a solution have defined their roles in various ocean habitats and have had a profound influence on the structure of pelagic communities. For example, the relationship between water turbulence and the plankton' sinking speed also helps drive the seasonal succession of phytoplankton in the sanctuary. Large chain-forming diatoms dominate much of the sanctuary's open waters during the spring and summer, when winds create turbulence that helps keep diatoms in suspension and upwelling water brings nutrients to the surface.

In winter, when there's less mixing, phytoplankton growth decreases, and dinoflagellates, cyanobacteria and microalgae play a larger role relative to diatoms. Smaller than diatoms, these forms can use low levels of nutrients more efficiently than the larger diatoms. These groups also account for most of the plant productivity in oceanic waters, where nutrients are generally scarce and where diatoms tend to sink into the depths.

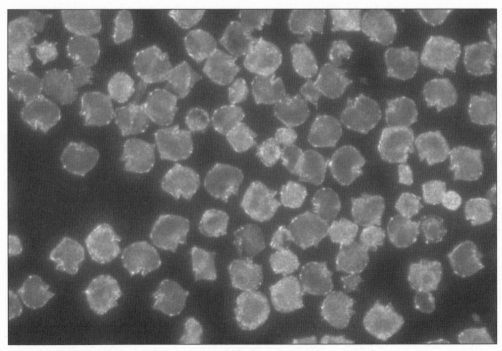

A group of dinoflagellates provides a rich source of food to a variety of animals in the open ocean.

THE ANIMAL MULTITUDES: HIGH SEAS DRIFTERS

THE OCEAN'S OPEN WATERS support an amazing variety of zooplankton—the drifting animals of the pelagic world. Nearly every phylum of animals has representatives that along with myriad protozoans, spend at least a part of their lives adrift in the ocean. Zooplankton live at all depths, though each species has its preferred depth range. Most are herbivores, which graze on phytoplankton in the upper waters. Predatory zooplankton prey on these grazers or on other predators. Some are omnivores and eat phytoplankton or other zooplankton depending on what's available. As with phytoplankton, our knowledge of zooplankton has been shaped by our methods of study. We've learned the most about those large enough and sturdy enough to be caught intact in plankton nets. Copepods and shrimplike euphausiids, both arthropods, make up the bulk of this netplankton. Now, using new tools, we've begun to expand our vision to include the very small protozoans and other micro-zooplankton along with the diverse groups of delicate gelatinous animals. Seven major groups form the nucleus of the sanctuary's zooplankton communities: protozoans, cnidarians, ctenophores, chaetognaths, molluscs, arthropods and chordates. Some zooplankton (holoplankton) live their whole lives as plankton. Others

Crab larvae feed on small, single-celled plants.

(meroplankton) merely spend part of their lives there as larvae before assuming benthic or nektonic lifestyles when they mature.

Throughout the year, the offshore waters host a succession of meroplankton—the eggs and larvae of crabs, barnacles, worms, sea stars, snails, fishes, sponges and others. By trusting their offspring to the currents they run the risk that their progeny will be swept away forever, but their eggs are small, and they can afford to produce millions of them so that a few survive. The risks are great, but the rewards are greater. A planktonic larval stage gives animals who, as adults, live on the seafloor or in the intertidal zone as adults a way to disperse and colonize new territory. And patches of phytoplankton and swarms of other zooplankton provide a rich source of food for larvae.

Animals with planktonic larvae can increase their reproductive success by timing their spawning to correspond with favorable currents or periods of abundant food. In the sanctuary, strong plumes of upwelling water push far offshore in summer and can sweep larvae away. For that reason, the main spawning area for the major species of pelagic fishes along our coast—including Pacific sardine, northern anchovy and Pacific hake—lies south of Point Conception where upwelling is less intense. Less-mobile species have other ways to avoid being carried offshore into unsuitable habitat. Rockfishes, the major group of predatory, bottom-dwelling fishes in our area, give birth to live young thereby reducing the amount of time their young spend in the plankton. They and others, such as brown Irish lords and greenlings, spawn in winter so their larvae enter planktonic life before intense spring upwelling begins. The onset of upwelling may also cause brown Irish lord and greenling larvae to quickly settle out of the plankton and take up the bottom-dwelling lifestyle of adults.

Like phytoplankton, zooplankton face problems of buoyancy and of surviving long enough to reproduce in an open world with no hiding places. They also need ways to find and capture food. Small size again offers many solutions. As mentioned, smaller objects tend to sink more slowly than larger ones of the same density because they have a larger surface area. There's also a relationship between the size of an animal and the size of the food it eats. Phytoplankton are small, so many of the animals who graze on them are small.

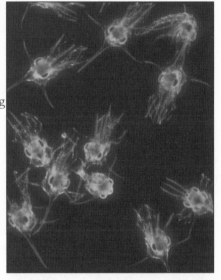

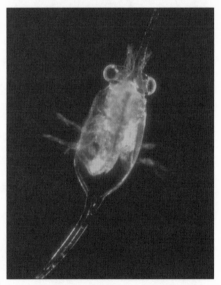

Crabs produce planktonic larvae (top & bottom) that develop adrift at sea.

Zooplankton have other ways to stay suspended in water. Like phytoplankton, many sport spurs or spines that help slow their downward movement and protect them from predators. Most can also swim at least well enough to keep from sinking. Copepods often have oil droplets under their shells that make them more buoyant and serve as energy reserves when food is scarce. Some siphonophores rely on gas-filled floats.

THE ADVANTAGES OF RUBBERY BODIES

PERHAPS THE MOST SIGNIFICANT ADAPTATION OF ZOOPLANKTON to pelagic life is the development of a gelatinous body. Other than the arthropods and a few other groups, most zooplankton have bodies with the consistency of rubbery gelatin. While these gelatinous creatures represent four major phyla and differ widely in what and how they eat, they share a basic architecture that ensures their success in the oceans. Their bodies are 95% water, which makes them nearly neutrally buoyant. Even their muscles are watery and weak compared to those of active swimmers like fishes. Since they don't rely on powerful muscles to propel them through the water, they don't need sturdy, heavy skeletons to anchor their muscles. These gelatinous animals truly belong to the oceans' open waters: their soft tissues would quickly be shredded in the rough-and-tumble intertidal zone; on land, they would collapse under the pull of gravity.

Watery bodies are also cheap to operate: there's not much to them, so it takes little energy to grow them and to keep them running. When food is abundant, gelatinous animals can grow and multiply quickly. When food is scarce, as it often is in open waters, many cope by simply "growing" smaller. Their

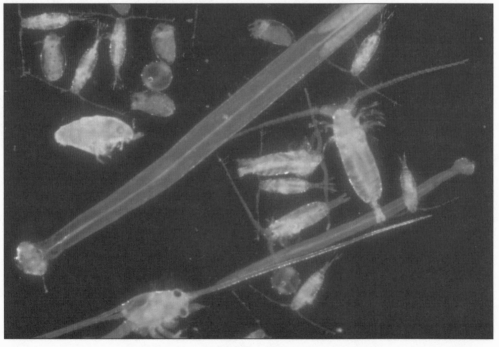

Zooplankton have adapted well to their watery environment.

tissues are also nearly clear, making them hard for predators to see.

Buoyancy and low food requirements also free them from the size restraints of arthropods. While copepods generally measure less than one centimeter long and euphausiids less than 10 centimeters, many gelatinous zooplankton grow much larger, with bodies sometimes several meters across and tentacles stretching three or four meters long. In the sanctuary's deeper waters, the siphonophore *Praya* sp. grows to 40 meters long.

Different groups have developed widely different ways of capturing food. Cnidarians, the "jellies," have tentacles armed with venomous stinging cells to subdue prey. Larvaceans, such as *Oikopleura*, and some pelagic snails, such as *Limacina helicina*, take advantage of the relative economy of producing mucus to spin elaborate webs to filter food from the water. Other pelagic snails are active hunters. The sea angel, *Clione limacina*, hunts and chases down its prey—*Limacina helicina*.

Purple-striped jelly
Pelagia colorata

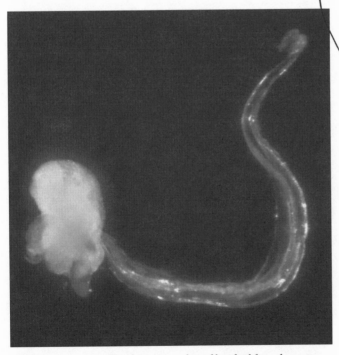

Larvaceans are capable of spinning webs to filter food from the water.

THE CONTROLLED WANDERING OF CAPABLE DRIFTERS

AS WE SPEND MORE TIME IN THE OCEAN OBSERVING the behavior of larger zooplankton, our views of them have changed. We now know, for example, that pelagic snails, pelagic worms, comb jellies like *Beroë ovata*, euphausiids and other zooplankton are active swimmers that blur the lines between "drifters" and "swimmers," between plankton and nekton.

We're also learning that plankton aren't at the mercy of the currents but have ways to use currents to their advantage. They can control their movements, stopping when they wish and often gathering in dense aggregations. Some copepods can sense the shift in the color of light shining through a patch of phytoplankton above them. They rise in response. When the color of the light shifts again, indicating they've reached the proper level, they begin swimming horizontally in pursuit of the drifting plants. Even such "simple" animals as jellies and comb jellies have complex behaviors and sophisticated mechanisms to find prey and avoid predators. Some zooplankton have the ability to make directional migrations and to follow "scent trails"–chemical traces left by the passage of phytoplankton or other zooplankton.

Every twenty-four hours in the sanctuary, uncountable millions of zooplankton, large and small, rise towards the surface then, hours later, sink back into the depths. Zooplankton of all groups (though not every species), make these daily vertical migrations. Between them, they form the largest mass movements of animals on earth. Their movements are timed to light. Most rise at dusk and return to the depths at dawn, keeping themselves in a consistently evenly dark world. Some follow a reverse pattern, rising by day and sinking at night. Copepods and other smaller species may travel several hundred meters a day; stronger-swimming zooplankton, such as euphausiids, 800 meters or more. It takes an effort for these small creatures to travel

Comb jellies have toothlike structures in their mouth that allow them to eat larger gelatinous animals.

such long distances, so there must be pay-offs that make their migrations worthwhile.

Since more food nearer the surface where phytoplankton grows, why would zooplankton go to the trouble to move back and forth? There are several theories. One holds that zooplankton retreat into deeper water by day to avoid predators like fishes, squids and birds which hunt by sight. The plankton move up to feed under the cover of darkness when these visual predators can't see to hunt.

Vertical migration may also be a way for zooplankton to reach other water masses. Currents vary in speed and direction at different depths. By sinking to another level, zooplankton could ride the

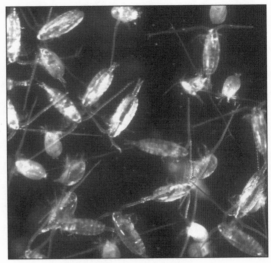

Copepods are found in abundance in open waters along the West Coast

currents there, then rise into a different volume of surface water. A swarm of zooplankton can quickly graze out a patch of phytoplankton so vertical migration can give them access to new patches of food. Some phytoplankton wield chemical defenses, releasing substances that are toxic to zooplankton or that inhibit their feeding. Vertical migration may be a way for zooplankton to avoid prolonged exposure to these toxins.

It's becoming clear that several different forces drive vertical migration. There's a whole range of variations on the "normal" pattern, even among a single species. Zooplankton adjust their behavior to fit the circumstances. The copepods *Calanus pacificus* and *Metridia lucens* live in abundance in open waters along the west coast. They're preyed on by planktonic predators—mainly arrow worms, predatory copepods and perhaps euphausiids—who migrate towards the surface and feed mostly at night. These predators don't hunt by sight, but instead sense movements or scents in the water around them. To avoid them, *Metridia* and *Calanus* would have to follow a reverse migration schedule, moving towards the surface by day. But this would expose them to danger from visually feeding predatory fishes. Studies in a bay in Washington have shown that these and another copepod change their patterns of migration depending on whether invertebrate predators or fishes are most abundant.

Why don't the invertebrate predators change their migrations to match those of the copepods? Since they're larger and more conspicuous, they're easier prey for fishes, so there's greater incentive for them to stay in the depths by day.

191

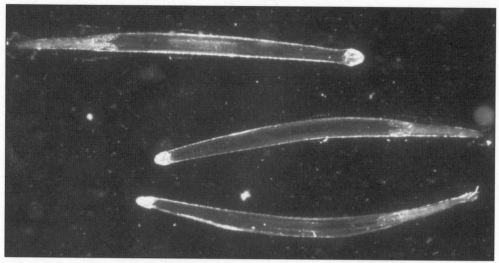

Arrowworms are fearsome predators of copepods and other animal plankton.

OCEAN SWIMMERS—
BUILT TO TRAVEL

IN CONTRAST TO THE GREAT DIVERSITY OF ZOOPLANKTON, there are very few kinds of nekton—powerfully swimming pelagic animals–in the sanctuary's open waters. Most are fishes, primarily sardines, anchovies, herrings, mackerels, salmon, hake, tuna, ocean sunfish and some sharks. And like the fishes, most of the other nekton, including marine mammals, seabirds and sea turtles, are vertebrates, the class of animals to which we also belong. Among the invertebrates, squid along with some euphausiids and pelagic crabs, are considered nekton.

We know generally more about nekton than plankton mainly because they're larger and (in some ways) easier to study and because we harvest many of them for food or other uses. Still, the vast size of the pelagic habitat and the difficulties we face in studying it leave many of our questions about the lives of these animals unanswered. Market squid (*Loligo opalescens*), for example, support a profitable fishery in the sanctuary and squid play a central role in the ecology of pelagic waters here. Yet, other than the fact that they come in close to shore to spawn in places in the sanctuary, we know little about their lives during the rest of their year.

Swimmers face the same challenges for life in a fluid, open habitat as drifters, but meet those challenges in very different ways. As with plankton, buoyancy is a central concern for nekton. But nekton also need to be streamlined to move

Green sea turtles are well suited for life at sea, with streamlined shells and paddlelike flippers.

efficiently through the water, so they can't rely on the spines and projections that help support many types of plankton. And in order to swim, they need powerful muscles and a strong skeletal framework for the muscles to pull against, not a watery gelatinous body, which is more suitable for less energetic lifestyles.

Many fishes, including northern anchovies and Pacific sardines, two of the most common epipelagic fishes in the sanctuary, can change their buoyancy by adjusting the amount of gas in their swim bladder. For speedier predators like Pacific mackerel and Pacific bonito, who often make rapid changes in depth, swim bladders take too long to adjust. The bodies of fishes contain deposits of fat (which, like the oil droplets in copepods, are less dense than sea water) that help make them more buoyant than they would otherwise be. Blue whales, harbor seals and most other marine mammals have a two-fold system for staying buoyant: a layer of blubber just under their skin along with air in their lungs and in special air sacs. (The blubber also helps insulate them against cold ocean water.)

Pacific mackerel
Scomber laponicus

Nekton also need protection from predators, mainly other kinds of nekton. Predation here is

Schools of mackerel travel along our coast, covering hundreds of miles a year.

fierce, and nearly any animal, from the smallest anchovy to a blue whale may fall victim. There are no hiding places in this transparent world, so most fishes and many marine mammals rely on camouflage coloration to disguise their presence–both from their predators and their prey. Fishes, like albacore tuna, are often countershaded. Their dark backs blend with the ocean depths when viewed from above. From below, their lighter bellies merge into the brightness at the surface. Rather than having rounded bellies which cast a dark shadow, many pelagic fishes, like Pacific herring, have flat sides that taper down to meet in a V-shaped keel. Most wear shades of silvery blue or green to match the color of ocean water.

Schooling offers another defense against predators. A school offers many pairs of eyes alert for danger, so a predator can't easily make a surprise attack. When a lone predator does attack, the school responds with complex evasive maneuvers. Sardines, anchovies and many other schooling fishes have reflective, silvery scales. As the school turns and whirls to escape, their scales flash like thousands of tiny mirrors, making it hard for a predator to single out any one fish. Schooling works for both predator and prey. Schooling predators can launch coordinated attacks designed to confuse their prey and separate individuals from the school.

Above all else, nekton are built to swim. Most have streamlined shapes designed for continuous, efficient movement through water. Speed becomes another strategy in the evolutionary game of survival between predators and prey. Predators need speed to chase down prey. This need has driven the evolution of predators like albacore tuna and Pacific bonito towards teardrop-shaped bodies and crescent-shaped tails that provide maximum thrust. To eliminate turbulence and drag, their fins fit flat against their bodies in special grooves. Their eyes, rather than bulging out as in many other fishes, also lie flush with their smooth skin.

The epipelagic nekton native to the sanctuary make full use of their mobility. Most range widely up and down the Pacific coast of North America. Albacore and other tunas cover thousands of miles as they crisscross the Pacific Ocean. Arctic terns migrate from pole to pole–a round-trip of 22,000 miles. Their restless movements are driven by the search for food and the irrepressible urge to reach suitable spawning areas. The boundaries of their travels, especially those of pelagic fishes, are often marked by ocean currents and temperature boundaries.

Swimming takes energy, and these active swimmers need large amounts of food to fuel their high metabolism. Adults seek out areas where food is abundant and often follow seasonally changing sources of food. But areas rich in food for adults may not be suitable for their larvae or newborn young, which is likely why sardines, anchovies and hake spawn in the Southern California Bight, where their larvae are less likely to be carried far offshore by upwelling currents. In those waters, their larvae are also more likely to find sufficient food of the right size (such as dinoflagel-lates) to sustain them during the critical early days of their life. As they grow, the adults move north to exploit rich crops of diatoms and zooplankton in the upwelling areas along the coast. Hake may travel 2,000 kilometers, as far north as Vancouver Island, on their journeys.

Gray whales move up and down our coast in winter on their way from their feeding waters off Alaska to the lagoons in Baja, California, where their calves (which lack the thick layer of insulating blubber of adults) can be born in warm water. The San Lorenzo and Pajaro rivers along with Aptos Creek and other creeks along the central coast once supported spawning runs of coho salmon which returned to these rivers to spawn after spending several years feeding in the ocean both here and far to the north. These long-distance migrations capture our imaginations,but most nekton, from squid to fish, turtles and marine mammals, make journeys of varying lengths unheralded and largely unnoticed by us. In the sanctuary, fishes, inverte-brates, mammals and birds make seasonal migrations up and down the coast, from the depths to shallower water and from the ocean into estuaries like Elkhorn Slough.

THE INVISIBLE BORDERS THAT STRUCTURE A WIDE-OPEN WORLD

THE WORDS "OPEN WATERS" may conjure up images of boundless tracts of ocean where plants and animals can freely swim or drift, and where a given species might be found anywhere and everywhere. But the real picture is very different. The sanctuary plays host to dynamic communities of phytoplankton, zooplankton and nekton. The roster of species present and their abundance changes daily, seasonally, yearly and on much longer cycles.

Far from being homogeneous, the ocean's open waters are divided into distinct water masses marked by differences in temperature, salinity and the amount of dissolved nutrients they carry. These physical factors determine the kinds of plants and animals who live in the water which, in turn, change the character of the water mass. Phytoplankton, for example, use up nutrients, but provide food for grazing zooplankton, who then serve as prey for various predators. Biological factors, like the availability or lack of food and the presence of predators or competitors, work along with the physical factors to influence the community of life that the water supports. Water masses, both large and small, can be identified by the groups of species that live in them.

In the North Pacific, scientists have identified four major water masses— Subarctic, Transition Zone, Central and Equatorial—marked by distinct groups of plankton and nekton. The sanctuary lies in the center of the Transition Zone. Characteristic zooplankton of this zone include the copepods *Eucalanus californicus* and *Pleuromamma borealis*; the euphausiids *Nematoscelis difficilis* and *Thysanoessa gregaria*; and the arrow worm *Sagitta scrippsae*.

But the boundaries of this zone shift and the sanctuary lies in a region of overlap between the three other zones. Subarctic species are common as far south as Cape Mendocino. Some Equatorial species range north to Point Conception. The waters of the Central region lie just a few hundred miles west of us, separated from the coast by the California Current. This current carries a tongue of cold, nutrient-rich Subarctic Water far south along the coast. Below this surface layer, a countercurrent of warmer, saltier Equatorial water flows north. The Central water mass flows sluggishly in a circular gyre that pushes against the westward edge of the California Current. The strength of the California Current and its countercurrent vary considerably over time. And the interactions of these water masses within the California Current shape pelagic life in the sanctuary.

Sea winds drive seasonal and shorter-term changes. In spring and summer, persistent northwest winds along the coast push surface water south and offshore. As coastal surface water flows seaward, water from below wells up to take its place, and in turn flows offshore. Cold and nutrient-rich, this upwelled water supports blooms of coastal diatoms and zooplankton. Plumes of upwelled water may stretch hundreds of kilometers offshore. These long fingers of water carrying coastal plankton penetrate into the oceanic plankton communities of the California Current.

When the northwest winds subside in late summer, this surface flow reverses and tongues of oceanic water, with their associated plankton, push towards the coast. Swarms of heteropods and pteropods, along with salps, moon jellies, eggyolk jellies and other oceanic plankton appear near shore. In summer, warm surface temperatures and an abundance of jellies lure warm-water nekton like ocean sunfish and leatherback sea turtles far north into the California Current. They, too, may appear along our coast at summer's end as warm, less saline surface water from the edge of the current pushes towards shore.

In winter, prevailing southerly winds push surface water north, and the warm-water Davidson current develops along the coast. This northward flowing current brings with it different species of plankton to sanctuary waters. Dinoflagellates like *Gonyaulax polyedra*, common in southern California waters, become abundant here.

Studies off the coast of Oregon show similar patterns there. Warm-water species of copepods, arrow worms and larvaceans, not present in summer, become common in winter, when they're carried north by the Davidson Current.

While these are seasonal trends, they can happen on a smaller scale at any time of the year with changes in the prevailing winds. Just as there may be warm spells on land in mid-winter, or sunny days during the "rainy" season, a few

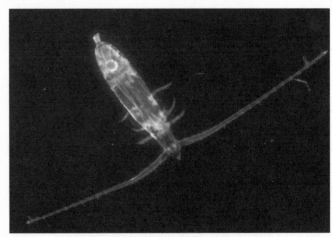

Copepods drift in the ocean's currents and can be found in abundance seasonally in the bay.

days of strong northwest winds in January can cause "unseasonable" upwelling. Likewise, even in spring and summer there are periods of calm when upwelling stops and oceanic water moves towards shore. The complexion of pelagic communities here can change in a matter of days.

Winds and plumes of upwelled water can also help create eddies of warm water, which bulge shoreward from the edges of the California Current, mixing different pelagic communities. One such eddy often sits at the outer edges of Monterey Bay. These mass movements of water—onshore and offshore, north and south—driven by winds and countercurrents, all work to stir together northern, southern and central water mass species in the sanctuary.

Dinoflagellate

The nature of pelagic communities here changes over longer cycles, as well. El Niño weather patterns can shift the ranges of pelagic species northward. During the El Niño of 1957-1958, southern species like the euphausiid *Nyctiphanes simplex* and the pelagic tunicate *Doliolum denticulatum* became abundant here along with blooms of tropical dinoflagellates.

Pelagic red crabs, *Pleuroncodes planipes*, normally found off Baja California, appeared in southern California waters that year. The next year, swarms of them appeared in Monterey Bay for the first time since 1859, an event that was repeated in 1984 after the El Niño of 1982-83.

The strength of the southerly flow of the California Current changes on a cycle of eight to sixteen years. Periods of strong flow may carry down large numbers of subarctic plankton like *Euphausia pacifica* and the pteropod *Limacina helicina*, greatly increasing local populations. Cold-water nekton, such as salmon, may extend their ranges southward. During periods of weak flow, and therefore warmer waters here, southern species like yellowfin, bonito and bluefin tuna expand their ranges northward. The ranges and abundance of northern anchovies and Pacific sardines also seem to shift in step with one another in these long-term cycles.

During years of warm water, populations of zooplankton, many of which depend on the lush crops of phytoplankton fueled by upwelling, may decrease to one-fifth of their levels during colder periods. Decreasing numbers of plankton may in turn affect populations of seabirds, marine mammals and commercially

Krill are a favorite food source for many open ocean animals.

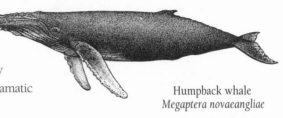

important fishes like sardines, salmon and hake. These changes in the California Current appear to happen rapidly in response to climate changes. If we are going through a period of global warming, as many scientists believe, we may see sudden and dramatic changes in pelagic life along our coast.

Humpback whale
Megaptera novaeangliae

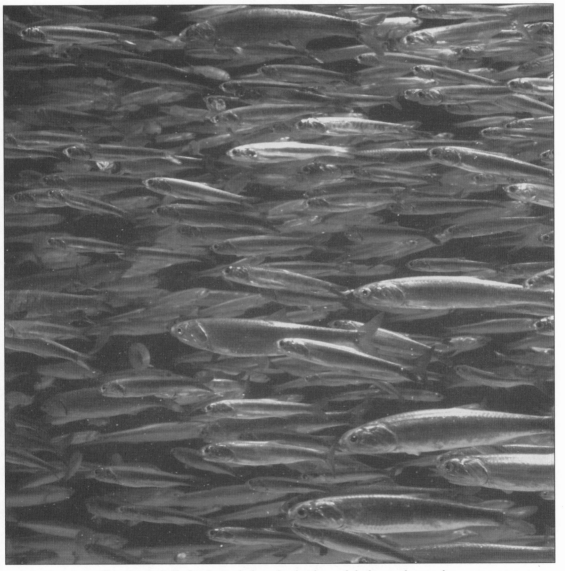

This silvery school of anchovies feeds on the abundance of plankton in the outer bay.

PATTERNS OF ABUNDANCE AND SCARCITY

PICK A SPOT IN THE OPEN WATERS of the sanctuary, go there and tow a plankton net behind your ship, then examine your haul under a microscope. Or dive in with scuba gear and have a look around. What will you find?

You might discover water made murky by dense blooms of diatoms or tinged red by uncountable numbers of microscopic dinoflagellates. You might find yourself surrounded by swarms of zooplankton: squadrons of gelatinous salps or doliolids perhaps, or clouds of copepods. A school of anchovies could swirl around you. You might even catch a glimpse of a huge blue whale. Or you could find nothing but clear water with some bacteria and protozoans visible only at the highest magnifications under your microscope. Go a few meters deeper, or come back a few days later, and you could find conditions completely different.

The outer reaches of Monterey Bay are home to a variety of plants and animals from microscopic plankton to huge whales.

Life isn't randomly dispersed through ocean waters, but is concentrated in patches. The four major North Pacific water masses recognized by scientists represent a type of large-scale patchiness. Each carries a "patch" of its own characteristic plants and animals. The large-scale patchiness defined by these water masses covers tens of thousands of square kilometers and persists for thousands of years. But patchiness occurs on much smaller and shorter-lived scales as well. Even within a larger water mass, one parcel of water may be virtually barren, while another nearby may teem with life. These smaller-scale patches can vary in size from aggregations of plankton a few meters or less across to ones covering hundreds of square kilometers. They change with time as well, some lasting less than a day, others persisting for weeks, months or years.

To get a mental picture of patchiness, imagine looking at an intricate tapestry. Viewing it from a distance, you might notice its overall pattern. Look more closely and you will begin to make out smaller elements–individual details within the broader pattern. Look more closely still, and you would begin to see even finer patterns within the fabric.

Patchiness also occurs on land as well. To see patchiness for yourself, take a drive along the Big Sur coast and look at the mountainsides. Grass balds alternate with scrubby chaparral and barren rocky outcrops. Forests of live oak, madrone and redwoods line sheltered ravines. Enter one of these groves and you'll find a different community of plants and animals than those on surrounding exposed slopes. Moving to an even finer scale, explore the stream tracing the ravine floor. There, under individual rocks, you may discover giant salamanders or insect larvae that live nowhere else in the surrounding mountains.

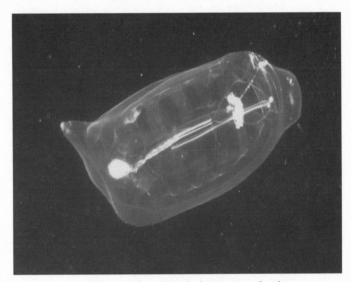

In the summer and spring when plant plankton is most abundant, soft-bodied salps graze on the harvest.

Now, transfer this image to the sanctuary's open waters. Instead of immense redwoods which live for centuries, there are patches of microscopic plants which persist for just days or weeks. Instead of solid ground, there is restless water, stirring and mixing the communities living in it.

The constant movement of water plays an important role in the formation and dispersion of patches. Wind-driven Langmuir circulation cells (see *Oceanography*), create short-lived patches of plankton that aggregate where the water from adjoining cells converges and sinks. Fishes and other nekton gather here as well to feed on the concentrations of plankton. When the winds die, the cells disappear, and the plankton disperse.

During periods of upwelling, plankton and nekton become concentrated at the fronts between plumes of cold upwelled water and the warmer surface waters around them. A dramatic example of this occurs seasonally in Monterey Bay. Cold upwelled water flowing south from near Pt. Año Nuevo doesn't penetrate into the northeast corner of the bay. The result is an "upwelling shadow," with a sharp change in temperature marking the front between the upwelled water and the warmer inshore water. The boundary between these two water masses is often marked by abrupt changes in water color, shoals of up to 100,000 large jellies (*Chrysaora* sp.) and surface slicks with accumulations of floating debris. Large numbers of fish eggs, crab larvae, copepods, arrow worms and other zooplankton become concentrated along the inshore each side of the front, with ten- to thousand-fold differences in abundance compared to the seaward side. This front often persists for several months through the upwelling season. Other upwelling fronts push offshore during intense upwelling and disappear or move shoreward during periods of calmer winds when upwelling relaxes, creating shorter-lived concentrations of plankton.

Even within water masses of similar temperature and salinity are often subtle differences that affect the distribution and abundance of the life found there. Each has its own complement of competitors, predators and prey. And each has a unique "water history": a history which includes among other things the origin of the water, the abundance of nutrients it held and how they've been used by a succession of phytoplankton. The history of a water mass helps determine the kinds and abundance of the phytoplankton living in it at any given time. This, in turn, affects the populations of zooplankton living in the water.

For example, more than a dozen species of salps may live in the sanctuary. Their ranges overlap and they all eat diatoms–they all seem to have similar lifestyles. Normally they live scattered through the water in low numbers, but occasionally some are found in large swarms. And it's here that species begin to show their differences. Studies of *Salpa fusiforma* and *Thalia democratica* have shown that each swarms in the presence of a different group of diatoms. That is, each has a habitat, identified by the abundance of a particular group of diatoms, to which it's best suited.

Salps seem to be opportunists. Small, isolated populations survive under a variety of conditions until they happen upon a rich patch of the right kinds of diatoms. Then, with the high growth rates and short generation times characteristic of these gelatinous zooplankton, they undergo a population explosion to reap the bounty of their new-found food source. They're adapted (as all pelagic creatures must be in one way or another) to a patchy environment where food is usually scarce, but may suddenly be encountered in abundance.

The adaptation of each species of zooplankton to patchiness affects where it lives. Like salps, herbivorous copepods and euphausiids also graze diatoms. But swarms of salps and dense concentrations of these slower-growing crustaceans aren't

The endless blue water of the open ocean is home to California barracuda, tuna and other ocean-going swimmers.

found together. The strategies of salps to deal with a patchy supply of food work best under different conditions than those of copepods and euphausiids.

Strategies vary even among different species of copepods. Some survive only a few days without food and reach their seasonal peaks of abundance at places, and times of the year, when patches of food are readily available. Others may live weeks without feeding and can survive where phytoplankton patches are fewer and farther between. Some copepods feed specifically on just a few types of food. But those, like *Calanus pacificus*, which live in waters with large seasonal changes in abundance of phytoplankton (as in the sanctuary) often can switch diets to take advantage of whatever types of plankton are most abundant at any time.

Scientists speak of "scales of patchiness," which refers, in part, to the size of patches, how far apart they are, how often they form and how long they last. For each pelagic plant and animal, the scales of patchiness of the nutrients or food it needs and of its predators and competitors profoundly effect its life. The critical limits vary for each, but in general larger and longer-lived creatures are less affected by small-scale variations in patchiness.

In the sanctuary, a fifteen-millimeter-long arrow worm, like *Sagitta scrippsae,* may be able to eat enough in a few minutes to last it for twenty-four hours. A five-meter-long white shark, in contrast, may be able to eat enough at one feeding to last it for weeks or months. As long as each finds food within the time it needs, it won't "notice" any shorter-term patchiness.

An animal foraging in the ocean is much more likely to find new patches of food by moving vertically a few meters deeper or shallower than by staying at one depth and traveling much longer horizontal distances. As it descends from the surface into the depths, conditions of light, temperature and salinity change rapidly and fairly predictably. Plankton tend to aggregate in thin, broad zones where they find conditions best suited to their needs, creating layers of patchiness at different depths.

The vertical migrations of many plankton provide a way for them to sample different layers of water for patches of food. The comb jelly *Leucothea* sp. eats copepods, pelagic snails and other zooplankton, which congregate in a layer at the thermocline. *Leucothea* makes short, rapid jaunts up or down in the water, then cruises more slowly at one depth. Its vertical forays may help it locate a layer of concentrated prey, and it then hunts along that layer. Individuals sometimes leave seemingly rich layers of plankton. It may be that once they've eaten their fill, they move elsewhere to avoid being eaten in turn by the larger comb jelly, *Beroë*, which also hunt in plankton-rich patches. *Beroë forskalii* also forages vertically, spiraling up through the water in search of concentrations of other comb jellies.

Phytoplankton also become concentrated in relatively thin, horizontal layers at boundaries marked by slight variations of temperature. There's usually one layer,

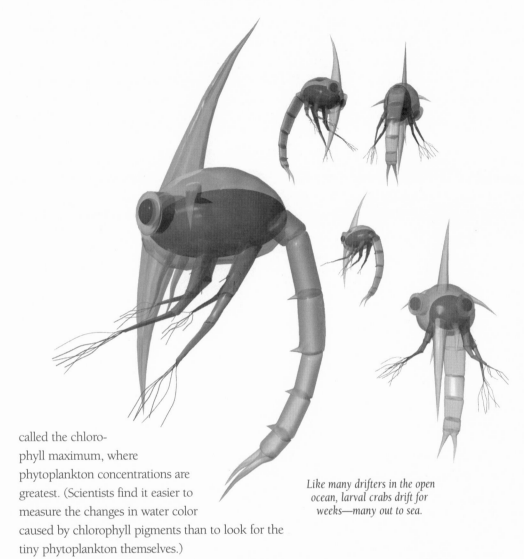

Like many drifters in the open ocean, larval crabs drift for weeks—many out to sea.

called the chloro-
phyll maximum, where
phytoplankton concentrations are
greatest. (Scientists find it easier to
measure the changes in water color
caused by chlorophyll pigments than to look for the
tiny phytoplankton themselves.)

The presence of this phytoplankton layer is vitally important to many zooplankton, including the larvae of anchovies. Anchovies spawn en masse in the Southern
California Bight south of Point Conception. Once their eggs hatch, the larvae live for
a while on food reserves stored in their yolk sacs. Once they exhaust those reserves,
they need to quickly locate rich layers of just the right-size dinoflagellates, such as
Gymnodinium splendens. The larvae seek out the temperature layer that marks the
chlorophyll maximum (often around twenty meters or so deep), then adjust their
buoyancy so they stay suspended to feast on this rich phytoplankton pasture. In
good years, when winds stay calm and food is plentiful, many of the larvae survive.
But in some years, untimely storms or strong winds stir the upper waters, destroying

the layers of temperature and scattering the patches of phytoplankton, and nearly all the uncountable millions of anchovy larvae perish.

Occasional catastrophic events like this are another form of patchiness to which anchovies and other pelagic life must be adapted. It's often boom or bust in the sanctuary's dynamic open waters. Along this eastern edge of the Pacific Ocean winds drive upwelling that fuels seasonal bursts of abundance. The same winds–too strong, or at the wrong time–can scatter that abundance and sweep it away. When the winds fade at summer's end, upwelling stops, the fields of phytoplankton dwindle and animals must move on or make do until the cycle begins again.

Patchiness, boom or bust, is a condition of life here with which plants and animal must deal if they are to survive. But it's patchiness that makes ocean life as we know it possible at all. The open ocean–and the deep sea below–are almost incomprehensibly vast, and the supply of available nutrients is low. If nutrients were distributed equally throughout the oceans, there wouldn't be enough in any one place to support profusions of life like those we find in the sanctuary.

Selected Outer Waters Species

BIRDS

Arctic tern, *Sterna paradisaea*
Brown pelican, *Pelecanus occidentalis*

INVERTEBRATES

Arrow worm, *Sagitta scrippsae*
Comb jelly, *Beroë* spp.
Copepod, *Calanus pacificus*
Copepod, *Eucalanus californicus*
Copepod, *Metridia lucens*
Copepod, *Pleuromamma borealis*
Cross jelly, *Mitrocoma cellularia*
Crystal jelly, *Aequorea victoria*
Diatom, *Chaetoceros*
Diatom, *Ditylum brightwellii*
Diatom, *Thalassiosira*
Dinoflagellate, *Ceratium*
Dinoflagellate, *Gonyaulax polyedra*
Dinoflagellate, *Gymnodiaium splendens*
Egg-yolk jelly, *Phacellophora camtschatica*
Euphausiid, *Nematoscelis difficilis*
Euphausiid, *Nyctiphanes simplex*
Euphausiid, *Thysanoessa gregaria*
Larvacean, *Limacina helicina*
Larvacean, *Oikopleura*
Lobed comb jelly, *Bolinopsis infundibulum*
Lobed comb jelly, *Leucothea* sp.
Moon jelly, *Aurelia aurita*
Pelagic red crab, *Pleuroncodes planipes*
Pelagic tunicate, *Doliolum denticulatum*
Plankton, *Euphausia pacifica*
Purple-striped jelly, *Pelagia colorata*
Salp, *Salpa fusiforma*
Salp, *Thalia democratica*
Sea angel, *Clione limacina*
Sea nettle, *Chrysaora fuscescens*
Siphonophore, *Praya* sp.

FISHES

Albacore, *Thunnus alalunga*
California barracuda, *Sphyraena argentea*
Bluefin tuna, *Thunnus thynnus*
Blue shark, *Prionace glauca*
Jackmackerel, *Trachurus symmetricus*
Market squid, *Loligo opalescens*

Northern anchovy, *Engraulis mordax*
Ocean sunfish, *Mola mola*
Opah, *Lampris guttatus*
Pacific bonito, *Sarda chiliensis*
Pacific hake, *Merluccius productus*
Pacific herring, *Clupea pallasii*
Pacific mackerel, *Scomber japonicus*
Pacific sardine, *Sardinops sagax*
Pelagic stingray, *Dasyatis violacea*
Soupfin shark, *Galeorhinus galeus*
Thresher shark, *Alopias vulpinus*
Yellowfin tuna, *Thunnus albacares*

MAMMALS

Blue whale, *Balaenoptera musculus*
Gray whale, *Eschrichtius robustus*
Harbor seal, *Phoca vitulina*
Pacific white-sided dolphin,
   Lagenorhynchus obliquidens

PLANTS

Cyanobacteria, *Synechococcus*

REPTILES

Green sea turtle, *Chelonia mydas*
Leatherback sea turtle,
   Dermochelys coriacea coriacea

The midwater octopus, Vitreledonella sp., *constantly roams the sea, unlike it's bottom-dwelling cousins.*

CHAPTER TWELVE

THE DEEP SEA

*Every part of the earth or air or sea has an atmosphere peculiarly
its own, a quality or characteristic that sets it apart from all others. When I
think of the deep sea...I see always the steady, unremitting, downward drift of
materials from above, flake upon flake.*

RACHEL CARSON

THE OPEN WATERS OF THE SANCTUARY stretch from
the surface to near the seafloor, in some places more than
10,500 feet (3,200 meters) deep. But beneath the shallow
sunlit surface layer (the epipelagic zone) living conditions
change dramatically.

If we could follow an animal into the depths, a diving elephant seal perhaps,
or a tiny lanternfish on its daily migration to the surface and back into deeper
water, we'd notice how quickly sunlight fades into a dim, blue twilight. By the time
we've descended just around 330 feet (100 meters) there's no longer enough light
to fuel the growth of phytoplankton. Below this changeable boundary lie the dark
reaches of the deep sea.

WHAT IS THE DEEP SEA?

THE TERM "DEEP SEA" encompasses several distinct habitats. The deep sea begins with the midwater (the mesopelagic zone). This is a twilight world where fishes, squid and prawns tend to have large, sometimes elaborate eyes to make the most of the faint downwelling sunlight. Between 1,970 and 3,280 feet (600 and 1,000 meters), twilight grades into total darkness. Animals living in the deeper midwater (the bathypelagic zone) that lies below often have very small eyes, or no eyes at all, and rely on other senses to hunt prey and avoid predators.

Other animals populate the deep seafloor and the walls of the many submarine canyons which cut the continental shelf in the sanctuary. In some respects, these bottom (benthic) communities have more in common with those of the shallower sandy seafloor and reef habitats than they do with the pelagic midwater communities just above them. But

Mushroom soft coral, *Anthomastus ritteri* (top)

Brownsnout, *Dolichopteryx longipes* (middle)

Midwater octopus, *Bolitaena microcotyla* (bottom)

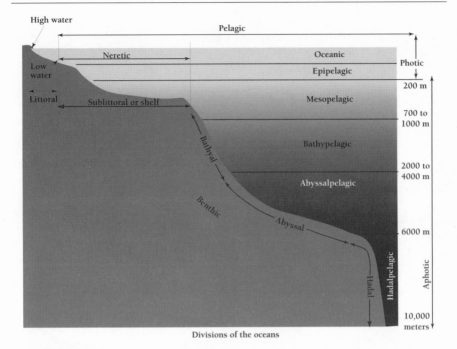

Divisions of the oceans

both deep benthic and midwater communities are bound together in the darkness that plays a key role in shaping life in the deep.

The deep sea encompasses nearly 98 percent (by volume) of all living space on Earth. (Land makes up less than one percent.) Yet in spite of its vast size, it remains the least known ecosystem on the planet. Huge, dark and remote, the deep sea poses many and difficult challenges to those who seek to fathom its secrets.

Much of what we know has been pieced together from net trawls pulled blindly through the water or drug across the seafloor. At best, they provide a view of deep sea life distorted by imprecision, limited scope and the fact that they destroy beyond recognition some of the most important members of deep sea communities, while allowing others to escape completely. More recently, manned and remotely operated research submersibles, along with other modern tools, have given us new ways of probing the depths. They've opened our eyes to a world we've never before been able to see and are dramatically changing our view of deep sea life.

But even these tools give us only murky and incomplete glimpses into the heart of the ocean. Our vision is limited to the narrow swath of a submersible's lights, a field of view something like that from an automobile on a foggy night. And the lights and noise frighten some animals away, while attracting others—biasing our perceptions. Our picture of the deep remains a patchwork with many missing pieces.

How do you count octopuses?

How do the methods scientists use to calculate the abundance of marine animals affect their estimates? Scientists used two different methods to calculate the abundance of red octopus, *Octopus rubescens*, on the sandy deep seafloor in the sanctuary. Based on trawl samples, a traditional tool for measuring the abundance of bottom-dwelling animals, red octopus were rare—fewer than one octopus were collected per 270,000 square feet of seafloor. In contrast, video observations using Monterey Bay Aquarium Research Institute's (MBARI) submersible, showed an abundance of red octopuses—about one every three square meters. Why the difference? The small, agile octopus were able to avoid the trawl, or slip through the mesh of the net and escape.

212

The pieces we do have reveal surprising diversity and complexity in a world we once thought to be without life or at most monotonous and sparsely populated. The deep waters of the sanctuary are home to giant squid and matchstick-size fishes. Anglerfish twitch glowing lures to entice smaller fishes within reach of their large, toothy jaws. Ropelike, 130-foot (40-meter) long, siphonophores wait in the darkness for jellies, salps and pelagic worms to blunder into their web of stinging tentacles. Whole communities of tiny animals— worlds in microcosm—live on the flakes of marine snow that drift steadily, unremittingly, downward.

Anglerfish,
Linophryne coronata

Siphonophore,
Apolemia sp.

Others make their homes on the deep seafloor and the flanks of underwater canyons. Glass sponges live anchored to rocky faces where currents wash ultra-fine food particles through their porous bodies. Rattail fishes probe the sediments, scavenging on the bodies of dead animals or straining worms and small molluscs from the mouthfuls of muck they suck from the seafloor. Beds of clams

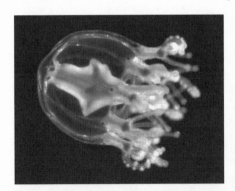

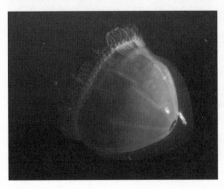

Hydromedusa, *Cladonema* sp. (top)
Bell jelly, *Polyorchis penicillatus* (right)
Midwater jelly, *Benthocodon* sp. (bottom)

213

thrive on the energy contained in anoxic, sulfide-rich fluids seeping through rock strata.

To our eyes, creatures of the deep may seem bizarre, improbable, and the physical conditions of their habitat hostile to the extreme. But, as for all creatures, evolution has shaped their remarkable forms and wondrous lifestyles to fit the demands of their habitat. To a deep sea animal, it's our dry world of land, sun and wind which would seem harsh and strange.

PHYSICAL CONDITIONS

A QUICK PASSAGE INTO DARKNESS isn't the only change we'd experience on our trip into the deep sea. As we descend below the well-mixed surface layer, warmed by the sun and stirred by winds, we'd feel the water growing steadily colder. The temperature drops most dramatically in the upper several hundred feet (few hundred meters), the zone of rapid temperature change called the thermocline. Temperatures at the surface vary between about 46°F (8°C) and 61°F (16°C). By the time we reach 3,280 feet (1,000 meters), the water is a frigid, yet relatively constant, 60°F or 5°C. Below this, the temperature declines more gradually to about 40°F in the sanctuary's deepest reaches.

While the temperature decreases with depth, the pressure of the water pressing in around us increases drastically. When we stand on land, the weight of the atmosphere pushes in on us with a pressure of 14.7 pounds per square inch (about one kilogram per square centimeter)—an amount known as one atmosphere. In the sea, pressure increases by one atmosphere for each 33 feet (10 meters) in depth. By the time we reach 660 feet (200 meters), the pressure is more

A white whelk, Neptunea amianter *and a red whelk,* N. antigua *are among benthic species found in the Monterey Canyon.*

than 20 times greater than at the surface; on the deep seafloor at the mouth of Monterey Canyon, the pressure is 320 times greater.

As a way of demonstrating the effects of such pressure, scientists sometimes carry Styrofoam cups into the deep on submersible expeditions. When the submersible surfaces, the cups have been squeezed into miniatures of themselves. But for deep sea animals, the problem is not one of

A featherstar, Florometra serratissima, filters tiny particles from the water as its kind has been doing for thousands of years.

being physically crushed. They must deal with the more subtle, but no less real, effects that the tremendous pressures have on their internal physiology—the operation of their cellular metabolism.

The amount of oxygen dissolved in the water also changes as we descend. Levels are highest at the surface, where wind stirs the waves. The amount drops gradually to about 2,300 feet (700 meters). There lies a region of very low oxygen levels called the "oxygen minimum zone." Below this, oxygen levels begin to rise again.

Unlike it's shallower cousins, this predatory tunicate, Megalodicopia hians, eats small animals trapped in its cavernous hood.

Cold Seeps

COLD SEEP COMMUNITIES were found in
Monterey Canyon in late 1988 (after being
first discovered off Florida in 1984), by
scientists aboard the research submersible,
Alvin. Their presence had been predicted
from earlier trawls which brought up the
shells of clams associated with seeps.

In contrast to other deep sea habitats in
the sanctuary, which depend on food from
above, cold seep communities are fueled by
the chemical energy contained in sulfide-rich
fluids seeping up through the seafloor. In
this, they share much in common with
hydrothermal vent communities like those
on the deep seafloor near the Galapagos
Islands. But where hydrothermal vents are
hot springs along volcanically active seafloor
spreading centers, the fluid oozing up
through cold seeps is the same temperature
as the surrounding sea water.

For most life on Earth, the food web
starts with plants, which use the energy in
sunlight to convert inorganic compounds
into organic compounds through photosynthesis. The food webs in vents and cold seeps
begin with bacteria which, through a process
called chemosynthesis, use the energy in

hydrogen sulfide or methane in a similar way.
Around seeps and vents, bacteria play a role
like that of plants in most other habitats: they
are the primary producers of food for other
members of the community.

Hot vents and cold seeps share similar
fauna: mats of chemosynthetic bacteria, and
specialized groups of large clams, mussels and
worms as well as various crabs, snails and
smaller worms. Bacterial mats and five species
of vent clams dominate our local cold seeps,
along with galatheid crabs, limpets and snails.
(One of the clams is a newly described species,
Calyptogena packardana, named in honor of the
Packard family who founded both the aquarium and MBARI.)

The first seeps in the sanctuary were
found at 10,500 feet (3,200 meters) in the fan
valley at the mouth of the Monterey Canyon.
Since then, more sites have been found and we
now recognize three other geologically distinct
seep areas here.

The shallowest of these, dubbed "Mount
Crushmore" by MBARI scientists, consists of
several seeps on the wall of the Monterey
Canyon near the mouth of Soquel Canyon
between 1,885 and 2,275 feet (580 and 700
meters) deep. There, fault movements have
pushed up the sandstone and mudstone of the

These cold seep clams, Calyptogena pacifica, *may take up to 100 years to reach adult size.*

Purisima Formation and seeps seem to form where fluid oozes from fractures in the porous layers of rock.

About 2,925 feet (900 meters) deep on the western wall of the Monterey Canyon at a site dubbed "Clam Field," fluids seep out along hundreds of yards of Monterey shale. The fluids seeping from these rocky outcrops may come from the hydrocarbon deposits in the shale.

Another site, "Clam Flats" sits on the continental slope about 3,280 feet (1,000 meters) deep. The seeps here may be driven by tectonic compression. As tectonic plates push against each other, fluid trapped in sediments in the accretionary wedge between them gets pushed upward until it seeps out from the seafloor. The chemistry of the seep fluids is different at each site, and these differences are reflected in the make-up of the seep communities.

At Mount Crushmore, seep fluids are low in sulfide and lack methane. Here, 85 percent of the clams are of the species *Calyptogena pacifica*.

At Clam Flats, where sulfide levels nearly 100 times higher, and the fluids also carry high levels of methane, 99 percent of the clams were the seep clam *Calyptogena kilmeri*. Fluids at Clam Field also have high sulfide levels (but only about half those at Clam Flats) and low levels of methane. Here, *C. kilmeri* makes up 85 percent of the population.

Seep clams rely on chemosynthetic bacteria within their tissues to harness the energy stored in hydrogen sulfide; and in turn to use this energy to covert dissolved carbon dioxide into organic compounds the clams can use. While each species of clam seems to have its own type of bacteria, the bacteria all have the same ability to use hydrogen sulfide. But the clams differ in their physiological abilities to bind and store sulfide, and scientists believe this accounts for the differences in their distribution.

Calyptogena pacifica seems to be able to concentrate sulfide in its tissues at levels ten times greater than *C. kilmeri*. This allows *C. pacifica* to survive in low-sulfide seeps and at the edges of higher-sulfide seeps, where sulfide flow is too low to sustain *C. kilmeri*. Researchers also suspect that *C. kilmeri* has a higher metabolism which allows it to grow rapidly and outcompete *C. pacifica*.

Scientists have found striking differences in the growth and average age of populations of different species of seep clams. The average age of populations of fast-growing *Calyptogena kilmeri* is three to five years, and these clams reach maximum size in about 15 years. In contrast, *C. pacifica* may take 100 years to reach adult size, and the average age of the population is 90 to 100 years.

This raises questions about how long individual seeps last, and how seep animals colonize new, widely scattered seeps. The very broad guess is that seeps last between 10 to 10,000 years. In the axial valley of the canyon, where turbidity currents deposit their load of organic sediments, MBARI scientists have found smaller seeps which seem to have variable fluid flow. Anaerobic bacteria feed on the buried sediments, producing energy-rich hydrogen sulfide which seeps up through the sediments. Here, clams move around more often, as if looking for places where the flow best meets their needs.

Gray mats of chemosynthetic bacteria are often scientists' first clue to the presence of a seep. These mats support a number of other animals including snails of the genus *Mitrella* which may graze on the bacteria. Also here are galatheid crabs, sometimes called squat lobsters. Members of this group of crabs are common in many benthic habitats, but several species are unique to seep and vent habitats. They're found only on rocks among and covered by the bacterial mats.

Animals from the surrounding seafloor forage around seeps. Crabs move through, including tanner crabs which eat large clams. Dover sole are frequent visitors; large octopuses often live nearby. Predatory snails also venture into seeps to prey on the clams. Seep communities seem to act as scattered oases of relative abundance on the otherwise food-poor seafloor.

Temperature, pressure, oxygen and darkness all play roles in shaping the nature of life in the deep. But the quality that sets the deep sea apart from all other habitats—the characteristic that most concisely defines its essence—is the scarcity of food. In nearly all other habitats, living communities include both plants and animals—producers and consumers. But plants can't grow in deep sea darkness, so there's no production of food here. With few exceptions, life here depends on what bits of organic material drift down, or can be harvested on nightly migrations to the productive surface waters. And the need to find and make the most efficient use of the limited resources available to them has shaped the bodies and behaviors of deep sea animals as well as their community interactions.

Even so, the surface communities don't give up their bounty easily. Much of the production there is recycled many times through complex food webs; little makes its way into deeper waters. In many areas of the ocean, it's estimated that less than five percent of the organic production of phytoplankton at the surface settles even 1,640 feet (500 meters) deep, and only one percent reaches the ocean floor. With less food available, fewer animals can make a living in the deep. And in contrast to the abundance at the surface, the deep sea is sparsely populated.

Yet, as with other habitats in the sanctuary, life in the deep sea here is exceptionally rich and varied in comparison to most parts of the ocean. With the narrow continental shelf along our coast, 3,280-feet (1,000-meter) deep water lies directly under highly productive nearshore surface waters. And some thirteen submarine canyons, most notably the Monterey Canyon, cut into the shelf in the sanctuary, bringing deep water even closer to shore. Along the eastern coast of the United States and other places where the continental shelf is wider, deep water lies under low-productivity surface waters much further offshore.

In the sanctuary, "organic energy"—food—moves into the depths in three main ways: through the active movements of animals back and forth between deep water and the surface; through the sinking of phytoplankton, fecal pellets of zooplankton and other organic particles; and through the transport of seaweed remains from nearshore kelp forests.

The Oxygen Minimum Zone

NEAR THE SURFACE, where plant plankton produce oxygen and restless waves mix water and air, ocean water is well-oxygenated. But below this surface layer, oxygen levels in the water begin to drop dramatically. Here animals and bacteria continue to use oxygen, but there are no plants nor atmospheric mixing to replenish the supply.

At around 1,970 (600 meters), the level of oxygen dissolved in the water has dropped to nearly zero. There lies a layer of water several hundred feet (a few hundred meters) thick known as the oxygen minimum layer. Around 3,280 feet (1,000 meters), oxygen levels begin to rise again. This boundary marks the beginning of the total darkness of the deep midwater (the bathypelagic zone). The sparse organisms at these depths use little oxygen, and cold, oxygen-rich currents provide a new supply.

The low oxygen levels in the oxygen minimum layer limit the distribution of midwater animals. Fishes, shrimps and others living here have adaptations to survive at low oxygen levels: well-developed gills to help extract oxygen from the water; an inactive lifestyle, which lessens oxygen use; and complex biochemical adaptations to make more efficient use of oxygen. Fast-moving fishes and squid are at most fleeting visitors to this zone.

One resident is the vampire squid, *Vampyroteuthis infernalis*, an unusual cephalopod once thought extinct. It may be that this "living fossil" has survived for eons in these oxygen-poor waters, where some active predators have trouble foraging.

Shining tubeshoulder
Sagamichthys abei

This 10-inch-long blackbelly dragonfish, Stomias atriventir may use its chin barbel as a lure. This deepsea fish bears tiny photophores all over its body and in two long rows on its belly.

VERTICAL MIGRATION

Midwater mysid *Boreomysis sp.*

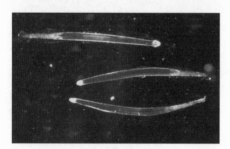

Arrowworms, *Chaetognaths*

Midwater shrimp, *Sergestes similis*

AS MENTIONED IN CHAPTER 10, *Open Waters,* many zooplankton and small fishes make daily vertical migrations between the surface and deeper water. These are creatures of two worlds which use the midwater as something of a bedroom community. They rise to earn their living feeding on the night shift near the surface. By day, they return to the quiet safety of the depths to rest. The most common migrators are lanterfishes, krill, midwater shrimps, squids and certain kinds of siphonophores and arrowworms.

Scientists have long been aware of the migrations of plankton. The magnitude of this daily mass vertical migration of animals in the ocean became clearer with the development of echo sounders during World War II. Echoes bouncing back from concentrations of midwater animals showed as reflective layers—or "scattering layers," as they came to be called—between 660 and 3,200 feet (200 and 700 meters) deep. Scattering layers are best developed in areas, like the sanctuary, where high surface productivity provides rich forage for midwater commuters.

Many, but not all, animals living in the scattering layers migrate. In a study in Monterey Bay, the bristlemouth fish, *Cyclothone signata*, and the arrowworm, *Pseudosagitta lyra*—both non-migrators—were among the most abundant animals in trawls taken through the scattering layers.

Also common in the trawls were krill, *Euphausia pacifica*, and the midwater prawn, *Sergestes similis*, both of which are migrators. The krill graze on phytoplankton and also eat copepods and other zooplankton. The prawns prey on krill as well as copepods and other crustaceans.

Many kinds of midwater fishes join the prawns and krill in the daily migration. Of the fishes, lanternfishes—nearly all of which are migrators—are one of the most successful families in terms of both numbers and diversity. In the sanctuary, two species of lanternfishes—northern lampfish, *Stenobrachius leucopsarus*, and the California headlightfish, *Diaphus theta*—are each very abundant at certain seasons. The headlightfish moves toward the surface at night to nibble on euphausiids and copepods, while the lampfish prefers young prawns and deeper-living copepods.

The depth and intensity of the vertical migration varies daily. The character of the scattering layers also varies seasonally as species change in abundance or move to different depths in response to changing water conditions or food supplies, or to reproduce. The Monterey Bay study found one layer between 820 and 980 feet (250 and 300 meters) deep in winter in which the headlight fish was the most abundant animal. By spring, these fish were gone and midwater prawns were abundant, along with lampfish and krill.

By early summer, the single scattering layer had become one solid band of reflections from the surface into the deep as the upwelling-fueled phytoplankton bloom fed a riotous explosion of zooplankton, large and small. Clouds of life hovering in the water and gray fog in the summer skies above cut the amount of light reaching the depths. Keyed to the darkening water, prawns, lampfish and krill shifted their level upward in response; some headlightfish reappeared. In fall, the layer shifted downward, a second layer formed and headlightfish began to increase in numbers.

A more recent study off southern California showed four distinct resident communities of midwater animals associated with different scattering layers interacting with a number of more ephemeral groups. Species, genera and families change with depth, but a similar cast of characters play key roles in each community: jellies, siphonophores, larvaceans, ctenophores, lantern-

Hatchetfish
Argyropeledus sp.

fishes, hatchetfishes, bristlemouth fishes, squids, prawns, euphausids and the ubiquitous copepods. About half of the fishes and crustaceans are vertical migrators. Fewer of the gelatinous zooplankton seem to be vertical migrators, but it's important to remember that we know generally less about the various jellies than about fishes and crustaceans. They may be moving in concert to other cues—other

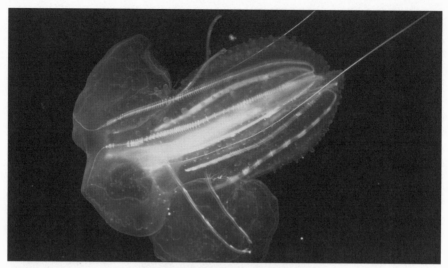

Midwater ctenophore, *Leucothea* sp.

Midwater narcomedusa, *Solmissus marshalli*

environmental rhythms. The midwater jelly, *Solmissus marshalli*, and the siphonophore, *Nanomia* sp., among others, seem to be partial migrators, moving between different depths, but not necessarily all the way to the surface. Differences in depth ranges and migration patterns allow species which might otherwise compete for similar resources to co-exist. These differences, along with seasonal variations, add a structure and complexity to the midwater world which we're only beginning to understand.

We still have much to learn about midwater community relations and the interactions between predator and prey in this twilight realm. But the daily feeding excursions of the vertical migrators to the surface and back help provide the energy which runs these communities.

Living Lights in a Midnight Sea

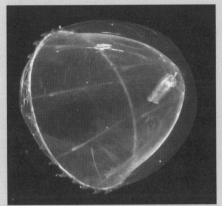

Midwater jelly, *Colobonema sericeum*

EVEN IN CLEAR OCEAN WATER, most downwelling light is absorbed as it travels through the water column. Because of this, the light which makes it into the depths is limited to a dim, blue-green color. However, downwelling sunlight is not the only source of light in the deep ocean: In the darkest depths of the ocean, most species use bioluminescence—light produced by living organisms—in their struggle to survive. Bioluminescence is highly developed and widespread among midwater animals. It is estimated that 90 percent of the species living below 2,300 feet (700 meters) are bioluminescent, including representatives from nearly every phylum found in the deep sea. The fact that this phenomenon is so highly developed and widespread among deep sea organisms suggests that it must be of great adaptive value.

The light-producing organs of bioluminescent fishes, squids and invertebrates are called "photophores." These organs emit light from various light-producing chemical reactions. In most animals, these reactions are carried out by the animals themselves; in some animals, however, light is produced by luminescent bacteria living within the light-producing organs. Photophores in various deep sea animals range from very simple structures to complex light-control systems equipped with lenses to focus light, tubes to control its direction, and colored filters or flaps to control its color and vary intensity.

Bioluminescent light may play a number of different roles in the deep:

CAMOUFLAGE: photophores on the underside of an animal are lit to match downwelling light and disguise the animal's silhouette from predators below. Lanternfishes and many squids use light in this way.

ESCAPE FROM PREDATORS: a blinding flash startles a predator long enough for an animal to escape. Some cephalopods and worms release a "smokescreen" of bioluminescence; some jellies (*Colobonema*) can shed glowing tentacles to throw pursuers off the track. The smokescreen of light and jettisoned glowing body part may look enough like the prey to attract the predator while the darkened animal flees.

"BURGLAR ALARM EFFECT:" some organisms light up in the presence of a potential predator—and they don't even have to see the predator to do this. Small algae on the sea's surface, dinoflagellates, flash when a grazer swims through them. The flashing alerts a predator, such as a fish, to the presence and exact location of the grazer. This type of light in the sea is the most familiar; the flashing of the dinoflagellates at the surface causes glowing wakes of passing boats and sparkling waves.

PREY ATTRACTION AND CAPTURE: light organs dangling on a line look like a good meal for a passing animal. But these act like lures and help catch a meal. Deep sea anglerfish, blackdragons and others use glowing lures to attract prey. Some fish (the Malacostiidae) use a special red light to illuminate and catch their prey.

SPECIES RECOGNITION AND COMMUNICATION: some animals use light to find a mate in the dark. Lanternfishes and squids have species-specific patterns of photophores that help them find mates of their own species. And in some, males and females have different patterns. So a light show will tell another fish which species and sex it is.

MARINE SNOW

VERTICAL MIGRATORS RISE TO EXPLOIT THE ORGANIC RICHES in the surface waters, then carry a portion of that energy—in the form of their living tissues—down into the midwater. But food also flows into the deep sea in the form of the sinking remains and waste from the swarming life at the surface. Much of what reaches the deep seafloor from above comes in the form of marine snow.

The amount and type of snow varies with the seasons, with peaks following the bursts of upwelling productivity in spring and summer. Other peaks occur during mass molts of euphausiids, when blizzards of empty exoskeletons sift downward, trapping and carrying smaller particles with them and changing the character of the midwater, at least temporarily. And a heavy sleet of fecal pellets follows the nightly surface feedings of the vertical migrators.

As noted in the *Open Waters* chapter, the nutrients in small particles are likely to be recycled through the actions of bacteria and dinoflagellates many times in the upper waters. But as small particles clump together into larger flakes of marine snow, they begin to sink more quickly. And the faster they sink, the more of the energy they contain is carried into the deep before being reprocessed. Snow or pellets that sink faster than 660 feet (200 meters) per day carry much of their energy with them to the deep seafloor. The fecal pellets of salps and pteropods sink most rapidly, as fast as 3,280 feet (1,000 meters) per day, so the wastes from these abundant herbivores help feed sea stars, sea cucumbers and other grazers and deposit-feeders on the seafloor.

The discarded houses of giant larvaceans, *Bathochordaeus* spp., sink nearly as fast—up to 2,625 feet (800 meters) per day. Scientists using submersibles have studied the houses of these larvaceans in the midwater of Monterey Bay between 330 and 1,640 feet (100 and 500 meters).

Giant larvaceans are relatively abundant, perhaps one per 264,200 gallons (1,000 cubic meters): slightly less than the volume of water in the Monterey Bay Aquarium's Kelp Forest exhibit. Their large houses, enriched with an accumulated load of fecal pellets and other detritus sink quickly to the seafloor once discarded, where they provide a major source of food for benthic animals.

The houses are also home to communities of protozoans, bacteria, copepods and other animals, and serve as feeding stations for midwater zooplankton. Up to 10 times as many animals were found associated with the houses than were present in the surrounding water. Copepods were the most abundant animals by far; many belonged to groups usually associated with bottom habitats rather than pelagic waters. For them, the houses provide worlds to colonize in the dark galaxy of the midwater.

The houses of giant larvaceans support a unique and newly discovered midwater community about which we know little. Further studies will likely show that similar communities live on other forms of marine snow as well. Each is an ephemeral island of life in miniature where animals take refuge, live and die, mate and lay eggs, graze and hunt. Each is a packet of energy drifting unremittingly downward toward the seafloor.

Whalefall

JUST AS COLD SEEPS AND HOT VENTS ARE OASES on the seafloor, so are the skeletons of whales that have sunk to the bottom. A whale carcass provides a feast of organic material for animals living on the seafloor. Like cold seep communities in the bay, whale falls are populated by free-living chemosynthetic bacteria and animals that have chemosynthetic symbiotic bacteria living inside them.

Off Santa Catalina island in southern California, Dr. Craig Smith and his colleagues have studied the communities that spring up around whale carcasses. The whale bones are covered by bacterial mats. At the sites, they have found clams (similar to those on cold seeps here) and mussels with chemosynthetic bacteria in their gills. Other grazing animals take advantage of this oasis on the seafloor: the snail, *Mitrella*, is found at whale falls as are galatheid crabs.

As whale carcasses are reduced to skeletons, the sulfide-based communities remain. Whale bones are rich in oils, and some bacteria use these oils as an energy source. These bacteria break down sulfates in the oil and in the process release hydrogen sulfide which diffuses to the outside of the bones. The hydrogen sulfide, in combination with oxygen in the water, in turn becomes the energy source for the chemosynthetic bacteria which support a community similar to those living on cold seeps.

Cold seeps are isolated and widely separated from each other by long stretches of seafloor. Scientists have wondered how the specialized types of cold seep animals colonize these scattered patches. Fallen whale carccasses offer one possible answer.

Presuming that there are many whale falls on the bottom of the ocean, they may act as "stepping-stones" between seeps. The drifting larvae of animals from a cold seep might be more likely to reach a nearby whale carcass than a more distant seep. As a community becomes established on the whale carcass, the residents in turn reproduce and release larvae which might then reach another carcass. Eventually, a series of short steps like this could lead to colonization of a far distant seep. The more we explore the deep seafloor, the more chemosynthetic communities we find. But there is still much we don't know.

To learn more about whale falls, Dr. Smith plans to sink a whale that has died and watch the colonization process to try to answer some of these questions: How long does it take? Where do the animals come from? How similar are they to vent animals? Jim Barry at the Monterey Bay Aquarium Research Institute is planning to do similar work here in the bay. He hopes to find the carcass of a whale and sink it, but so far, there hasn't been a dead whale to sink.

Selected Deep Sea Species

MIDWATER

INVERTEBRATES

Arrowworm, *Pseudosagitta* spp.
Barrel amphipod, *Phronima* sp.
Black-eyed squid, *Gonatus onyx*
Black prince copepod, *Gaussia princeps*
Cockatoo squid, *Galiteuthis phyllura*
Cock-eyed squid, *Histioteuthis heteropsis*
Comb jelly, *Beroe forskalii*
Crystal amphipod, *Cystisoma fabricii*
Dancing bristle worm, *Tomopteris* sp.
Giant larvacean, *Bathochordaeus* sp.
Giant ostracod, *Gigantocypris* sp.
Giant red mysid, *Gnathophausia ingens*
Glass shrimp, *Pasiphaea pacifica*
Hammerhead larvacean, *Oikopleura* sp.
Krill, *Euphausia pacifica*
Lobed comb jelly, *Bathocyroe fosteri*
Midwater jelly, *Atolla vanhoeffeni*
Midwater jelly, *Atolla wyvillei*
Midwater jelly, *Colobonema sericeum*
Midwater narcomedusa, *Solmissus marshalli*
Midwater octopus, *Vitreledonella* sp.
Nermertean worm, *Nectonemertes* spp.
Orange siphonophore, *Halistemma* sp.
Pacific sergestid, *Sergestes similis*
Pelagic worm, *Alciopa* sp.
Rabbit-eared comb jelly, *Kiyohimea usagi*
Red octopus, *Octopus rubescens*
Rocket ship siphonophore, *Chuniphyes* sp.
Sea gooseberry, *Hormiphora* sp.
Siphonophore, *Apolemia* sp.
Siphonophore, *Nanomia bijunga*
Siphonophore, *Praya* spp.
Sword-tail squid, *Chiroteuthis calyx*
Umbrella comb jelly, *Thalassocalyce inconstans*
Vampire squid, *Vampyroteuthis infernalis*

FISHES

Blackdragon, *Idiacanthus antrostomus*
Bristlemouth, *Cyclothone signata*
California headlightfish, *Diaphus theta*
Dollar hatchetfish, *Sternoptyx* sp.
Gulper eel, *Eupharynx pelecanoides*
Midwater eelpout, *Melanostigma pammelas*
Northern lampfish, *Stenobrachius leucopsarus*
Owlfish, *Bathylagus* spp.
Pacific dreamer anglerfish, *Oneirodes acanthias*
Pacific viperfish, *Chauliodus macouni*
Pallid eelpout, *Lycodapus mandibularis*
Ribbonfish, *Trachipterus altivelis*
Shining tubeshoulder, *Sagamichthys abei*
Silver hatchetfish, *Argyropelecus* sp.

MARINE MAMMALS

Northern elephant seal, *Mirounga angustirostris*
Sperm whale, *Physeter macrocephalus*

BENTHIC

INVERTEBRATES

Apple anemone, *Stomphia* sp.
Basket star, *Gorgonocephalus* sp
Benthic jelly, *Benthocodon pedunculata*
Benthic jelly, *Ptychogastrea polaris*
Benthic siphonophore, *Dromalia alexandri*
Bottlebrush sponge, *Asbestopluma* sp.
Brachiopod, *Terebratulina* sp
Brittle star on sea pens, *Asteronyx loveni*
Brisingid sea star, *Brisinga* sp.
Club-tipped anemone, *Corallimorphus profundus*
Cold seep clam, *Calyptogena kilmeri*
Cold seep clam, *Calyptogena pacifica*
Cold seep clam, *Calyptogena packardana*
Cold seep snail, *Mitrella permodesta*
Deep sea cucumber, *Pannychia* sp.
Deep sea cucumber, *Scotoplanes globosa*
Deep sea hare, *Pleurobranchaea californica*
Deep sea star, *Poraniopsis* sp.
Dumbo octopus, *Grimpoteuthis* sp.
Feather star, *Florometra serratissima*
Fish-eating star, *Stylasterias* sp.
Flapjack octopus, *Opisthoteuthis californica*
Giant isopod, *Bathynomas* sp.
Glass sponge
Golden eye mysid, *Mysinae* sp.
Heart urchin, *Brisaster latifrons*
Multi-arm sea star, *Rathbunaster californicus*
Mushroom soft coral, *Anthomastus ritteri*
Peppermint gorgonian, *Paragorgia* sp.
Pink sea urchin, *Allocentrotus fragilis*
Platinum topshell, *Calliostoma platinum*

Pom-pom anemone, *Liponema brevicornis*
Predatory tunicate, *Megalodicopia hians*
Red sea fan, *Psammogorgia* sp.
Red sea star, *Hippasteria spinosa*
Sea cucumber, *Parastichopus johnsoni*
Sea cucumber, *Psolus squamata*
Sea pen, *Ptilosarcus* sp.
Sea whip, *Halipteris* sp.
Seep tube worm, *Lamellibrachia* sp.
Snail, *Neptunea amianta*
Spider crab, *Chorila longipes*
Spiny king crab, *Paralithodes rathbuni*
Spot prawn, *Pandalus platyceros*
Squat lobster, *Munida quadrispina*
Sun star, *Solaster dawsoni*
Tanner crab, *Chionoecetes tanneri*

FISHES
Big fin eelpout, *Lycodes cortezianus*
Big skate, *Raja binoculata*
Black hagfish, *Eptatretus deanii*
Brown cat shark, *Apristurus brunneus*
Deep sea sole, *Embassichthys bathybius*
Dover sole, *Microstomus pacificus*
Filetail cat shark, *Parmaturus xaniurus*
Longspine thornyhead, *Sebastolobus altivelis*
Pacific grenadier rattail, *Caryphaenoides acrolepis*
Pacific hagfish, *Eptatretus stoutii*
Pacific sleeper shark, *Somniosis pacificus*
Pigmy poacher, *Odontopyxis trispinosa*
Sablefish, *Anoplopoma fimbria*
Shortspine thornyhead, *Sebastolobus alascanus*
Spotted ratfish, *Hydrolagus colliei*
Starry skate, *Raja stellulata*

GLOSSARY

abyss: deep sea region from 8,000 to 19,000 feet deep and temperatures below 39°F

abyssal: referring to the deep sea or abyss

acrylic: plastic used to make many large aquarium exhibit windows

adaptation: a characteristic (body part, behavior, etc.) that helps a plant or animal survive

aggregate: to cluster together to form a dense mass

algae (singular—alga): simple non-seed-bearing plants, including one-celled diatoms and multicellular seaweeds

algin: a carbohydrate extracted from brown marine algae; widely used for its water-binding, thickening and emulsifying properties

amphipod: any member of the taxonomic group (Order Amphipoda) of small, laterally compressed (thin) crustaceans with one set of feet for jumping and another set for swimming; includes whale lice, skeleton shrimp and beach fleas

anaerobically: to live life nearly or completely without oxygen

anal: near or at the opening of the lower end of the intestines; anus

annelid: any member of the taxonomic group (Phylum Annelida) of worms with ringed or segmented bodies, like earthworms

aphotic zone: zone without light; that portion of the ocean where light is insufficient for plants to carry out photosynthesis

aquatic: living or growing in or on the water

arthropod: any member of the taxonomic group (Phylum Arthropoda) with jointed legs and a segmented body, like insects, crustaceans, spiders, etc.

ascidian: any member of the taxonomic group (Class Ascidiacea) of tunicates, usually sac-shaped with a tough outer covering, like a sea squirt

asexual: sexless; having no evident sex or sex organs

asexual reproduction: reproduce without sex by fragmentation or budding

baleen: horny plates that grow down from the upper jaw in a baleen whale through which water is strained in feeding to capture plankton. They are used to strain their food, krill from the sea water.

basalt: a tough, dark, fine-grained to dense volcanic rock commonly occurring in sheetlike lava flows

bends: a painful and dangerous condition caused by the formation of nitrogen bubbles in the blood or body tissues created by a rapid lowering of pressure, as when a diver returns too quickly to the surface after a deep or long dive; decompression sickness

benthic: near or on the bottom (of the ocean, lakes, rivers, etc.)

berm: a ledge or shoulder; the flat portion of the beach

binomial: a two-word (genus and species) scientific name for an organism

bioluminescence: the production of visible light by living organisms

biomass: amount of living organisms in a given area or volume

biosonar: the production and reception of sound waves by animals for finding food, determining surroundings, etc. (see echolocation)

bivalve: any member of the taxonomic group (Class Bivalvia) of molluscs having two valves or shells hinged together, like a mussel, clam, scallop or oyster

blade: the leaflike part of a seaweed

blubber: layer of fat beneath the skin of whales and other marine mammals

brackish water: water that is somewhat salty, but less salty than sea water

broadcasting: the releasing of sperm and egg into the water where fertilization and development will occur

calcareous: containing calcium carbonate

California Current: cold ocean current that flows southward along the west coast of the U.S. to the northern part of Baja California

camouflage: a behavior, shape, coloration and/or pattern that helps a plant or animal blend in with its surroundings

canopy: the top layer of the kelp forest where fronds float on the sea surface and shade the forest floor

carnivore: any animal or plant that eats the flesh of other animals

cartilage: a firm but flexible connective tissue

caudal: posterior; toward the tail

caudal peduncle: fleshy portion of body just in front of the tail or caudal fin

cephalopod: any member of the taxonomic group (Class Cephalopoda) of molluscs having a distinct head with a beak and muscular tentacles near the mouth, like octopus, squid and cuttlefish

cetacean: any member of the taxonomic group (Order Cetacea) of marine mammals, like whales, dolphins and porpoises

chlorophyll: the green pigment found in plants which is essential in the use of light energy in photosynthesis

chordate: any member of the taxonomic group (Phylum Chordata) of animals having at some time in their development a notochord, gill slits and dorsal nerve cord, including vertebrates and tunicates

cilia: minute hairlike strands some animals use to produce a current to move themselves or to feed

claspers: modified pair of appendages on male sharks, skates and rays used to pass sperm to the female

Cnidarian: any member of the taxonomic group (Phylum Cnidaria) having a sac-like body with a mouth surrounded by stinging tentacles, like jellyfishes, anemones, hydroids and corals

commensal: an organism that lives in close association with another organism, benefiting from the association without helping or harming the other organism

community: all of the plants and animals living in a specific area (habitat); often described by the most abundant or obvious organisms (kelp forest community, mussel bed community, etc.)

consumer: an organism that feeds on other organisms

continental shelf: an old, wave-cut terrace gently sloping seaward from the exposed edge of a continent to where the steeper descent of the continental slope begins

continental slope: beyond the shelf, the slope descends more steeply into the ocean depths

copepod: any member of the taxonomic group (Subclass Copepoda) of crustaceans, some free-living, others parasitic

Coriolis effect: the deflection of a moving body, like the oceans, to the right in the Northern Hemisphere and to the left in the Southern Hemisphere caused by the Earth's rotation

Costanoans: the original human inhabitants of the Monterey Bay area from ca. 30,000 B.C. to 1875

countershading: a type of protective coloration (camouflage) in which an animal is dark on the back or top and lighter on the underside

countercurrent heat exchange: a way to conserve body heat by exchanging heat from warm blood flowing to the body surface with cool blood flowing to the body core

creosote: a colorless or yellowish oily liquid containing a mixture of phenolic (white, poisonous, corrosive crystals) compounds obtained by distilling tar; used to preserve wood

cross-fertilization: fertilization in which the gametes (egg or sperm) are produced by separate individuals

crustacean: any member of a taxonomic group (Class Crustacea) of arthropods with a hard outer shell, jointed legs and gills for breathing, including crabs, beach hoppers, pill bugs, shrimps and barnacles

crustal plates: individual plates or pieces which make up the solid, rocky outer portion or shell of the Earth

cryptic: camouflaged, fitted for concealment

Davidson Current: warm ocean current flowing northward between the shoreline and the California Current along the west coast of the U.S. during winter months

davit: a pair of cranelike structures invented by the Genovese for removing their feluccas (boats) from the water to avoid damage by unpredictable storms

debilitate: to weaken, deprive of strength

decimate: to destroy or kill a large part of the population

decomposer: an organism, like a fungus or bacterium, that causes the decay of dead plants and animals

delayed implantation: a process by which the fertilized egg does not attach to the uterine wall for weeks or months after fertilization. This delays development so that the young is not born at an inappropriate time or location.

deposit-feeder: an animal that feeds by consuming debris (detritus) on or in the seafloor

dermal denticles: the toothlike scales of elasmobranchs (sharks, etc.) embedded in their skin (dermis); placoid scales

detritus: particles of debris from decaying plants and animals

diatom: a group of microscopic single-celled algae (plants) with cell walls of silica

dimorphism: having two different and distinct forms in the same species, as in sexual dimorphism where males and females have different characteristics

disruptive coloration: a type of camouflage where color patterns break up or disrupt body form to make an animal unrecognizable to predators or prey

dorsal: pertaining to the back or upper surface of an animal

drift algae: pieces of seaweed that break free of their attachment and drift

echinoderm: any member of the taxonomic group (Phylum Echinodermata) of invertebrates, usually with a hard spiny skeleton, radial body and water vascular system, including sea stars, sea urchins, sand dollars and sea cucumbers

echolocation: a process of using echoes (sounds reflecting off distant objects) to locate objects like prey (see biosonar)

ecology: scientific discipline involving interrelationships among animals, plants and their environment

eelgrass: grasslike, aquatic seed-bearing plant

El Niño: an unusual, warm, tropical surface current flowing north and south along the west coasts of North and South America

elasmobranch: any member of the taxonomic group (Class Chondrichthyes) of fishes with cartilaginous skeletons, toothlike scales and no air bladder, including sharks, skates and rays

embryo: the young of an organism at its early stages of development

endangered: threatened with extinction

endoskeleton: an internal skeleton, like the bony or cartilaginous skeletons of vertebrates

erosion: a wearing down and reshaping process of the continents caused by wind, rain, water and humans

estrus: a regularly recurrent period of ovulation and sexual excitement in female mammals other than primates

estuary: where river currents meet and are influenced by oceanic tides

excurrent: pertaining to a current that flows outward

exoskeleton: an external skeleton, like the "shell" of a crab

extinct: no longer existing

fauna: animal population of particular location, region or period

felucca: Genovese (Italian) fishing boat used for catching rockfishes, barracuda and salmon

filter-feeder: an animal that eats by passing surrounding water through a filtering device (like barnacle legs, clam gills, etc.) and filtering or straining out small particles of food

flagellum (plural—flagella): a slender, whiplike strand used to move the body, produce a current or sense the surroundings

flora: the plant population of a region, period or location

fluke: one of the two horizontally flattened divisions of the tail of a whale

fog: a large mass of water vapor suspended at or just above the Earth's surface; thick, obscuring mist

food chain: sequence of living organisms in which members of one level feed on those in the level below it and are in turn eaten by those above it

forage: food for animals, especially when taken by browsing or grazing; to search for food

fossil: the hardened remains or traces of plant or animal life of a past geological period

fouling: a mass of living and non-living bodies and particles attached to a submerged object

frond: a kelp stipe (the stemlike part) and the attached blades (the leaflike parts)

fusiform: shaped like a torpedo—rounded, broadest in the middle, and tapering toward each end

gamete: a mature sperm or egg, capable of participating in fertilization

gametophyte: a plant that produces gametes or sex cells

gastropod: any member of the taxonomic group (Class Gastropoda) of molluscs including snails, slugs, limpets and periwinklesgenera (singular—genus); a biological ranking between family and species

generic: pertaining to the biological rank of genus

gestation: the carrying of young in the uterus; pregnancy

234

gill: the body part used by aquatic animals for respiring (breathing under water)

gill rakers: small, bony structures on the inside edge of fishes' gills that support the gills, prevent solid particles from injuring the gills and prevent food from escaping into the water

granite: a hard igneous rock that makes up the Earth's continents; weathered down, it's one substance that eventually becomes beach sand

gravid: pregnant; bearing eggs or young

habitat: the place where a plant or animal lives; home

halophyte: plant that can grow in soil with a high salt content

haptera (singular—hapteron)**:** a rootlike structure forming parts of the holdfast of certain brown algae and attaching the plant to the substrate

hemoglobin: an iron-containing pigment in red blood cells, which conveys oxygen to tissues

herbivore: any animal that eats plants

hermaphrodite: an animal with both male and female sex organs

holdfast: the part of a seaweed that holds the plant to a firm surface (substrate) by rootlike branches called haptera

hydrodynamics: the branch of physics that studies fluids in motion and the forces which affect motion

hydroid: a cnidarian, often with a well-developed polyp stage and often living in colonies; a hydrozoan

incurrent: pertaining to a current that flows inward

inert: unable to move or act

inorganic: being or composed of matter that is not plant or animal

intertidal: the area of the shore between the highest and lowest tidal levels

intraspecific: within a single species

invertebrate: an animal without a backbone or spinal column

iridescent: having or displaying rainbowlike colors

isopod: any member of the taxonomic group (Order Isopoda) of aquatic crustaceans with six pairs of legs and a flat oval body like that of a garden sowbug or pill bug

junk: a high-sterned boat 30 or more feet long used by the Chinese for long-distance travel

kelp: any of the large brown seaweeds, like *Macrocystis* (giant kelp)

keratin: the protein in skin, nails and hair

krill: shrimplike crustaceans (mostly of the genus Euphausia); large populations live in certain seas and are the principal food of some whales and fishes

labyrinth: any body structure full of intricate cavities and canals

lampara net: two-person net used by the Sicilians in the 1890s to catch sardines in the early stages of the sardine fishery

larvae (singular—larva)**:** the young and immature form of an animal that is unlike the adult and must change to become an adult

lateral line: a line of minute pores along the heads and sides of many fishes and some amphibians for sensing vibrations and pressure

leach: to remove unwanted parts of a substance by a percolating or filtering liquid

lichen: a small plant composed of a fungus and an alga living symbiotically

littoral: of, on or along the coastline or shore

littoral drift: the transporting of sand along a beach by wave action striking the beach at an angle

locomotion: the act of moving; the ability to move from place to place

mammal: any member of the taxomonic group (Class Mammalia) that are warm-blooded, have hair and nurse their young, including whales, otters and humans

mantle: the portion of the body wall in snails and other molluscs that lines and secretes the shell; in shell-less molluscs (octopus and squid) it forms the body wall

mantle: the portion of the earth's interior between the molten core and the thin surface crust

mean sea level: the average level of all the tides

medusa: jellyfish; the free-swimming, jellyfishlike sexual form in the life cycle of cnidarians

melon: the forehead of a whale, used during echolocation

metabolism: physical and chemical changes within a living organism involved in the maintenance of life

midden: a refuse heap; a dump, especially referring to Indian kitchen middens

migrate: when animals move en masse to and from feeding and reproductive or nesting areas

mollusc: any member of the taxonomic group (Phylum Mollusca) of invertebrates with a soft unsegmented body often enclosed wholly or partially by the mantle and a shell, including chitons, clams, snails, slugs, octopuses and squids

molt: to shed part or all of a coat or outer covering and replace with a new one

morphology: the body structure and form of an organism

mudflat: muddy or sandy coastal strip usually submerged by high tide

myoglobin: the oxygen-carrying pigment found in vertebrate muscles

neap tide: tides during the quarter and three-quarter moon when the difference between high and low tides is the smallest because the Sun and Moon are at right angles to one another

nekton: open-ocean animals that are active swimmers powerful enough to move against ocean currents (e.g., tuna)

nematocyst: the stinging capsule of cnidarians used for protection and capturing food

nestler: an animal that lives sheltered or partly hidden

neutral buoyancy: weightless in the water, neither rising nor sinking

niche: the role of an organism in its community

nudibranch: any member of the taxonomic group (Order Nudibranchia) of marine gastropods without a shell; sea slug

nutrient: any of a number of inorganic or organic compounds or ions that promotes growth or provides energy

oceanic period: the short season (September and October) when upwelling stops, sea surface temperatures rise and clear water flows in from offshore

oceanography: study of the physics, chemistry, biology and geology of the world's oceans

omnivore: any animal that eats both animals and plants

opportunistic feeder: an animal that feeds on whatever is available

organic: derived from living organisms; relating to or containing carbon compounds

organism: a living thing

oxygen minimum layer: an area where oxygen is depleted, just above the seafloor and at mid-depth zone

Pangaea: a large single supercontinent formed about 280 million years ago

paralytic shellfish poisoning (PSP): a toxin harmful to humans, especially found in mussels during the warm months of the year when mussels eat certain dinoflagellates

parasite: a plant or animal that lives in or on another plant or animal and obtains nourishment from it at the host's expense

pectoral: pertaining to anterior or upper thoracic region, as pectoral fins of fish; in chest region

pelage: hairy covering of a mammal; fur

pelagic: of the open oceans

pelvic: relating to, or located in or near, the pelvis

peripheral: the outermost region or parts

peristalsis: a rhythmic progressive wave of muscular contraction; used by the fat innkeeper worm to pump water through its burrow

phalarope: small swimming and wading shorebirds resembling sandpipers

pholad: a clam of the family Pholadidae that bores into shale and similar substrate

photic zone: the surface layer of an ocean or lake that is penetrated by sunlight and in which phytoplankton flourish

photosynthesis: the process by which green plants use energy from sunlight to produce sugar and oxygen from carbon dioxide and water

phylum (plural—phyla): broad, principal division of the animal kingdom displaying one of the 35+/-basic body plans

physiology: all the vital processes and activities within an organism

phytoplankton: plant plankton, including diatoms

pilings: long, heavy timbers or beams driven into the seafloor with tops projecting above the waterline to support a wharf or bridge

pinniped: any member of the taxonomic group (Suborder Pinnipedia) of marine mammals having finlike feet or flippers, including seals, sea lions and walrus

plankton: plants and animals that swim weakly, or not at all, and drift with ocean currents; most are tiny

plankton bloom: a rapid growth and multiplication of plankton

plate: "islands" of granite floating around on a semi-liquid mantle making up the Earth's crust

pod: a group of animals like whales swimming or moving closely together

polychaete: any member of the taxonomic group (Class Polychaeta) of mostly marine annelid (segmented) worms, having on most segments a pair of fleshy leglike appendages covered with bristles, like scale worms, feather-duster worms, tube worms, etc.

polygynous: relating to or practicing polygyny, the mating of a male animal with more than one female

polyp: a body form of coelenterates characterized by a more or less fixed base and a baglike body, with a mouth/anus at the top surrounded by a ring of tentacles

porifera: any member of the taxonomic group (Phylum Porifera) of primitive invertebrates; sponges

predation: the act of capturing prey for food

predator: an animal that kills and eats other animals

prenatal: preceding birth

prey: an animal that a predator kills and eats

proboscis: an elongated or protruding organ or tubelike structure located in the mouth region of many animals and commonly used while feeding

producer: an organism (plant, diatom, some bacteria) that produces its own food through photosynthesis

productivity: the sum of organic matter produced by living organisms in a given area or volume in a given time

promontory: a high ridge jutting out into the sea

purse seiner: a fishing boat with a large net drawn around a school of fish by a smaller boat

radula: a tonguelike band of teeth used by snails and most other molluscs to scrape, tear, bore, etc.

raft: a large number of sea otters or sea lions together in the water

rasp: to scrape or rub, as with a file

ray: any member of the taxonomic group (Order Myliobatidiformes) of cartilaginous fishes with a stinger on the tail and which bear live young, like bat rays and stingrays

red tide: red or reddish-brown discoloration of surface waters, most frequently in coastal regions, caused by concentrations of certain microscopic organisms, particularly dinoflagellates

respiration: breathing; the act of assimilating oxygen and releasing carbon dioxide and other products

rete (plural—retea)**:** an interlacing network of vessels or nerve fibers

saltmarsh: a transition between terrestrial and marine ecosystems

sampan: a flat-bottomed boat 18 to 26 feet long sculled by a single fisherman; used by the Chinese for shore fishing

scavenger: an animal that eats dead plants and animals or their parts

scuba: (initials that stand for self-contained underwater breathing apparatus) a device that lets a diver breathe air while under water

seaweed: any of the large plants that grow in the sea, especially marine algae like kelp

sedimentary: formed by the deposit of sediments (matter that settles to the bottom of liquids)

sedimentary rock: rock formed by layers of sediment subjected to tremendous pressures over long periods of time

semi-diurnal: occurring twice a day, as in semi-diurnal tides

sessile: stationary; attached to the seafloor or an object such as a pier piling

shellfish: any aquatic animal with a shell, like shelled molluscs or crustaceans

shunt: to divert something onto another course

siliceous: containing silica (a hard glassy mineral found in quartz, sand, opal, etc.)

siphon: a tube or tubelike part of an animal through which water, air or food passes

skate: any member of the taxonomic group (Order Rajiformes, Family Rajidae) of rays with a broad flat body, no stinger and a tail with two dorsal fins

slough: a swamp, marsh, bog or pond which is part of an inlet or backwater

spawn: to produce and deposit eggs

species: a basic taxonomic group consisting of individuals with common attributes who, upon breeding, produce fertile offspring

spiracle: an opening in the head area of some sharks, skates and rays through which water is drawn and passed over the gills

spore: a single or multicellular asexual reproductive structure capable of giving rise to a new organism without the union of sexual cells

sporophyll: special fronds growing at the base of a holdfast that bear reproductive parts

sporophyte: in plants with alternating generations, the individual or generation that bears asexual spores

spreading centers: plate boundaries where new oceanic crust is created.

spring tide: tides during the new and the full moon, when the difference between high and low tides is the greatest because of the combined "pull" of the Sun and the Moon

stipe: the stemlike part of a kelp plant connecting the holdfast to the blades (the leaflike parts)

subduction: one of the Earth's crustal plates "diving" beneath the surface of another crustal plate

subsistence: the barest means needed to sustain life

substrate: any surface on which a plant or an animal lives or on which a material sticks

subtidal: below the intertidal, or below the level of the lowest tide

surfline: the area near shore where the waves break

surge: a movement of a mass of water

surge channel: a channel along the edge of rocks or reefs in which the water level fluctuates with wave or tidal action

suspension-feeder: an animal that removes debris (e.g., detritus) or other particles suspended in the surrounding water

sustenance: that which sustains life; nourishment; food

swell: an ocean wave that moves steadily without breaking

symbiotic: a mode of living where two different species live in intimate association with each other resulting in an advantage for at least one of the species

taxonomy: scientific classification of animals and plants

tectonic: pertaining to the movement of major sections of the earth's crust

terrestrial: pertaining to the Earth; of the land

test: the endoskeleton of various animals like sea urchins or sand dollars

thermocline: a zone of rapid temperature change as one descends deeper into the water

thorax: portion of body between the head and abdomen; the chest

tide: the daily rise and fall of sea level along a shore caused by the gravitational pull of the Sun and Moon and the rotation of the Earth

tidemark: the highwater mark left by tidal water

tide pool: a pool of water left along the shore as the tidal level falls

topographic: the physical features of a place or region, like mountains, canyons, etc.

trophic: pertaining to growth or nutrition

tsunami: Japanese term for a large wave caused by seismic disturbances like submarine landslides, earthquakes, volcanic eruptions, etc.

tube feet: an extension of the water vascular system of echinoderms (sea stars, sea urchins, etc.) which aids locomotion, grasping and feeding

tunicate: any member of the taxonomic group (Subphylum Urochordata) of solitary or colonial chordates

turbid: stirred up sediment; cloudy

turf: plants and animals forming a thick mat on a substrate

unicellular: one-celled; single-celled

upwelling: cold, nutrient-rich waters that rise to the surface

vasculated: having numerous blood vessels

ventral: pertaining to the underside of the body

vertebrate: any member of the taxonomic group (Subphylum Vertebrata) of chordate animals having a segmented spinal column, like mammals, fishes, birds, reptiles and amphibians

vestigial: usually a nonfunctioning remnant of a body part that once existed as a fully functioning part of an organism, like vestigial hipbones in whales

vibrissae (singular—vibrissa)**:** a mammal's whiskers

volcanism: volcanic activity and earthquakes deep within the earth.

vortex: a whirl or whirlpool of water or air

water vascular system: in echinoderms (sea stars, sea urchins, etc.) a system of water-filled canals and structures that aids in locomotion and food gathering

wetlands: land or areas (as tidal flats or swamps) containing high levels of soil moisture

wrack (beach wrack)**:** drift algae that has washed up onto the shore

zero tide: the average of the lower low tides

zonation: the distribution of the plants and animals in a community into recognizable zones

zooplankton: animal plankton

SUGGESTIONS FOR FURTHER READING

Akeman, T. 1994. SANCTUARY IS WORK IN PROGRESS. *The Monterey (CA) County Herald,* 8 May.

American Fisheries Society. 1991. COMMON AND SCIENTIFIC NAMES OF FISHES FROM THE UNITED STATES AND CANADA. 5th ed., special publ. no. 20. Bethesda, MD.

Barnes, R.D. 1980. INVERTEBRATE ZOOLOGY. Philadelphia: W.B. Saunders and Co.

Barry, J.P., B.H. Robison, H.G. Green, C.H. Baxter, C. Harrold, R.E. Kochevar, Dan Orange, S. Lisin, P.J. Whaling and J. 1993. INVESTIGATIONS OF COLD SEEP COMMUNITIES IN MONTEREY BAY, CALIFORNIA, USING A REMOTELY OPERATED VEHICLE. American Academy of Underwater Sciences, P Proceedings. 17-23.

Boolootian, R.A. (ed.) 1966. PHYSIOLOGY OF THE ECHINODERMATA. New York, NY: Wiley Interscience.

Broad, W.J. 1997. THE UNIVERSE BELOW: DISCOVERING THE SECRETS OF THE DEEP SEA. New York, NY: Simon and Schuster.

Brusca, R.C., and G.J. Brusca. 1990. INVERTEBRATES. Sunderland, MA: Sinauer Assoc., Inc.

Burton, M., and R. Burton. 1984, c. 1975 ENCYCLOPEDIA OF FISH. S.I.:BPC Publishing.

Canby, Thomas Y. National Geographic Society. 1990. EARTHQUAKE—PRELUDE TO THE BIG ONE? *National Geographic.* May 177(5):76-105.

Carey, Francis G. 1992. Through the thermocline and back again: Heat Regulation in Big Fish. *Oceanus* Fall: 35(3):79-85.

Castro, J.I. 1983. THE SHARKS OF NORTH AMERICAN WATERS. College Station, TX: Texas A&M Press.

Castro, P., and M.E. Huber (eds.) 1997. MARINE BIOLOGY. Dubuque, IA: William C. Brown Publishing.

Chipping, D.H., and R. McCoy. 1982. COASTAL SAND DUNE COMPLEXES: PISMO BEACH AND MONTEREY BAY. CALIFORNIA Geology, Sacramento, CA.

Clark, A. 1962. STARFISHES AND THEIR RELATIONS. London: British Museum.

Connor, J., and C. Baxter. 1989. KELP FORESTS. Monterey, CA: Monterey Bay Aquarium Foundation.

Connor. J. 1993. SEASHORE LIFE ON ROCKY COASTS. Monterey, CA: Monterey Bay Aquarium Foundation.

Safina, Carl. 1993. BLUEFIN TUNA IN THE WEST ATLANTIC: NEGLIGENT MANAGEMENT AND THE MAKING OF AN ENDANGERED SPECIES. *Conservation Biology* 7(2):229-234.

Davis, C. 1994. SECRETS, TREASURES OF UNDERWATER PARK ATTRACT ECOTOURISTS. *The Monterey County (CA) Herald,* 22 May.

Deriso, R. B., and W.H. Bayliff (eds.). 1991. WORLD MEETING ON STOCK ASSESSMENT OF BLUEFIN TUNAS: STRENGTHS AND WEAKNESSES. SPECIAL REPORT NO. 7. Inter-American Tropical Tuna Commission. La Jolla, CA.

Dybas, C.L. 1993. BEAUTIFUL, ETHEREAL LARVACEANS PLAY A CENTRAL ROLE IN OCEAN ECOLOGY. *Oceanus* Summer:36(2):84-86.

Dybas, C.L. 1995. SEAGOING SPACESHIPS: EXPLORING THE MARINE WORLD BY THE LIGHT OF SEA SPRITES CALLED LARVACEANS. *Wildlife Conservation.* September/October 98(5):30–34.

Dymond, J. 1992. PARTICLES IN THE OCEAN. *Oceanus* Spring 35(1):60–67.

Emory, J. 1989. THE MONTEREY DUNES: A RELIC ON THE EDGE. *Pacific Discovery.* California Academy of Sciences. Summer: 42(3):22-31.

Eschmeyer, W.N. 1983. PACIFIC COAST FISHES. Boston, MA: Houghton-Mifflin Co.

Eschmeyer, W. N., and E. S. Herald. 1983. A FIELD GUIDE TO THE FISHES OF NORTH AMERICA. Boston, MA: Houghton-Mifflin Co.

Fast, T. N. 1957. THE OCCURRENCE OF THE DEEP-SEA ANGLERFISH, *CRYPTOSARAS COURESII*, IN MONTEREY BAY, CALIFORNIA. *Copeia* (3):237–240.

Ferguson, A., and G. Calliet. 1990. SHARKS AND RAYS OF THE PACIFIC COAST. Monterey: Monterey Bay Aquarium Foundation.

Fitch, J.E., and R.J. Lavenberg. 1968. DEEP WATER TELEOSTEAN FISHES OF CALIFORNIA. Berkeley, CA: Univ. of CA Press.

Fitch, J.E., and R.J. Lavenberg. 1971. MARINE FOOD AND GAME FISHES OF CALIFORNIA. Berkeley, CA: Univ. of CA Press.

Florkin, M., and B.T. Sheer (eds.). 1976. CHEMICAL ZOOLOGY. New York, NY: Academic Press.

Food and Agriculture Organization of the United Nations. Prepared by: Collette, B.B and C.E. Nauen. 1983. SCOMBRIDS OF THE WORLD. FAO species catalogue. vol. 2. Rome: United Nations.

Gage, J.D., and P.A. Tyler. 1991. DEEP-SEA BIOLOGY. Cambridge: Cambridge Univ. Press.

Garrison, Tom. 1993. OCEANOGRAPHY. Belmont, CA: Wadsworth Publishing Co.

Gordon, B.L. 1977. MONTEREY BAY AREA: NATURAL HISTORY AND CULTURAL IMPRINTS. Pacific Grove, CA: Boxwood Press.

Gordon, D.G., and A. Baldridge. 1991. GRAY WHALES. Monterey, CA: Monterey Bay Aquarium Foundation.

Gordon, D.G. 1994. SEALS AND SEA LIONS. Monterey, CA: Monterey Bay Aquarium Foundation.

Gore, Rick. National Geographic Society. 1990. BETWEEN MONTEREY TIDES. *National Geographic,* February 177(2):2-43.

Gotshall, D.W., and L.L. Laurent. 1979. PACIFIC COAST SUBTIDAL MARINE INVERTE-BRATES. Monterey, CA: Sea Challengers.

Gotshall, D.W. 1989. PACIFIC COAST INSHORE FISHES. 3rd ed. Monterey, CA: Sea Challengers.

Greene, H.G., and K.R. Hicks. 1989. GEOLOGY OF MONTEREY SUBMARINE CANYON SYSTEM AND ADJACENT AREAS, OFFSHORE CENTRAL CALIFORNIA: RESULTS OF NOAA SEA BEAM SURVEY DESCRIPTIVE REPORT FOR SURVEYOR CRUISE, US Geological Survey Open-File Report: 89–221.

———. 1990. ASCENSION-MONTEREY CANYON SYSTEM: HISTORY AND DEVELOPMENT. GEOLOGY AND TECTONICS OF THE CENTRAL CALIFORNIA COAST REGION, SAN FRANCISCO TO MONTEREY. American Association of Petroleum Geologists, Bakersfield, CA.

Griffin, J.R. 1975. MARITIME CHAPARRAL AND ENDEMIC SHRUBS OF THE MONTEREY BAY REGION. *Madrono* 25(2):65–112.

Griggs, G., and L. Savoy. 1985. LIVING WITH THE CALIFORNIA COAST. Durham, NC: Duke Univ. Press.

Griggs, G., and M. Silver. 1994. MONTEREY BAY MARINE SANCTUARY: A NATURAL LABORATORY FOR SCIENTIFIC RESEARCH. AAAS Annual Meeting, San Francisco, CA, 18–23 February.

Halstead, B.W. 1965. POISONOUS AND VENOMOUS MARINE ANIMALS OF THE WORLD. Washington, DC: US Government Printing Office.

Harbison, G.R. 1992. THE GELATINOUS INHABITANTS OF THE OCEAN INTERIOR. *Oceanus* Fall 35(3):18–23.

Hardy, A. 1965. THE OPEN SEA. Boston, MA: Houghton Mifflin.

Hart, J.L. 1973. PACIFIC FISHES OF CANADA: Fisheries Research Board of Canada. Ottawa.

Herald, E.S. 1972. FISHES OF NORTH AMERICA. New York, NY: Doubleday and Co.

Hochachka, P.W., and G.N. Somero. 1973. STRATEGIES OF BIOCHEMICAL ADAPTATION. Philadelphia, PA: W.B. Saunders and Co.

Howard, A. D. 1979. GEOLOGIC HISTORY OF MIDDLE CALIFORNIA. Berkeley, CA: Univ. of CA Press.

Hunt, J.C. 1996 OCTOPUS AND SQUID. Monterey, CA: Monterey Bay Aquarium Foundation.

Hyman, L.H. 1940–1967. THE INVERTEBRATES. 6 vols. New York, NY: McGraw-Hill.

Reserves at Fort Ord, Fremontia, 4(2):25–28.

Irion, R. 1992. MONTEREY BAY: A SANCTUARY FOR LIFE. UC Santa Cruz Review Fall: 18(1):6-11.

Jensen, G.C. 1995. PACIFIC COAST CRABS AND SHRIMPS. Monterey, CA: Sea Challengers.

Jones, M. Guil. 1993. BIOLUMINESCENCE. *The Science Teacher.* January 60(1):19–21.

Joseph, J., and W. Klawe, P. Murphy. 1988. TUNA AND BILLFISH—FISH WITHOUT A COUNTRY. Inter-American Tropical Tuna Commission, La Jolla, CA.

Kovacs, D., and K. Madin. 1996. BENEATH DEEP WATERS: MEETINGS WITH REMARKABLE DEEP-SEA CREATURES. New York, NY: Viking Press.

Kukowski, G.E. 1972. A CHECKLIST OF THE FISHES OF THE MONTEREY BAY AREA INCLUDING ELKHORN SLOUGH, THE SAN LORENZO, PAJARO

AND SALINAS RIVERS. MOSS LANDING, CA: Moss Landing Marine Laboratories.

Lalli, Carol M. and Ronald W. Gilmer. 1989. PELAGIC SNAILS. Palo Alto, CA: Stanford Univ. Press.

de Laubenfels, M. 1932. MARINE AND FRESHWATER SPONGES OF CALIFORNIA. US Natl. Mus. 81:1–140.

Leet, W.S., and C.M. Dewees, C.W. Haugen. 1992. CALIFORNIA'S LIVING MARINE RESOURCES AND THEIR UTILIZATION. California Sea Grant. UCSGEP-92-12. SH 222 .C2 C34.

Lemonick, M.D. 1995. THE LAST FRONTIER. *Time* vol. 146, issue 7, August 14:52–60.

Love, R.M. 1991. PROBABLY MORE THAN YOU WANT TO KNOW ABOUT THE FISHES OF THE PACIFIC COAST. Santa Barbara, CA: Really Big Press.

Love, R.M. 1994. *MOLA MOLA.* Dolphin Log. July:12.

Love, R. M., and T. Thys. 1993. MOLAS. *Ocean Realm.* November:43.

Love. R.M. 1992. MARINE BIOLUMINESCENCE. *Ocean Realm.* July/August:54-59.

Lydon, S. 1985. CHINESE GOLD. Capitola, CA: Capitola Book Co.

Lydon, S. 1984. MANKIND AND MONTEREY BAY. Monterey, CA: Monterey Bay Aquarium Foundation.

Manton, S. 1977. THE ARTHROPODA: HABITS, FUNCTIONAL MORPHOLOGY, AND EVOLUTION. New York , NY: Oxford Univ. Press.

Margolin, M. 1978.THE OHLONE WAY. Berkeley, CA: Heydey Books.

Marshall, N.B. 1979. DEVELOPMENTS IN DEEP SEA BIOLOGY. London: Hutchison.

Martin, B.D. 1964. MONTEREY SUBMARINE CANYON, CALIFORNIA: GENESIS AND RELATION-SHIP TO CONTINENTAL GEOLOGY. PhD diss., Univ. of Southern California, Los Angeles, CA.

MBNMS EIS/MANAGEMENT PLAN. 1990. Prepared by Marine and Estuarine Management Division, Office of Ocean and Coastal Resource Management, National Ocean Service and National Oceanic and Atmospheric Administration. August.

MBNMS PERMIT ACTIVITY REPORT, September 19, 1994. NOAA.

McClane, A.J. 1978. MCCLANE'S FIELD GUIDE TO SALTWATER FISHES OF NORTH AMERICA. New York, NY: Henry Holt and Co.

McNutt, S. R., and R. H.. Sydnor (eds.). 1990. THE LOMA PRIETA (SANTA CRUZ MOUNTAINS), CALIFORNIA EARTHQUAKE OF 17 OCTOBER 1989. Dept. of Conservation, Div. of Mines and Geology, special publ. 104, Sacramento, CA.

Meglitsch, P.A. 1972. INVERTEBRATE ZOOLOGY. New York, NY: Oxford Univ. Press.

Miller, D., and R. Lea. 1972. GUIDE TO THE COASTAL FISHES OF CALIFORNIA. California Fish Bulletin, no. 157.

Monterey Bay Dunes Coalition. 1991. MONTEREY BAY DUNES: A STRATEGY FOR PRESERVATION. Monterey, CA.

MONTEREY BAY NATIONAL MARINE SANCTUARY: SUMMARY OF REGULATIONS. May 1993, NOAA.

Morris, R.H., and D.P. Abbott, E.C. Haderlie. 1980. INTERTIDAL INVERTEBRATES OF CALIFORNIA. Stanford, CA: Stanford Univ. Press.

Moyle, P.B., and J.J. Cech Jr. 1988. FISHES—INTRODUCTION TO ICHTHYOLOGY. Englewood Cliffs, NJ: Prentice-Hall.

National Geographic Society. 1985. OUR RESTLESS PLANET EARTH. *National Geographic,* August 168(2):142-181

Nelson, G. 1975. ENCYCLOPEDIA OF FISHES. Washington, DC: American Museum of Natural History.

Nybakken, J.W. 1993. MARINE BIOLOGY: AN ECOLOGICAL APPROACH. 3rd ed. New York, NY: Harper Collins College Publishers.

Pearse, V., and J. Pearse, M. Bushsbaum, R. Buchsbaum. 1987. LIVING INVERTEBRATES. Boston, MA: Blackwell Scientific Publications and The Boxwood Press, Pacific Grove, CA.

Peden, A. E., and G.S. Jamieson. 1988. NEW DISTRIBUTIONAL RECORDS OF MARINE FISHES OFF WASHINGTON, BRITISH COLUMBIA, AND ALASKA. *Canadian Field Naturalist* 102(3):491–494.

Perry, F.A. 1977. FOSSILS OF SANTA CRUZ COUNTY. Santa Cruz, CA: Santa Cruz City Museum.

Phillips, J.B. 1931. UNUSUALLY GOOD FISHING IN AND OFF MONTEREY BAY. CA Dept. Fish and Game 18(1):21–24.

Rees, W.J.(ed). 1966. THE CNIDARIA AND THEIR EVOLUTION. New York, NY: Academic Press.

Richardson, S. 1994. WARM BLOOD FOR COLD WATER. Discover 15(1):42.

Ricketts, E.F., and J. Calvin. 1985. BETWEEN PACIFIC TIDES. 5th ed. Palo Alto, CA: Stanford Univ. Press.

Riedman, M. 1990. SEA OTTERS. Monterey, CA: Monterey Bay Aquarium Foundation.

Roberson, D. 1985. MONTEREY BIRDS. Carmel, CA: Monterey Peninsula Audubon Society.

Robison, B. 1976. DEEP SEA FISHES. *Natural History* 85(7):38–46.

Robison, B. 1995. LIGHT IN THE OCEAN'S MIDWATERS. *Scientific American,* July 273(1):60-64

Roedel, P.M. 1953. THE JACKMACKEREL, *TRACHURUS SYMMETRICUS:* A REVIEW OF THE CALIFORNIA FISHERY AND OF CURRENT BIOLOGICAL KNOWLEDGE. CA Dept. of Fish and Game 39(1):45-68.

Saunders, R.T. 1992. CREATING AN OCEAN CONSTITUENCY: CITIZEN INVOLVEMENT IN THE NATIONAL MARINE SANCTUARY PROGRAM. *Current: The Journal of Marine Education.* 11(2):27.

Schmitt, W.L. 1965. CRUSTACEANS. Ann Arbor, MI: Univ. of MI Press.

Sharp, G.D., and A.E. Dizon. 1978. THE PHYSIOLOGICAL ECOLOGY OF TUNAS. New York, NY: Academic Press.

Silberstein, M., and E. Campbell. 1989. ELKHORN SLOUGH. Monterey, CA: Monterey Bay Aquarium Foundation.

Smith, J. P. Jr., and K. Berg (eds.). 1988. CALIFORNIA NATIVE PLANT SOCIETY'S INVENTORY OF RARE AND ENDANGERED VASCULAR PLANTS OF CALIFORNIA. California Native Plant Society. Sacramento, CA.

Smith, M.M., and P.C. Heemstra. 1986. SMITH'S SEA FISHES. Berlin: Springer-Verlag.

Smith, R.I., and J.T. Carlton. 1975. LIGHT'S MANUAL: INTERTIDAL INVERTEBRATES OF THE CENTRAL CALIFORNIA COAST. 3rd ed. Berkeley, CA: Univ. of CA Press.

Sommer, F., J. Christiansen, P. Ferrante, R. Gary, B. Grey, C. Farwell and D. Powell. 1989. HUSBANDRY OF THE OCEAN SUNFISH, *MOLA MOLA.* AAZPA Regional Conference Proceedings FR 35(1):410–417.

Staff/California Coastal Commission. 1990. REPORT TO THE CITY OF SAND CITY ON THE IMPLEMENTATION OF ITS LOCAL COASTAL PROGRAM. Santa Cruz, CA.

Thys, T. 1994. SWIMMING HEADS. Natural History 94(8): 37.

Trombley, J. 1992. CAST A COLD LIGHT. *Pacific Discovery* Fall 45(4):8-18.

US Army Corps of Engineers. 1985. COAST OF CALIFORNIA STORM AND TIDAL WAVES STUDY: GEOMORPHOLOGY FRAMEWORK REPORT Monterey Bay. Ref. No. CCSTWS 85-2. Menlo Park, CA.

US Department of Commerce. 1985. ELKHORN SLOUGH NATIONAL ESTUARINE SANCTUARY MANAGEMENT PLAN. Prepared by Elkhorn Slough Estuarine Sanctuary Advisory Committee, The Resources Agency California Department of Fish and Game, National Oceanic and Atmospheric Administration Sanctuary Programs Division. August.

US Department of Commerce. 1992. FINAL ENVIRONMENTAL IMPACT STATEMENT AND MANAGEMENT PLAN FOR THE PROPOSED MONTEREY BAY NATIONAL MARINE SANCTUARY. Prepared by Sanctuaries and Reserves Division, Office of Ocean and Coastal Resource Management, National Ocean Service and National Oceanic and Atmospheric Administration. June.

US Department of Commerce/National Oceanic and Atmospheric Administration. 1990. MONTEREY BAY NATIONAL MARINE SANCTUARY, DRAFT ENVIRONMENTAL IMPACT STATEMENT/MANAGEMENT PLAN. Washington, DC.

US Geologic Survey. 1985. Geomorphology framework report: MONTEREY BAY: COAST OF CALIFORNIA STORM AND TIDAL WAVES STUDY. US Army Corps of Engineers, Los Angeles District, Planning Division, Coastal Resources Branch. December.

Vaeth, J. Gordon. National Geographic Society. 1992. MACON: LOST AND FOUND. *National Geographic,* January 181(1):114-127.

Valiela, I. MARINE ECOLOGICAL PROCESSES. Berlin: Springer-Verlag.

Walford, L. A. 1937 (reprinted 1974). MARINE GAME FISHES OF THE PACIFIC COAST FROM ALASKA TO THE EQUATOR. Neptune, NJ: T.F.H. Publications.

Wheeler, A. 1975. FISHES OF THE WORLD. New York, NY: MacMillan Publishing Co.

Williams, T. 1992. THE LAST BLUEFIN HUNT. *Audubon,* Jul-Aug. 94(4):14–20.

Yonge, C., and T.E. Thompson. 1976. LIVING MARINE MOLLUSCS. London: William Collins Sons and Co., Ltd.

Young, P. H. 1969. THE CALIFORNIA PARTYBOAT FISHERY 1947–1967. CA Dept. of Fish and Game Fish Bull.145. SH 473 .Y685.

INDEX

249

INDEX

251

ILLUSTRATIONS

*Adapted from EARTH, Press & Siever, 2nd Edition, W.H. Freeman and Company, 1978: 34, 35

*Adapted from Engineering Science Inc., Regional Sewer Facility Plan, Vol. VI, 1976: 42

*Adapted from LIVING WITH THE CALIFORNIA COAST, Griggs & Savoy, Duke University Press, 1985.: 47,80

*Adapted from Castro and Huber, MARINE BIOLOGY, Wm. C. Brown, Inc. 2nd Edition, 1997: 14.

*Adapted from Nybakken, MARINE BIOLOGY, AN ECOLOGICAL APPROACH, Harper and Row Publishers, Inc. 1988:19,24,180.

*Adapted from P.T. Strub, Oregon State University, unpublished: 22

*After InterNetwork, Inc.; REPORTS TO THE NATION/ THE CLIMATE SYSTEM: published by the National Oceanic and Atmospheric Adminstration and the University Corporation for Atomspheric Research, Vloume 1, 1991: 26,27

*Redrawn, by permission, from Carefoot, PACIFIC SEASHORES, A GUIDE TO INTERTIDAL ECOLOGY, University of Washington Press, 1977: 88

Caudle, Ann/Monterey Bay Aquarium: 57, 58 (bottom), 60, 63, 64 (bottom), 65 (middle, bottom), 66, 67, 70, 71, 86 (top), 87 (top), 88 (top, middle), 89, 90 (top), 94, 98 (top), 103, 104 (left), 106, 108, 109 (top), 111 (top, bottom), 114, 116, 117, 127, 137 (top, bottom), 138, 142 (bottom), 143 (top), 145 (top), 148, 150 (bottom), 151, 154, 155, 158 (bottom), 168, 169 (middle), 170, 171, 173 (bottom), 174 (bottom), 175, 176

Cruttenden, Carla: 97, 107, 111 (middle) 126 (top), 150 (2nd from top), 158 (top)

Folkens, Pieter A./Monterey Bay Aquarium: 225

Kells, Valerie/Monterey Bay Aquarium: iii, 1, 29, 83 (top), 104 (right), 123, 141, 149 (middle, bottom) 150 (1st from top, 3rd from top), 189 (top), 199 (top), 209, 213, 219, 221

King, Jane/Monterey Bay Aquarium: 77, 83 (bottom), 84, 85, 105, 118, 130 (top), 163, 164

Kopp, Kathy/Monterey Bay Aquarium: 135 (bottom right), 169 (top)

Leggitt, Marjorie C./ Monterey Bay Aquarium: 214

Maher, Norman M. /Monterey Bay Aquarium Research Institute, ©June 1995: 51, ©1997: xii

McCann, Andrea/ Monterey Bay Aquarium: 179

Monterey Bay Aquarium: 39, 40, 58 (top), 73, 79, 100, 124, 126 (bottom), 131, 143 (bottom)

Monterey Bay Aquarium Research Institute © 1997, Courtesy of: 50, 54

Ormsby, Lawrence: i, vii, 11, 17, 20, 32, 36, 37, 68-69, 86-87 (bottom), 90-91 (bottom), 95, 102, 109 (bottom), 153, 181, 183 (top), 184 (bottom), 186, 205

Ormsby, Lawrence/Monterey Bay Aquarium: 64-65 (top), 80, 98 (bottom),

Tatko, Thom/Monterey Bay Aquarium: 193 (top)

PHOTOGRAPHS

Cover: Kip Evans, Monterey Bay Aquarium, Charles Seaborn

Back cover: Kip Evans, Monterey Bay Aquarium

*Balthis, Frank: 96

Barry, Jim, Courtesy of: 119 (bottom)

Browne, Rick/Monterey Bay Aquarium: 79, 125 (top left, bottom), 134, 135 (bottom left), 136

Evans, Kip: vi, viii, 3, 7, 12, 76, 200

Hayes, Dawn/Monterey Bay Aquarium: 93

Hopkins Marine Station/Jim Barry, Courtesy of: 119 (top)

Keimel, Bridget/Monterey Bay Aquarium: 193 (bottom)

Leet, Mark./Monterey Bay Aquarium Research Institute © 1997, Courtesy of: 212

Mayer, Melanie: 60

Monterey Bay Aquarium: v, x, 10, 56, 59, 72, 81, 83, 125 (top right), 128, 129 (bottom), 130 (bottom), 132, 133, 135, 142 (top), 144 (top), 145 (bottom), 157, 162, 165, 166, 167 (top), 172, 182, 184 (top), 185, 187 (middle), 188, 194, 198 (top), 199 (bottom), 201, 203, 213 (left), 214, 219, 220 (bottom, top), 223

Monterey Bay Aquarium Research Institute, Courtesy of: 222 (bottom)

Murrell, Michael, Courtesy of: 64 (bottom left)

Ocean Imaging/Monterey Bay Aquarium: 18, 23

Olsen, Kathleen/ Monterey Bay Aquarium: 82, 107

Our Lady of Refuge, Parish, Castroville, Courtesy of: 62

Racicot, Craig W./Monterey Bay Aquarium: 210 (top), 215

Rigsby, Michael: 105 (bottom), 115

Robinson, George A./Dept. of Special Collections, Stanford Univ. Libraries: 101

Seaborn, Charles: 103, 110, 122, 129 (top), 137 (middle right), 140, 144 (bottom), 147, 149 (top), 156 (top), 159, 167 (bottom), 169 (bottom), 173, 174 (top)

Seaborn, Charles/Monterey Bay Aquarium: ii

Silberstein, Mark: 66

Webster, Steven K.: 105 (top), 111, 152

Wrobel, Dave: 84, 190, 208, 213 (right), 220 (middle)

Wrobel, Dave/Monterey Bay Aquarium: 178, 183 (middle), 187 (top), 189 (bottom), 191, 192, 197, 198 (bottom), 210 (middle, bottom), 216, 222 (top)

Monterey Bay Aquarium Press
886 Cannery Row / Monterey, CA 93940
http:// www. mbayaq.org

UNDERWATER WILDERNESS Charles Seaborn 48277	$29.95

NATURAL HISTORY BOOK SERIES

OCTOPUS AND SQUID James C. Hunt. 47155	$9.95
SEALS AND SEA LIONS David George Gordon 23624	$9.95
SEA OTTERS Marianne Riedman 14746	$9.95
SHARKS AND RAYS Ava Ferguson & Gregor Cailliet 14745	$9.95
GRAY WHALES David G. Gordon & Alan Baldridge 16515	$9.95
SEASHORE LIFE ON ROCKY COASTS Judith Connor 18813	$9.95
KELP FORESTS Judith Connor & Charles Baxter 13717	$9.95
ELKHORN SLOUGH Mark Silberstein & Eileen Campbell 13716	$9.95

FOR KIDS

YOUNG EXPLORER'S GUIDE TO UNDERSEA LIFE Pam Armstrong 92508	$16.95
SEA SEARCHER'S HANDBOOK: ACTIVITIES FROM THE MONTEREY BAY AQUARIUM 47138	$16.95
SEA LIFE COLORING BOOK Deborah A. Coulombe 47104	$3.95
FLIPPERS & FLUKES COLORING BOOK Deborah A. Coulombe 47121	$3.95

EXHIBIT-RELATED BOOKS

THE OUTER BAY Michael Rigsby 92491	$4.95
A GUIDE TO THE WORLD OF THE JELLYFISH Eileen Campbell 17212	$5.95
MONTEREY BAY AQUARIUM Michael Rigsby 18503	$6.95

VIDEOS

BEHIND-THE-SCENES AT THE MONTEREY BAY AQUARIUM 47172	$24.95
JELLIES AND OTHER OCEAN DRIFTERS 22964	$19.95
THE MONTEREY BAY AQUARIUM VIDEO TREASURY 12815	$24.95

SUBTOTAL	
Shipping	
(CA deliveries add 7.25% sales tax) Sales Tax	
TOTAL	

How to order:

Individuals: You may order books and videos directly from the aquarium by calling our Gift and Bookstore.
Monterey Bay Aquarium Gift and Bookstore
TEL (408) 648-4952   FAX (408) 648-4994   EMAIL giftstore@mbayaq.org   E-QUARIUM www.mbayaq.org

Trade, Wholesalers and Libraries: Books (except for *The Outer Bay*) are available through our distributor Roberts
Rinehart Publishers. Videos and The Outer Bay may be ordered directly from the Monterey Bay Aquarium Gift
and Bookstore.

Roberts Rinehart Publishers
(800) 352-1985

Rush delivery? Alaska, Hawaii, or
International destinations?
Please call for appropriate shipping charges

For shipping and postage charges for US
address only, add the following amounts:

$0-$15.00	$3.95
$15.01 - 30.00	$5.95
$30.01 - 50.00	$6.95
$50.01 - 75.00	$8.95
$75.01 - 100.00	$9.95
$100.00+	$12.95

NATURE/NATURAL HISTORY

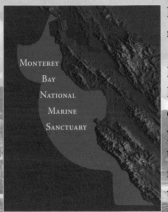

Explore the nation's largest marine sanctuary

From the famed San Francisco coast to the bluffs of Big Sur, this book takes you beneath the waters of the nation's largest national marine sanctuary to explore the breathtaking habitats and incredible sea life in this crown jewel of sanctuaries. Playful sea otters tumble in nearshore kelp forests. Mysterious vampire squid hunt in the dark depths of the mysterious Monterey Bay deep sea canyon. The first complete natural history of one the most popular dive and tourist meccas in this country features lively writing and a wealth of illustrations.

Includes species lists, suggestions for further reading, glossary, index and over 300 photographs, scientifically accurate diagrams, and maps.

MONTEREY BAY
AQUARIUM

Monterey Bay Aquarium...Inspiring conservation of the world's oceans

Developed with support from Monterey Bay National Marine Sanctuary office of the National Oceanic and Atmospheric Administration

ISBN: 1-878244-11-6
$19.95

51995

9 781878 244116